THE
SUPREME
COURT
AND
ADMINISTRATIVE
AGENCIES

The
Supreme Court
and
Administrative
Agencies

MARTIN SHAPIRO

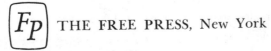 THE FREE PRESS, New York

Collier-Macmillan Limited, London

217848

TO

ROBERT G. McCLOSKEY

Preface

Perhaps all of us, or at least those of us who attempt the social sciences, ought to follow the practice of Henry Adams and entitle our books, *The Education of. . . .* Certainly this book is a record of my struggle to understand a difficult subject. At best it signals a few promising leads rather than the ultimate synthesis that is the dream of scholars. It once seemed relatively easy to grasp the Supreme Court by a chain of outstanding decisions running from *Marbury v. Madison* to the latest major pronouncement on grave constitutional issues. A sufficiently subtle articulation of the links would fulfill the responsibility of the teacher and scholar. Our students went forth, their minds well stocked with memorized briefs and their hearts uplifted by their acquired skill at the manipulation of precedent. The chains are now broken, and, without relief from our responsibility for mastering *Marbury* and his rapidly multiplying decendants, we now find that the Court slips away from us down the byways of admiralty and patent, organi-

zational behavior, decision-making theory, the psychology
of attitudes, small-group analysis and, worst of all, finally
falls into that endlessly subtle flux of interactions we call
the American political system.

It was bad enough when we had to know how to distinguish *United States v. E. C. Knight* from *Swift & Co. v.
United States*. How much worse to be required to specify
precisely how much influence the Court has over patent
policy, or even precisely what our patent policy is. With
increasing momentum in recent years the books and articles
and the new and amended courses in the college catalogues
have been moving us further toward that same state of
breathless questioning and wide-eyed uncertainty about the
Supreme Court that is to be found among other students
about the portions of politics they study. I hope, and fear,
that this book takes us another step along this path—
whether toward heaven or hell is another matter. In any
event I doubt that we shall shortly be able to say what
Adams finally did, that his "Education had ended. . . ."

This book is dedicated to someone who has had a great
deal to do with my education, but I must add a note of
regard for those to whom that education is currently entrusted, the faculty of the Division of Social Sciences of
the University of California, Irvine. I must acknowledge
the kindness of the editors of the *Law in Transition Quarterly* who have given me permission to reprint some materials that originally appeared there, and the even greater
kindness of my secretary, Miss Dorothy Donatone, who
managed to translate all of these materials from manuscript
to typescript. To my wife and to John Wilkins, a frequent
house guest, I owe formal acknowledgment of their quiet
support.

M. S.

Irvine, California
August, 1967

CONTENTS

THE
SUPREME
COURT
AND
ADMINISTRATIVE
AGENCIES

Introduction

             A book about the Supreme Court and administrative agencies must necessarily be directed at several audiences. One is composed of experienced students of law and courts already familiar with much of the basic data covered here. For them this book will, I hope, offer a fresh point of view and, perhaps more important, a compact treatment of the subject. Materials on the relations between the Court and the agencies are widely scattered through the literatures of federal jurisdiction, administrative law, constitutional law, civil procedure, and public administration—and through each of the substantive areas of law such as antitrust, patent, and labor that are of common concern to agencies and courts. Because there is a natural tendency to treat each of these subjects independently, students, practitioners, and scholars are likely to run across the Supreme Court here and there within the context of other problems. It is to be hoped that focusing directly on the Court and the agencies will make somewhat clearer the political relation between them which is frequently obscured by fragmentation into traditional legal categories.

A second audience consists of those who have come, or are coming, to their knowledge of the Supreme Court through the study of constitutional law. This book is designed to give them a brief introduction to some of the nonconstitutional work of the Supreme Court, work that claims a major share of the Court's time and attention and that has a major impact on areas of public policy which are only rarely or marginally touched by the Court's constitutional pronouncements. The point is not only that the student of Court *cum* constitution has an incomplete knowledge of the Court, but that, given the fact that the Court is only nine men who cannot rigorously segregate their various jobs into thought-tight mental compartments, it is likely that their non-constitutional efforts color their constitutional thinking. The student of constitutional law must, therefore, know something of the problems treated here not only to gain a fuller view of the court he is studying but also to increase his understanding of the process of constitutional judgment itself.

Finally, there is an audience that is relatively unfamiliar with legal materials of any kind, and is basically concerned not with law in particular but with politics and government in general. This book is very much designed for them, and the remainder of this introduction will introduce them to some of the vocabulary and phenomena that it is necessary to understand to pursue the subject.

JUDICIAL REVIEW

The place to begin, I suppose, is with the term "judicial review." Judicial review has both a general and a particular meaning. The particular meaning, and the one most often invoked in the United States, is the power to declare statutes and the regulations and acts of government officials and agencies unconstitutional. This power does affect the relations between the Supreme Court and administrative agencies when a citizen's dispute with an agency raises constitutional questions. But such occasions are rare. Much more frequently the dispute is about the meaning of the words in a statute or regulation or previous court opinion. Each party interprets the words to favor his position, and someone must determine which interpretation shall prevail. Judicial review in the more general sense is the power of a court to review the interpretations made by government agencies and officers (including other courts and judges) in order to determine what interpretation of the statute, regulation or previous ruling, and/or findings of fact supporting them shall be taken as binding upon the parties. In this sense judicial review is the power to declare an act or decision of a government official not unconstitutional but simply illegal—not beyond the totality of powers that government may legitimately exercise, but simply beyond the authorization of the statute or other legal rule by which he is supposed to conduct himself.

Judicial review in this sense is a very common and indeed almost inevitable phenomenon in modern society. Today there are a great number of government activities, and most of them are established and circumscribed by statute and governed in their details by various rules and regulations. Given the limitations of language to convey precise meanings, and the magnitudes of the interests affected by government activity defined by law, it is inevitable that many disputes arise over the meaning of various laws. Judicial review is a convenient device for resolving those disputes before they become conflicts that disrupt society.

Judicial review, however, is not simply the institutional acknowledgment of the failure of legal language to convey exact meaning. In many instances the legislature must pass laws of very general wording whose precise meaning in each particular circumstance must subsequently be filled in. Otherwise legislatures would get so bogged down in details that they could never complete their work. For instance, Congress may be concerned that there be enough trucklines in operation to insure prompt transportation services for shippers, but not so many as to lead to ruinous competition. It might attempt in a statute to specify, in precise detail, under exactly what circumstances a new truckline should be licensed. But to do so Congress would have to say things in a statute like

> Keokuck, Iowa, needs four trucklines unless that new superhighway that they have been talking about for ten years gets built. Then they will need five unless, of course, Uncle Charlie's Speedy Express gets rid of its Model T and gets two new tractors and vans. Then they will only need three as long as two freight trains a day also stop there.
> On the other hand Smithville, Tennessee, needs eight trucklines unless . . .

Congress does not, and probably could not, choose to write statutes like this which would require thousands of pages and millions of words describing every possible situation for every community. Instead it simply writes a statute which declares that it is the policy of Congress to maintain the health of the trucking industry and also to provide enough service to meet shippers' needs. Then, in the same statute, it empowers the Interstate Commerce Commission to license new trucklines when such action would be warranted by "public convenience and necessity." The I.C.C. then examines the situations in Keokuck and Smithville as they arise and tries to determine how many trucklines each really needs.

Statutory interpretation, then, not only entails discovering the correct meaning of certain words used in statutes, but filling in the details of statutes that provide only general statements of congressional intention. Judicial review in turn frequently, indeed typically, involves deciding whether the details filled in by agencies that administer statutes are consonant with the statute's general wording, or whether they are illegal in the sense of being out of harmony with the general provisions. The bulk of judicial review does not involve courts as superdictionaries carefully defining vague words, but rather judges as reasonably detached men seeking to discover whether the policies to be found in the agency-provided details are the policies that are or should be those to be found in the broad outlines of the statute.

REGULATORY AGENCIES

Having spoken of judicial review as basically the supervision of administrative-agency activities, we might next turn to the agencies themselves. The easiest of these to identify and categorize, and the ones that receive a large share of the Supreme Court's attention, are the independent regulatory commissions. There are ten such commissions ranging from the Civil Aeronautics Board to the Securities and Exchange Commission. These commissions exhibit quite complex and varying patterns of statutory subordination. Basically they operate under very broadly drawn statutes that assign them very great powers of supplementary lawmaking. For instance under a statute entitled the National Transportation Policy the Interstate Commerce Commission is directed to "provide for fair and impartial regulation of all modes of transportation subject to the provisions of this Act, so administered as to . . . preserve the inherent advantages of each. . . ." And it is told very little about exactly what these high-sounding phrases are to mean in detail.

The commissions have two basic means of filling in general statutes by their own detailed lawmaking. First they have what are often (and not particularly helpfully) referred to as quasi-judicial powers. They themselves make decisions whether or not to prosecute particular parties. (This is technically I suppose "quasi-administrative.") The prosecutions are then conducted before their own hearing officers and appeals are taken to their own commissioners. Thus each commission can make case law, just as courts do. The legal principles enunciated in the written opinions of hearing officers and commissions, and the general legal positions that can be discerned in the directions their decisions take, become part of the law.

Secondly, the commissions are usually empowered by the statutes establishing them and governing their activities to make rules and regulations spelling out in greater detail how the statutes will be applied in various classes of situations. This is frequently called their quasi-legislative power, and these rules and regulations become an important form of the statute. For instance, whereas the Securities Act prescribes in general the goal of honest and aboveboard stock sales based on full information to the customer, it is Securities and Exchange Commission regulations that specify exactly what procedures are to be followed and what information offered in connection with a new stock issue. These are not mere technical details, but questions of vital interest to corporations, brokers, and buyers.

One peculiar form of supplementary lawmaking power that is exercised by most commissions, and does not fall neatly into "quasi-judicial" or "quasi-legislative" pigeonholes, is the power to grant or withhold licenses frequently conferred upon them by statutes requiring such licenses for commercial undertakings. (The Supreme Court generally holds licensing to be quasi-legislative.) For instance, trucklines that offer their services to the public cannot operate without a license from the I.C.C. As we have already seen, the Commission is empowered to grant such a license when it suits the "public convenience and necessity," and refuse it otherwise. The written opinions of the I.C.C. in granting or withholding a license, and the general pattern of who gets and who doesn't get licenses under what circumstances, come to define what "convenience and necessity" mean. (There are infinite variations of the license power—for instance, the N.L.R.B.'s approval of the designation of a certain union as bargaining agent for certain workers.)

So far we have been speaking of commissions as operating under very broad mandates. Frequently, however, for one reason or another—indeed, sometimes because of unfavorable responses to earlier exercises of commission discretion—Congress will spell out in great detail some section of the statute the commission administers. Most commissions, therefore, operate within complex statutory schemes in some parts of which they are relatively free and in others relatively constricted. And, of course, every intermediate degree and combination of freedom and restriction upon the commissions can also be found. Within this complex of statutory provisions the commissions, by their words and actions in choosing whom to prosecute, whom to find legally wrong, whom to grant a license, and what regulations to issue, become an important part of the statutory scheme they administer.

LINE AGENCY

The other major form of administrative agency is the "line" agency of the executive branch. The independent regulatory commissions are independent in the sense that they are not subordinated to one of the great executive departments, like Treasury, State, Defense, or Agriculture. Instead they report directly to the President and Congress. The more typical administrative agency is a bureau within one of these major departments. Each is part of what we think of as the great Washington bureaucracy and each carries out a certain range of tasks assigned to it by statute and by its superiors. There are several hundred bureaus and comparable subunits within the executive branch. Nearly every one of these engages in some form of rule making. About 120 of them adjudicate private rights under various statutory provisions.[1] There is no particular advantage here in offering a systematic and exhaustive set of categories into which these agencies might be sorted. A few general introductory comments will suffice.

Many of the agencies issue regulations that become a part of the law. For instance, the Coast Guard, an agency

---

1. Krislov and Musolf, *The Politics of Regulation* 2 (1964)

of the Treasury Department, issues rules for small-boat operation under a general statute assigning to them the responsibility for safe coastal traffic. Internal Revenue Service rulings
are an integral and important part of the tax statutes. In
many instances the regulations are not commands directly
binding on individuals, but requirements that must be
met before federal funds will be expended. With the great
and ever-increasing dependence of other governmental units
on federal funds, however, such regulations are virtually
mandatory. For instance, no state can afford to ignore the
regulations of the Bureau of Public Roads in building a
highway that will be 90 per cent supported by federal funds.

Some line agencies also exercise a licensing power. The
Bureau of Land Management of the Department of Interior
grants licenses to stockmen to graze their animals on public
lands and in the process specifies how many of what kind
of animals may be grazed where, by whom, and for how long.
The Patent Office and the Copyright Office grant a peculiar
and very valuable kind of license to the recipients.

More important than licensing in the strictest sense may
be the planning powers of many agencies. Federal funds for
urban renewal for instance cannot be spent until the locality
has submitted a plan and had it approved by one of the
agencies of the Department of Housing and Urban Development. In the process of planning and approving or disap-
proving the plans of others, administrative agencies make
a great deal of public policy that could not have been fully
spelled out in a statute.

Another group of administrative agencies, largely but
not entirely clustered in the Justice Department, conduct
the business of law enforcement and prosecution. The antitrust policies of the United States, for instance, are set down
only very generally in statutes. The courts have always been
assigned the basic responsibility for filling out their meaning. But it is the Antitrust Division of the Justice Department that decides what firms to prosecute and sometimes
advises businessmen whether their proposed actions are likely
to violate the Sherman or Clayton Acts. Since the Division

has very limited funds, it can prosecute only a few suspected violators. Obviously what kinds of firms it chooses to prosecute and under what circumstances, and the general sequence and tempo of its prosecutions, are important factors in determining what the antitrust laws actually mean to the business community.

Perhaps special attention should also be called to the line agencies that must decide on a very large volume of claims by individual citizens. The Social Security Administration and the Veterans Administration pass upon millions of individual applications for pensions, loans, medical care, and other government services. Few of their decisions, however, reach the stage of judicial review. The Internal Revenue Service also considers millions of individual claims for deductions, exemptions, and the like, and many of their decisions are reviewed in the courts.

THE REVIEW PROCESS

It might be well then to turn briefly to the question of how administrative decisions get into courts for review before treating such complex questions as *Standing* more completely in Chapter 2. First, and probably most importantly, most administrative agencies cannot enforce their own decisions. In most instances where the agency decides that an individual or business firm must do something or refrain from doing something, it must go into a federal court and request the judge to issue an order to that effect if the individual or firm refuses to obey the agency voluntarily. Before issuing such an order the judge will consider the validity of the agency's decision in a trial in which the agency is one of the parties and the individual the other. Should the court find the agency decision valid and issue the appropriate order, disobedience to the order can be punished as contempt of court.

Sometimes, however, what an individual must do in order to get into court is refuse to conform his behavior to the agency's view of the law and wait for the agency to obtain a prosecution against him in a federal ˉcourt for breaking the federal law that the agency administers. In the course of this criminal prosecution the court must decide whether the agency's or the individual's interpretation of the law was valid. If the court finds the agency to be correct, then the individual is guilty and suffers fine or imprisonment. If the individual's interpretation of the law was correct, he is acquitted. This may seem a particularly harsh and risky way of getting one's legal rights tested in court, but the "test case" is one of the most traditional ways of defending individual rights. Its principal advantage is that it discourages dilatory, frivolous, and "legalistic" obstructions to agency actions because the individual will not risk prosecution unless he sincerely believes he has a relatively sound and justly legal position against the agency.

In certain instances, Congress has felt that it would be unfair to force the citizen to take the risk of losing a court case in order to get judicial review of agency actions affecting his rights. Under the Declaratory Judgment Act, in a few limited circumstances the citizen may request a court decision on the legality of his position vis-à-vis the agency before he is prosecuted.

There are, however, a great many circumstances in which agencies need not resort to courts at all, for either orders or prosecution, in order to enforce their decisions. For instance, if you must have a license from a government agency in order to conduct a business like a television station, and if the agency refuses you the license and grants the channel to someone else, then the agency need not go to court to effectuate its decision. It simply refuses to give you what you require. Similarly the Veterans Administration does not have to go to court to deny a veteran's pension claim. It simply doesn't send him his check the following month. In short, many agency decisions are self-enforcing.

In most instances where agency decisions are self-enforcing, however, Congress has provided for appeal to the courts in the statute establishing the agency or the program the agency is administering. Where the statute so provides, the individual may bring an action in the federal courts against the agency. If the court finds that the agency's decision was legally impermissible, it may either reverse the agency's decision and decide that the position taken by the individual was correct, or require the agency to decide the question again, using more equitable procedures or taking into account new facts or legal interpretations. Of course the second agency decision may also be appealed to the courts under the same statutory provision as the first.

Finally in any litigation before a court, the court must decide the relevant legal questions, and these questions often revolve around an agency action even when the agency is not a party to the litigation. When one manufacturer sues another for patent infringement, the court must decide whether the patent held by the first was valid, otherwise there can be no infringement. In doing so it in effect reviews the Patent Office's decision in issuing the patent. Many points of law and fact that are determined by an agency in one setting and at one time are "reviewed" by courts in quite a different time and setting in the course of performing their routine duties of deciding cases between individuals.

All of this has been a rather simple-minded introduction to the ground to be covered by a book on the Supreme Court and administrative agencies. It should now be possible to get to the heart of the matter. What is a court, and what, if anything, makes it desirable for courts to make all over again decisions that administrative agencies have already made?

1

Courts and Agencies

Because this book is about the Supreme Court
and administrative agencies, it would seem natural to begin
with some general comments about the functions of two of
the three great branches of American national government—
the executive and the judiciary—and then to proceed to the
constitutional relation between these branches. Yet such
a beginning would tend to freeze the mind into certain
long-taught clichés about three great branches facing one
another as brave champions, each behind the embattled
barrier of his constitutional position. Far more understanding can be obtained from viewing courts and administrative
agencies as coparticipants in the rather fluid, indeed often
amorphous, process of lawmaking as it is actually conducted
in American politics, without excessive concern for fitting
these fluid relationships into the frozen molds of traditional
constitutional doctrine.

In proposing to discuss the Supreme Court's relation

to administrative agencies in the context of the *lawmaking* process, I avoid not only the traditional constitutional setting of such discussions but also what for many will seem the crux of the problem. For is not judicial review of administrative action essentially designed as a check by courts on the way agencies *administer?* We shall see shortly that it is actually very difficult to distinguish lawmaking from administration. But even leaving this point aside, courts provide almost no effective check on what we typically think of as administration. When the Corps of Engineers builds a dam or when the Department of Health, Education, and Welfare prepares a research study on overcrowding in urban schools, there is almost no opportunity for judicial check on how efficiently, accurately, or fairly these agencies conduct their actual operations. The planning, research and development, spending and physical operation—hauling mail, printing money, storing grain—of administrative agencies are largely beyond the realm of judicial inspection. Indeed, most of the business of administrative agencies is conducted in the same way as the business of large corporations—by correspondence, consultations, interoffice memos, and telephone calls, all of which rarely rise to legal significance. A very large share of even those agency decisions that do directly affect the legal rights of individual citizens cannot be appealed to the courts, and an even larger share are not so appealed. Thus courts do not provide much of a check on the general operations of administrative agencies, the millions of decisions, actions, and physical operations that turn the words on the statute books into tuberculosis vaccines, hot meals for school children, rockets, national parks, and college dormitories.

Yet courts indubitably do something about administrative agencies. Roughly 20 per cent of the Supreme Court's written opinions concern administrative decisions. What then do the courts do, and what check if any do they provide? To answer these questions we must turn to an even simpler question, simpler in form at least: What is a court?

I begin with the premise that courts are political agencies.[1] It would take a very long book to adequately defend that premise alone, and I have other fields to cultivate. Here I must content myself with saying that those who do not accept the premise are relieved from reading any further. Yet they might stay with me awhile, because much of what follows, while assuming the premise, will I think go fairly far toward supporting it as well. For my purpose is to suggest in what ways courts might be differentiated from other agencies of government. In the course of running up one blind alley after another in the attempt to make such differentiations, it should become clear why the courts, to me at least, seem to be sufficiently similar to their brethren in government to be admitted to the political fraternity.

WHAT DO COURTS DO?

When we observe the persistence of a social institution we assume until convinced otherwise that it has some useful role in society that is in some sense peculiar to itself. Similarly, when we observe a segment of government that persists over time, we assume it to have some useful function of its own. We have long been familiar with the persistence of courts as an institution in Western societies and with court systems as a segment of Western governments.[2] It might, therefore, be assumed that courts performed tasks that are not being fully performed by other social institutions or segments of government. Is there indeed some special social or political utility in courts that warrants (or at least explains) their preservation as identifiable entities?

Having stated the problem in the broadest possible way, let me hasten to narrow it to a scope more suitable to a

---

1. See Shapiro, *Law and Politics in the Supreme Court* (1964)
2. Note that I deal not with law, but only with courts. While some readers may find this disjunction artificial, it is certainly true that law (at least in the sense of relatively general, relatively well-known, and relatively well-obeyed social norms) can and frequently has existed as an important social institution without courts, and that many areas of law today can be, and some are, administered without the use of courts.

political scientist and more appropriate to the scope of this book. Courts might have a wide variety of social functions relatively unrelated to their operations within government or their relations to other segments of government. For instance, their mere presence, quite aside from what they actually do, may provide symbolic assurance to a population that its regime seeks justice. Sending a man to confinement by means of a black robe in a walnut-paneled room may put him in a frame of mind more receptive to rehabilitation than if he had been sent to the same place by means of a blue suit in a civil-service green room. In short, courts may serve a wide range of symbolic functions in society that are peculiarly subtle and difficult to measure in isolation, and I do not wish to speculate on those functions here.

I do, however, wish to concern myself with what, if any, distinctive part the segment of government generally called courts plays vis-à-vis other segments of government. Put another way, it is not enough to say that the Pope and the President are both politicians. It is the task of students of politics to systematically describe both the similarities and differences between the various phenomena he labels political. In recent years considerable attention has been paid to describing the similarities between courts and other political agencies as part of the movement to overcome the view that courts are unique, apolitical bodies and to incorporate knowledge of them into the rest of what we know of the political process. Indeed much of the resistance to that movement surely comes from those who see in it an excessive preoccupation with making the judge look just like any other politician. More awareness of the differences between various kinds of politicians might make it clearer that in calling a judge a politician we do not necessarily mean that he kisses babies and worries about the voters back home. We proceed then to attempt to canvass the various ways in which we might be able to differentiate judges and courts from other political actors and agencies.

This attempt will be limited, however, to a consideration of appellate courts. The drawbacks of such a limitation are obvious. It may well be that the unique quality of courts lies at the trial level. We almost instinctively think of the "judicial function" in terms of judging between the legal positions of two parties under the existing law. It may be that the whole structure of appellate courts and appellate court lawmaking are only an incidental, and perhaps unfortunate, concomitant of this basic judicial function. I think this was basically the position of Learned Hand.[3] Nevertheless, so long as appellate courts exist, we are faced with the problem of differentiating them from other agencies.[4]

COURTS AS IDENTIFIABLE STRUCTURES

We begin our study of appellate courts with the fact that courts are courts and judges are judges; in short, that there is an identifiable government structure labeled courts and an identifiable office labeled judge.[5] If the proverbial man from Mars appeared among us and said, "Show me your courts," a few weeks or months of frantic travel would allow him to see a number of buildings, offices, chambers, filing cabinets, papers, and people addressed as judge, marshal, clerk, stenographer, or juryman. When the tour was over, we would say, "Now you have seen our courts."

Even at this level, however, it is not always easy to maintain a distinct boundary line between courts and other governmental structures. The French administrative courts present something of a puzzle for instance. They are, to be sure, called courts and follow procedures that have much in common with other courts, but it is not clear whether their leading personnel are considered by the French them-

---

3. See Hand, *The Bill of Rights* (1960)
4. It may be, of course, that the appellate court structure survives not because it has a peculiar utility of its own, but only because it is convenient or necessary to the trial court structure which may have such a utility.
5. The use of the word *structure* here should not be taken as indicating that I am engaging in the "structural-functional" analysis currently fashionable in political science. My use of the term is drawn from common usage, not from anthropology and sociology.

selves as judges or senior supervisory administrators in the bureaucratic chain of command. The American case is probably the clearest, with its traditions of not only an independent judiciary but a separate judicial branch of government. The English provide something of a halfway house with dual traditions of an independent judiciary and the judge as servant of the crown. Even the Americans have had a Court of Tax Appeals, an Interstate Commerce Court, and other "legislative courts"[6] that seem far less separable from other parts of government than our traditional courts.

Thus a kind of common-sense approach, which at bottom argues that everyone knows a court when he sees one, and that we all know that courts do exist, is a good starting point but does not solve all our problems. Not only do many agencies seem to fall on the borderline between courts and administrative offices and many government officials on the line between judge and administrative executive, but the courts do not even have a form of organization peculiar to themselves. For the internal structure of courts essentially follows the pyramidal form that we associate with Weberian bureaucracy.[7]

There are typically three or four levels of courts.[8] A dozen or so courts of the lowest level are supervised by one of the courts at the next higher level, and in turn a number of those courts are supervised by one at the next level until a single highest court controls all those below it—by virtue of controlling the courts immediately below it, which control the courts immediately below them, and so on. This is, of course, precisely the form taken by the typical administrative agency in business or government with its well-known organizational chart upon which the least important employees and units appear at the bottom with lines of command running upward and converging upon a single point,

---

6. See "Legislative and Constitutional Courts," 71 *Yale Law Journal* 979 (1962)

7. Weber, *The Theory of Social and Economic Organization* 329-30 (1947)

8. Jacob, *Justice in America* (1965). Mayers, *The American Legal System* (1964)

the agency head, the President of the corporation or the commanding general.

The correspondence of bureaucratic and judicial pyramids is hardly a coincidence, since the pyramidal form is adopted in both instances to insure that all subordinates will faithfully govern themselves by a consistent set of policies and norms established by their superiors. The organizational anatomy of courts is so similar to that of many other parts of government that we are certainly not going to be able to identify and separate courts by examination of governmental skeletons.

Moreover, even assuming that a separate and observable structure of courts does exist no matter how fuzzy some of the boundaries and how typical its skeleton, to what extent does this separable structure in fact perform some set of operations uniquely different from those performed by other governmental structures?

THE STATUTE MAKER

We might begin with a more careful statement of one of the major traditional propositions distinguishing courts from other agencies: Courts do not make law; they simply apply existing law to individual cases. As stated, this proposition is fundamentally incorrect. It may be possible to restate it, however, in the following form: Courts do not initiate major governmental programs. Such programs are initiated by a combination of legislative and executive branch agencies that we might call for the moment the "statute maker."

The reader should be aware, however, that the adoption of the term "statute maker" covers over a wide variety of difficulties and ambiguities. The word "statute" is used to distinguish generally between the major lawmaking symbolized by the appearance of new provisions on the statute books, which proclaim themselves to be laws, and the lawmaking done by courts and administrative agencies which proclaims itself to be secondary, supplementary, and interstitial and appears in the context of case decisions and agency rules. In a sense, using the term statute maker to distinguish one part of the national government from others may simply be assuming what is to be proved—that there is a difference between these two kinds of lawmaking. For the moment it is enough to say that there is a tangible difference between the passage of the Taft-Hartley Act and the decision that Pismo Packing Company did not violate Section 7 of that act when it discharged its employees for holding a clambake on company time. The term "statute maker" is meant to reflect this difference while admitting that at the margins no clear boundary exists between statute making and other forms of lawmaking.

The other major problem involved with an expression like "statute maker" is that it does not have a single, unified referent in the real political world. I do not mean Congress, and particularly I do not mean a Congress visualized as a unified democratic body expressing with one voice the command of a popular majority. There is a great debate over whether congressional processes actually reflect the public interest or the sentiment of the people, or whether they are bargained compromises between interest groups and the large number of committees, subcommittees, leadership structures, and individual leaders who fragment the powers of Congress.[9] There is no question, however, that most congressional statutes are at least partially a result of compromise and that even the congressional majorities that pass them are rarely of a single mind. This point will become particularly important later when we speak of statutory interpretation, where it is frequently impossible to discover "the intent" of a statute whose passage was participated in by many different subsets of Congress, each with a different intent from the rest.

Moreover, the "statute maker" is not even limited to

9. See Gross, *The Legislative Struggle* (1953); Matthews, *U.S. Senators and Their World* (1960); Peabody and Polsby, eds, *New Perspectives on the House of Representatives* (1963); Bauer, Pool, and Dexter, *American Business and Public Policy* (1963)

this very complex phenomenon we label Congress. The term includes certain actions of the President and the executive branch. Today Presidents are expected to have legislative programs, and the impetus behind most major legislation is Presidential. The President is thus a major aspect of the statute maker. Since executive agencies do most of the bill drafting today, the initial form of proposed statutes, and thus inevitably a major portion of their final thrust, is provided by the Department of Agriculture, the Treasury, and other executive departments, and more precisely by the partially autonomous bureaus that are their component parts.

The term "statute maker," then, is a simplifying device reflecting a complex reality. But it can be helpful in putting the work of courts and some aspects of the work of administrative agencies in a useful perspective.

COURTS AS SUBORDINATE
AND SUPPLEMENTARY LAWMAKERS

Certainly when we look at the nonconstitutional jurisdictions of the federal courts—that is, those areas in which the courts simply interpret and apply federal statutes whose constitutionality is in no way challenged—it is possible to say that the courts act in a subordinate and supplementary way to what is done by the statute maker. The law of taxation, labor, business regulation, agriculture, and the like is governed by major statutes whose passage were landmark events in the course of public policy. These major statutes have typically begun life as, or later become, major codes, great complexes of statutes which are periodically reviewed and modified by the statute maker. The codes tend to set the major direction of public policy. No court can independently declare as a matter of public policy that there shall be an income tax, or that electricity rates shall be regulated in the public interest, or that labor unions and management shall have available to them a special governmental mechanism to facilitate collective bargaining, yet the statute maker can, and has, done these things.

Courts, to be sure, do make a certain amount of policy within all these areas. As we shall see later, their decisions in certain instances may even constitute major amendments, deletions, or additions to an existing statutory scheme. Nevertheless such judicial policy making typically takes place within broad limits set by the statutes and can rarely move public policy more than a few degrees off the directional line set by the statute itself. Or perhaps it might be better to say that what the courts can do is to choose the exact degree of heading after the statute has specified the general compass direction. Courts make law—but federal courts, when not exercising their powers of judicial review of constitutionality, make supplementary law within the boundaries set by the statutes.

Nevertheless several considerations make it difficult to use this notion of supplementary or subordinate lawmaking as opposed to statute making as a final and definitive core around which to build a theory differentiating courts from other political agencies.

COURTS AS MAJOR POLICY MAKERS IN THE CONSTITUTIONAL SPHERE

In the first place, within the constitutional area courts may and frequently do initiate major governmental programs, even programs of a positive kind requiring significant public expenditure. For instance, if the Supreme Court had maintained the "separate but equal" rule in public education and then really enforced it, it would have compelled many Southern states to double and triple their educational budgets and embark on enormous programs of school building and teacher training. As it turned out, the Court initiated quite a different major program for the states by requiring integration. In the right to counsel cases, the Court has recently created an enormous new legal-assistance program in the sense that its decisions will force all jurisdictions to provide legal counsel to indigent accused persons at public expense or face the prospect of having all convictions of undefended indigents reversed on appeal.

There is, however, a double anomaly present in such positive programs. Judicial review of the constitutionality of statutes is a peculiarly American phenomenon[10] which even Americans admit to be remote from the normal or routine functions of courts. Secondly, while the Supreme Court may declare acts of Congress unconstitutional, the truly major positive programs initiated by the Court under the guise of review have always been those forced upon the states, not upon the central government. Such positive court programs thus may be viewed as peculiar to the operation of central courts in a federal system rather than a central feature of court behavior per se. Most nations have neither judicial review of constitutionality nor federal systems, yet they typically do have courts. In attempting to construct a general answer to the question, What is a court? we might then ignore certain American anomalies.

On the other hand, an American student may find the anomalies so overwhelming that any general theory which ignores them would be inapplicable to American politics. At the minimum it may certainly be said, however, that Americans have a peculiar talent for using a governmental institution for many different purposes, and that while the Supreme Court may play the part of major, positive-policy initiator in the constitutional federal segment of its jurisdiction, in another and far larger portion of its jurisdiction, and in one where it seems to act far more like other appellate courts both at home and abroad, it does seem to be a supplementary lawmaker.

THE COMMON LAW

A second difficulty with viewing courts as primarily supplementary lawmakers derives from our common-law heritage. Many portions of Anglo-American law were first created by series of court decisions, not statutes. The law

---

10. Although it has been copied, with degrees of success ranging from none to very partial by such nations as West Germany, Japan, and India.

then is to be found in the opinions not in any statute book. In such areas, statutes, even when they exist, frequently only codify previous judicial decisions or are themselves minor amendments or additions to the predominant body of case law. In those areas of law that are still essentially common law, the governing laws to which the courts subordinate themselves are laws of their own creation. In such areas the courts cannot be considered subordinates but are themselves the "statute maker."

It might be argued that common-law areas are now rapidly becoming a special case. Most segments of law in most Western jurisdictions are now governed by statute or code. The old common-law court hostility to statutes has largely dissipated and been replaced by considerable deference to the intent of the legislature even where codes are recent and are basically legislative summaries of the old case law. This is peculiarly true of the federal appellate courts where, with some curious exceptions to be noted shortly, common law today exists largely in the interstices of the statutes. The movement toward codes and model statutes is increasingly marked in the states as it is in Great Britain, where the common law nominally retains the greatest authority. Today it may actually be an anachronism, perpetuated by the historical orientation and case method of law-school instruction, to view common law—that is, judge-made case law—as the foundation or central portion of Anglo-American structures of law. Whatever their origins, most of the governing laws of British and American jurisdictions are today statutory.

Such a statement may seem to be contradicted by the vast amount of judicial lawmaking that can be observed today at both the state and federal level as well as in British courts. My point is, however, that by far the largest part of this lawmaking is not continued modification of a body of law created and maintained by previous judicial decisions, but is precisely that supplementary lawmaking elaborative of statutes that I am designating as the hallmark of courts. It may be difficult to isolate the point at which a legal system

changes from one in which the judges make the law, the
legislature codifies the decisions in statutes, and the judges
then go on to make more law until the legislature catches
up again, to one in which the legislature codifies past law
and the courts then go on to make subordinate law under
the codes until the legislature modifies them again in the
light of court experience. Indeed, the distinction between
the two systems may be, particularly in periods of transition
from one to another, a distinction without a difference. Yet
if like the man from Mars we were to take a simple-minded
view of American and British courts, surely today we would
find that most judges in most instances are subordinating
their creative legal tasks not basically to the historical evolution of the common law but to the wording and intent of
the last statute passed by the legislature. At the very minimum it surely must be conceded that where a legislature
chooses to pass a statute, the statute does today supersede the
previously existing common law and will be enforced and
interpreted by most courts in accordance with the intent of
the legislature. The old days of narrowly construing (or
ignoring) statutes in derogation of the common law are
pretty much gone.[11] And I think it must also be conceded
that there are increasingly few areas of law in which legislatures have not chosen to pass such statutes.

The alert reader will be conscious, I am afraid, that by
labeling the common-law activities of courts an anomaly,
along with their constitutional judicial review activities I
am piling up the anomalies, at least in the American instance, until they may overtop my view of courts as essentially
supplementary lawmakers. Certainly the continental reader
who sees very little judicial review, who probably blinds
himself to the common-law elements of his system, and who
above all perceives appellate judicial activity as the interpretation of statutes acknowledged by all to be the major

---

11. See Pound, "Common Law and Legislation," 21 *Harvard Law Review*
    383 (1908); Frankfurter, "Some Reflections on the Reading of Stat-
    utes," 47 *Columbia Law Review* 527 (1947)

enunciations of law, will be more at home with my views.
Nevertheless my common-law reader should check himself
to see how much of the judge-made law which looms so
large in his vision is today common law in the traditional
sense, and how much is in reality statutory interpretation.
The balance is surely tipping more and more toward the
latter.

It would be misleading to leave this aspect of the problem without briefly examining two areas of federal court
jurisdiction that seem to be peculiarly dominated by judge-
made law and thus appear to be major common law enclaves
in the increasingly statutory business of the courts. The first
is antitrust. The wording of the major antitrust statutes is
so vague, and the real-world problems to which the wording
must be applied so complex, that the Supreme Court has
actually made most of our antitrust law including the initiation of major changes in policy direction. It was the Court
which for many years decreed that antitrust policy would
not apply to the sector of the economy in which it was obviously most relevant—manufacturing—and it was the Court
that later did apply the law in that area. It was the Court
that decided that vertical as well as horizontal mergers fell
within the cognizance of the law. It was the Court that has
constantly defined and redefined such concepts as "control
of the market," "share of the market," and, most crucially,
"market" itself in order to shift federal policy to meet new
problems and new economic theories.

The second area of law requiring brief acknowledgment
is that of the federal law of labor contracts under the National Labor Relations Act. While the strike and other
labor-management tactics are regulated in some detail by
the statutes, the Act does not establish a substantive body
of law to govern the interpretation of the contracts entered
into by labor and management as a result of those tactics.
Since the Act does give the federal courts certain responsibilities in relation to the enforcement of such contracts, the
Supreme Court has read the intent of Congress as empower-
ing the federal courts to create, case by case, a federal com-

mon law of labor contracts.[12] The federal courts are now
proceeding to do so. In both of these areas, then, the major
rather than supplementary share of policy making seems to
lie with the courts.

Nevertheless both these areas do in fact correspond to
the notion of courts as supplementary lawmakers. There had
indeed been a common law of antitrust in the United States,
and the Sherman Act of 1890 was one of those acts which
incorporates the earlier common law into statute law. But
today it is surely the Sherman, Clayton, Federal Trade
Commission, and Wright-Patman Acts that are the primary
law of antitrust, not the common law of old. The courts
fill in the meaning of these broadly drawn ordinances by
statutory interpretation—that is, by subordinate lawmaking.
To be sure, on many occasions the interpretation may contribute more to the policy than the statutes themselves. This
is true, however, because the statute maker has deliberately
chosen to write his statute in broad language and thus
deliberately chosen to delegate large chunks of policy making
to the courts. The statute maker is free when he chooses to
withdraw the delegation or to correct its substantive results.

In the modern world the statute maker has increasingly
chosen to delegate large areas of policy making to administrative agencies. In some the delegation is so large and so un-
confined that it may be analytically correct but politically
unrealistic to view the administrator as subordinate. Antitrust represents an equivalent delegation on the judicial side.
As such it is less a survival of the old common-law power
of courts than a reflection of the modern trend of legislative
bodies to delegate their power. It is, moreover, a borderline
case compared to many of the delegations to administrators
that Congress has made in recent years. The courts are
surely far more subordinated to the antitrust statutes and
the statute maker's potential for changing them than is, for
example, the Defense Department in wielding the delegated
power of Congress to raise an army and a navy.

---

12. *United States v. Lincoln Mills,* 353 U.S. 448 (1957)

Similarly in the area of labor contracts it is precisely because the statute maker chooses not to make policy in this area and delegates this power to the courts that they exercise it. It is the terms of the statute that create the delegation and, viewed in the prospective of the entire statutory scheme of labor regulation, the law of contracts that the courts will develop is a very subordinate part.

To some of my readers much in the preceding paragraphs will seem legalistic and artificial. After all, where major policy initiative is vested by a statute in someone other than the statute maker, why call the "someone else" a subordinate lawmaker simply because he initially received his formal grant of power by statute? It may be true that the statute maker can change the terms of or withdraw the grant at some future time, but in many instances, at the moment and for practical purposes, the administrative or judicial delegate is the real source of the major policies.

THE STATUTE MAKER REVISITED

All of this is of course closely tied to our original rather artificial construction of the statute maker to which it is now necessary to return briefly. If we look closely at our predicated "statute maker" to whom the courts are subordinated, we may find that he does not exist, or rather that he encompasses all the Washington agencies, including the courts. An initial statute is likely to be the product of multiple influences. Each committee of Congress that handles the draft bill is likely to change it somewhat. The administrative agency which drafted it probably consulted various pressure groups during the drafting process, and the agency itself appears as a witness before the congressional committees, as do the groups. Individual congressmen seek to amend the bill in the interests of their constituents. The President or party leaders may intervene to protect interests of which individual congressmen seem insufficiently aware.

Even more important for our purposes, few statutes are

brand new. Most are revisions of past statutes. A major influence on such revisions will, of course, be the experience with the old statute. Administrative and judicial actions and attitudes toward the old statute naturally influence what the new one will be like. The courts merge with other government agencies. They lobby not by directly testifying to congressional committees but by their opinions and decisions in past cases under the old statute—opinions and decisions that may have more influence on Congress than the direct testimony of pressure groups and administrative agencies.

As with agencies too, the lawmaking of courts may move the statutory scheme in certain directions and statutory revision by Congress may frequently be simply another step in that direction no larger than the steps the courts have been taking. It is not always correct to see things in terms of "big" statutes followed by little court decisions. The policy changes effectuated by each may be about the same size, so that a chain of roughly equal links of court decision–legislative revision–court decision–legislative revision occurs in which no clear superior–subordinate relationship emerges between the "statute maker" and the courts.

It is too simple or too useless, however, to reduce all politics to intergroup and interagency struggle, or to stress the complex interactions of the legislative process and thus reduce all groups and agencies to equal and homogeneous units whose only characteristic is participation in the struggle. It is true that in the infinite variety of politics we can find instances in which the action of courts in interpreting and filling in a statute have had policy consequences far greater than those of the statute itself. Similarly, there have certainly been times when past judicial practice under a statute has been a major influence on the subsequent amendment of that statute, and sometimes it has been clear that the courts have consciously shaped their practice to achieve such amendment. Nevertheless, if we agglomerate the law proposing activities of the Executive and the law-passing activities of Congress on the one hand and similarly agglomerate the influence of courts in the process of lawmaking on the other, we must find that the executive-congressional axis makes the major governing statutes, whereas the total influence of the courts is comparable to that of a pressure group or single administrative agency influencing the statute maker at some points but not at others, and with varying degrees of success.

In short, in the context of group politics, the courts or a court—particularly the Supreme Court—may be viewed as one agency among many executive bureaus, legislative committees, regulatory agencies, and trade associations that participate in the "legislative struggle."[13] From a broader view, however, the courts tend generally to participate in this struggle in the role of subordinate lawmaker serving under the statute maker.

Perhaps the point will be clearer if put still another way. Every group and agency in Washington participates in legislation. Therefore each is in a sense part of the "statute maker." "Statute maker" is thus an artificial construct designating the sum total of the influences and procedures that culminate in major policy decisions. While each political actor is, at least in some of his behavior, a part of the statute maker, it is also possible to distinguish the various actors by distinguishing between the general relation of each to the statute maker as a whole. The House Committee on Agriculture and the Association of American Railroads are both political actors, both participate in statute making, but they certainly have far different relations to the statute-making process taken as a whole. The courts participate in the statute-making process and influence other participants. They can be distinguished from other participants in that they participate through their subordinate role in interpreting existing statutes. That they do participate sometimes marginally and sometimes quite centrally in making major policy decisions enunciated in statutes does not change the fact that they participate through their role of interpreting the earlier products of the statute maker.

---

13. See Gross, *op. cit. supra* note 9

LARGE AND SMALL-STEP CHANGES

Even maintaining the conceptual scheme of statute maker and subordinate lawmaker, however, it is possible to seriously challenge the distinction between major policy change supposedly left to the statute maker and marginal change in the keeping of subordinate lawmakers like courts. Later we will have occasion to examine at length the "incremental" decision-making technique shared by all public policy makers. But it must be admitted at this point that statutes rarely spring from the blue. New statutes are likely to represent relatively small changes in older statutes, sometimes changes no larger than those made by the courts in the process of statutory interpretation. Thus the distinction between statute maker and court is again likely to crumble. On the other hand, statutes can and sometimes do make major changes of which courts, again ignoring their constitutional decisions, are incapable. The Wagner Act (first National Labor Relations Act) and the Unemployment Act of 1946 are pioneering pieces of legislation setting up new policies and new agencies that no court could create by statutory interpretation. While most statute making is likely to be incremental, it can fairly be said that the statute maker can and sometimes does take longer steps than the courts can and do take.

This proposition in turn can help rid us of the anomaly that common law seemed to present in our argument that courts are essentially subordinate lawmakers. Even if the courts can use the processes of common law to create certain major governmental programs, the traditions of the common law require that they do so by very small and gradual steps, each deviating as little as possible from the previous state of the law. I am aware that the history of the common law contains some very big steps, but were these not themselves considered anomalies in the common law? And did they not largely cease to occur when we became accustomed to taking our big legal steps by statute? Indeed, did they not occur in the first place because the common-law system was so antagonistic to statutes that rather than leave an opening for them by leaving the need for major changes unsatisfied, it surreptitiously violated its own rules and took the big steps itself?

While we are discussing the relative amount of positive initiative courts and statute makers may take, it will be convenient to take up another phenomenon that is sometimes used to distinguish courts from legislatures. It is frequently said that the statute maker has the final say, that, after all, courts only interpret to the litigants the words the statute maker uses and thus perform only an intermediate task. This is rather like the old quarrels about who was sovereign—who had "the last word."[14] Such arguments are largely metaphysical rather than empirical, for they deal with potentials rather than realities. The sovereign may potentially have the last word on all political questions within a society. But since no single individual or governmental unit has the time or energy to deal at all with more than a fraction of the policy issues raised in any society, it matters not so much who theoretically would have the last word if all questions reached him, as who actually has the effective word on questions that in fact do reach him—and what questions in fact reach whom.

It is logically true that the statute maker potentially has the last word, since courts only interpret the words of a statute. If the statute maker does not like the interpretation, he may amend the statute to correct the court's interpretation and the court is bound to accept this new instruction. However, what in fact happens is a constant stream of statutes followed by court interpretations followed by amendments to alter those interpretations, followed by interpretations of the amendments followed by amendments in reaction to those interpretations. Over time during this process both the courts and the statute maker keep changing their minds as to what they really want the statute to mean, so that it

---

14. See Friedrich, *Constitutional Government and Democracy* 18, 190, 224, 260 (1941)

is often impossible to tell who is winning. A legislature that passes an amendment confirming a past court interpretation may be announcing its new independent judgment, not acquiescing to a court which may at the very moment be attempting to overthrow its own past interpretation. In this spiral of statute–interpretation–amendment no one has the final word. About all that can be said is that once the statute maker has specifically said that a certain interpretation of its intent by the courts is absolutely wrong, the courts are debarred from using that specific interpretation again, although they are free to resort to any one of the hundreds of other interpretations of the statutory words available to fertile minds trained in the dialectical skills of the law.

This returns us, however, to our main point that courts are, after all, limited to picking among at least moderately plausible alternative interpretations of the statutes passed by the statute maker. Therefore they are likely to be taking the smaller, more intermediate steps in between the strides of the statute. My point is not logical but empirical. Observation of actual court behavior will show that courts on the whole make smaller changes in policy than the statute makers and initiate far fewer new directions in governmental activity.

Nevertheless it would be impossible at this point to build a precise and systematic set of distinctions between courts and "statute maker" on the basis of policy initiative. We are concerned here only with the comparative length of decision-making steps among decision makers all of whom act incrementally. At most we are dealing in differences of degree, and we are doing so without any system of measuring the length of steps. There is currently no way of saying that courts on the average take 12-inch policy steps and statute makers 24-inch.

Indeed the legislative steps taken by the statute maker are usually much shorter than they might appear to a superficial observer. We have already noted that the bulk of statutory activity consists of minor amendments to previous statutes and that even major statutes usually constitute extensions of existing legislation. Perhaps even more important most legislative proposals, and particularly major ones, have been considered over many sessions of Congress and through many consultations between drafters in the executive branch. Typically they have been repeatedly modified before being enacted so that there is an internal process of short-step incremental decisions which has brought the statute maker from the old state of the law to the new. The statute books record only the occasional surfacing of the subterranean stream and leave the impression of a series of isolated and distant incidents where there is really a continuous flow of new but small change decisions. Conversely the law reports, since they note every decision, and every one as equal to every other, tend to exaggerate the impression of continuous flow and submerge really major decisions in the wash of precedent. Thus not only are we dealing with degrees of policy initiation for which we have no standard system of measures, but must confess that the differences between courts and statute maker we are trying to measure are not as great as they often superficially appear.

THE EXPECTATION OF JUDICIAL SUBORDINATION

The difference is there, however. Perhaps it is easiest to see at the level of expectations or role constraints. There is a general expectation, shared by the public, other politicians and the judges, that *any given judicial decision should be as close to the existing state of the law as circumstances will permit*. Admittedly "as circumstances will permit" is a vague phrase. What is really involved are two sets of expectations— one that judges will maintain the existing state of the law, the other that they will do substantial justice to the parties. These two expectations are at least potentially conflicting, and judicial behavior must be directed toward reconciling them.

If we consider the structure of the law and the social

structure to which it is to be applied, it is possible to give a somewhat more precise formulation of the expectation that judicial decisions shall whenever possible reflect the existing state of the law. Where the structure of the law is relatively clear, and when its application to existing circumstances yields acceptable but not optimal results, the judge should not change the law. This is in contradistinction to the statute maker who is expected to seek actively best (or at least better) results. In reality, of course, the statute maker frequently settles not for the best but for the best he can get the votes for, but this is only one way of defining the best. The statute maker is expected to make whatever law is necessary to achieve the public interest. The judge is expected to accept the existing state of the law when it is clear, unless it is positively unsatisfactory.

Where the structure of the law is clear and its application to existing circumstances is unsatisfactory, the judge is expected to change the law only to the extent necessary to achieve minimally acceptable results. Where a court is faced with two equally small changes one of which will yield far better results than the other, it is free to go for the best result it can get on the smallest change. The statute maker, however, is left to make the further and more drastic changes necessary to an optimal solution. Where the structure of the law is not relatively clear, complete, or precise, or is self-contradictory, courts are expected to make only that amount of law necessary to the efficient administration of the statute, and in doing so they are expected to choose the direction of alteration that the statute maker would have desired. Of course where the desires of the statute maker are not clear—and often they are not—the judge must willy-nilly (and is expected to) choose his own direction. The more unclear, incomplete, or contradictory the statutes, and the more unsatisfactory the social results of its application, the larger steps the court may take.

This emphasis on expectations will help clear up the anomaly that the courts' constitutional jurisdiction seemed to create when we began with the notion of courts as supplementary lawmakers. Constitutional judicial review exists because the Constitution is believed to be a statute written by a primary statute maker—in this instance "We the people." It is a peculiarly unclear, incomplete, and imprecise statute. Bearing this in mind, I think it can be shown that the courts in their constitutional jurisdiction continue to act as supplementary, small-step lawmakers bound by the expectation of minimal activity. But the statute they are interpreting is precisely the sort that allows, and is supposed to allow, a supplementary lawmaker the greatest range of discretion. Moreover, the nature of the Constitution as a "higher law" tends to elevate each of the distinctive features of a supplementary lawmaker under it at least one level above the same phenomenon in the context of routine statutory interpretation.

Thus while on an absolute scale the lawmaking accompanying constitutional judicial review may be of a magnitude equaling or exceeding much congressional-executive statute making, it is still governed by the expectation that the judges' decision is not an independent one, but one making more precise the wording of the existing "statute." Even within the constitutional setting, courts may from time to time appear to take very long steps, but such steps are permitted by the extremely general wording of the statute they are expected to fill out. It should also be noted that aside from the national and state supreme courts, appellate courts are likely to be overly cautious in introducing constitutional change, and that even the supreme courts are expected to make only the minimal constitutional changes necessary to acceptable results. Moreover, as we have already noted, those areas in which even the Supreme Court of the United States has taken the biggest steps on an absolute scale—reapportionment and segregation—are essentially matters of federalism. We should not allow the double anomaly that some courts in one area act as supplementers of a peculiarly elevated and vague statute, and that the Supreme Court of the United States has been assigned a peculiar role in coordinating and disciplining a federal system, to obscure the fundamental expectations of minimal changes that exist in relation to appellate court decision making in general and even within the field of constitutional interpretation.

The courts may not only continue to be viewed in terms of expectations demanding supplemental, relatively small-step lawmaking in the constitutional sphere but in the common-law sphere as well. For even the common-law judge is constrained by the expectation that he will undertake only that minimal change in the existing law necessitated by its vagueness, self-contradiction, or unworkability in the face of changing social and economic conditions. Surely this is a necessary and sufficient definition of the rule of *stare decisis* in common law. While there may be no statute maker, each court is supposed to act as a supplementary lawmaker to those which have gone before.

EXPECTATIONS AND JUDICIAL BEHAVIOR

The crucial question is whether these professional and public expectations about judicial behavior are reflected in the behavior itself. It is sometimes argued that the very function of a judicial opinion is to satisfy these expectations of minimum change while leaving the judge free in his decision—i.e., in decreeing which party wins and which loses—to pursue whatever policies he pleases, whether or not they deviate sharply from past practice. Opinions frequently do seek to minimize or camouflage judicial lawmaking. But this very fact tends to confirm the effect of expectations on behavior. First of all, it would be the most naïve psychology to believe that the judicial profession, paying constant, written, and public obeisance to the propriety of small-step judicial lawmaking, could divorce this central orthodoxy from its actual conduct. Secondly, politicians are generally punished if their actions deviate sharply from popular expectations and even more importantly from the expectations of the politicians with whom they are interdependent. A Supreme Court, for instance, which repeatedly and grossly violated the expectation of Congress that the Court seeks to satisfy the legislative will in interpreting statutes would be faced with a constant stream of legislative corrections to past judicial decisions. These corrections would reduce the Court's prestige, and the increased watchfulness of Congress resulting from such violation of expectations would materially reduce the freedom of maneuver which the Court now enjoys because of the relative inattention of Congress.

Moreover, a sharp distinction between opinion and decision is misleading. There are many theories about the nature and function of judicial opinions ranging from the camouflage notion at one extreme to the pretense at the other that a written opinion is a true and literal representation of the thought processes through which a judge passes in reaching his decision. Somewhere in between is the position that a judicial opinion is, or ought to be, the presentation of logically satisfying reasons for the decision, no matter what the judge's actual, conscious, and subconscious reasons for deciding as he did. There is obviously some truth in each of these theories, but they neglect what is actually the most vital function of an appellate opinion—the communication to others of what the law is. The lawmaking that appellate courts do is not embodied in who wins but in the statement of what the law is to be found in their opinions. For appellate courts intervene only sporadically in the affairs of private citizens and government agencies. If the same appellate court made every final decision on every matter that could potentially come before it, then what that court said would make no difference. It would set the real workings of the law by its patterns of actual reward and punishment of all the litigants. Since the judge would decide in every instance who won and who lost, his decisions would quite literally be the law. But courts as a whole (and more particularly any given court) decide only an infinitesimal number of the potential problems arising under a given statute. For this reason, if they are to make law they must communicate their legal propositions to those who apply the law day-by-day—to the private individuals and government agencies con-

cerned. The statute maker conveys his law by the words of his
statute, the court conveys its law by the words of its opinions.
Thus a court which by its language constantly subordinates
its lawmaking to the statute in order to satisfy expectations
will be satisfying those expectations because the law it conveys by that language will be subordinate, small-step law.
There will be occasions when courts can manage to find
small-step subordinate language to convey large-step non-
subordinate new law, but such occasions are likely to be
exceptions to the general run of court lawmaking. It would
take more double-think and far more efficiency of communication than we currently possess to allow the judges to
constantly say to others that they are making small and subordinate additions to the law while somehow actually com-
municating to them an entirely different quantitative and
qualitative level of new law.

Some of what I have said here may appear, at least
superficially, to be undercut by the recent attitudinal literature that indicates that certain justices of the Supreme Court
more or less consistently vote prolabor or probusiness or
progovernment no matter what the cases or what the Court's
opinions look like. The most ambitious and informative of
these works, Professor Schubert's *The Judicial Mind* indicates that the court is divided into subgroups of justices
characterized by quite stable political and economic attitudes
and ideologies, that these attitudes and ideologies largely determine the votes of the justices, and that, therefore, the legal
outcomes produced by the Court are a function of the relative
voting strength at any given moment in the Court's history
of the various attitudinal groups. Attitudinal studies are
basically designed to answer the question "to what extent
are . . . [men's] . . . public acts influenced by their personal
beliefs?"[15] Professor Schubert concludes that the public act
of a justice in casting his vote is highly correlated with his
personal beliefs.

Judicial opinions are not typically confessions of the
judges' personal beliefs but generally purport to be state-

15. Schubert, *The Judicial Mind*, 15 (1965)

ments of what the law and its attendant reasoning require.
It might appear, therefore, that opinions are irrelevant to
judicial behavior, and if opinions are the vehicle and response to outside expectations then those expectations too
may be irrelevant to behavior. Here again it must be repeated that the opinions themselves, not who won or lost,
are the crucial form of political behavior by the appellate
courts, since it is the opinions which provide the constraining
directions to the public and private decision makers who determine the 99 per cent of conduct that never reaches the
courts.

ATTITUDES AND DOCTRINE

Aside from this, and probably more important, attitudinal studies may appear to yield consistently prolabor and
probusiness attitudes on the part of a given judge, or even
majority of judges, and yet the overall impact of the Court
may not be simply a function of the prolabor decisions of
such a majority but may basically be a reflection of the state
of the doctrine embodied in the previous cases.

Let me offer a simple illustration. Let us say that at a
given point in time the doctrine of a court is that zoning
laws are sometimes unconstitutional, and that it in fact declares about half the zoning laws it reviews unconstitutional.
Such a doctrine will invite a wide range of business claims
that various zoning laws are unconstitutional. A simple chart
may be in order. The vertical axis represents the whole range
of claims of unconstitutionality of a zoning ordinance that
businessmen might make with the most plausible claims at
the top and least plausible at the bottom.

The horizontal axis represents time. Line A is the court's
doctrinal position that some zoning ordinances are unconstitutional and others are constitutional. The arc crossing
the line represents the distribution of judges on a multi-
judge court toward the doctrine. The dot represents the most
conservative judge. On all cases that arise he votes probusi-

ness. In other words, the most probusiness judge will vote
for business even on the least plausible business claim of
zoning unconstitutionality, while the most antibusiness judge
will vote against business even when its constitutional claims
are most plausible.

The concept of plausibility is the crucial one here.
Given the existing state of the doctrine (A), only cases fairly
close to A will ever get to the court. Where, for instance,
the businessman is confronted with a narrowly drawn, fairly
administered zoning law that meets all of the constitutional
hurdles that the Court has previously established, about all
he can do is argue that no zoning laws are constitutional—i.e.,
that zoning laws are unconstitutional per se. His doctrinal
stance is a point X. Given the doctrinal stance of the court,
which is that zoning laws are not per se unconstitutional, the

Chart

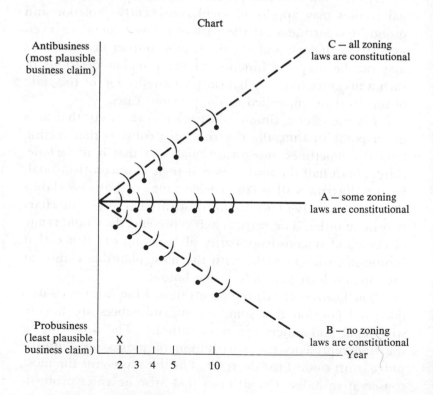

Antibusiness   C — all zoning
(most plausible   laws are constitutional
business claim)

                                                      A — some zoning
                                                      laws are constitutional

Probusiness   B — no zoning
(least plausible   laws are constitutional
business claim)   X   Year

                  2 3 4 5   10

businessman's claim is so implausible that it will never reach an appellate court. It probably will never reach a trial court, since he will be advised by counsel against pressing it. Thus the probusiness justice, even if we were to make the simplistic assumption that he will always vote probusiness no matter what, will not be able to favor the claim at X.

We can visualize the range of attitudes of the justices of a given Court sweeping out on both sides of the general line of doctrine then in play. That doctrinal line determines the plausibility of claims, and the attitude of an individual justice may determine the decision (who wins) but only in cases presenting plausible claims. The Court's written opinions, following expectations about *stare decisis,* will seek to minimize the distance between the collective decision in the given case (the point on the arc where the collective judicial attitude falls) and the decision demanded by the previously established doctrine (line A). If all the justices on the court, or a consistent majority, are probusiness, the line of doctrine may gradually drift down toward the entirely probusiness position that all zoning laws are unconstitutional (line B). If the justices are antibusiness the doctrinal line may move up to A. Of course many things besides judicial attitudes—ranging from public opinion to new statutes—may also determine the drift of the doctrinal line. For instance, in the face of universal public acceptance of zoning laws, no court, no matter how probusiness could drift back to line B.

From my point of view at the moment, however, what is most important is that our probusiness justice, represented on the diagram by the dot, has consistently voted probusiness in every case; yet depending on which way the line of doctrine has moved, he will be voting far more or far less probusiness. In year five, if doctrine has moved along line C, he will only be voting to give legal effect to about one-third of the potential probusiness zoning claims, for the other two-thirds are not plausible enough to reach the Court. If the doctrine had stayed on A, he would be attempting to give legal effect to slightly over half the claims; if it had moved to B, to over two-thirds.

This phenomenon shows how attitudinal analysis may indicate that some justices' voting behavior in future cases can be predicted with a high degree of certainty on the basis of a single attitude dimension (probusiness, procivil liberties), yet doctrinal analysis will still be necessary in order to predict and understand how and why the Court is satisfying some segments of the universe of potential business or civil rights claims in the society and not others.

Although the studies showing that some or most justices vote on the basis of rather fixed attitudes toward business or civil rights, rather than as a result of autonomous legal reasoning, may superficially suggest that who wins has nothing to do with what doctrines are pronounced, this is not actually true. For the state of the past law (statutes, doctrines, and so forth) determines in what kinds of cases and on what range of claims the justices will be able to exercise their attitudes by deviating slightly in one way or the other from the past law.

This is of course a somewhat oversimplified explanation. The doctrinal lines should probably not be represented by thin lines, but by shaded bars, inasmuch as the main doctrine is rarely so clear and precise as a single line suggests. Moreover two lines of quite contradictory precedent may exist at once (diagrams I, II, and III) and, depending on the judge's attitude, he may choose one line or the other. Or a single line may not move neatly in one direction but may wander as conditions, court personnel, and attitudes change (diagram IV). Nevertheless the main point remains the same. Our probusiness justice is never going to get to vote for the extreme probusiness claims represented by points X, no matter how much he wants to, because such claims are never plausible enough in terms of the proclaimed doctrine to ever reach the court.[16]

---

16. To simplify, I have assumed a judge who is absolutely probusiness. As Glendon Schubert has recently pointed out, attitude studies that show a consistently probusiness attitude on the part of a given judge actually only mean that in comparison to his fellow judges *and within the range of claims that reach the Court*, the judge votes for business with marked frequency. Thus, in fact, my case is even stronger than

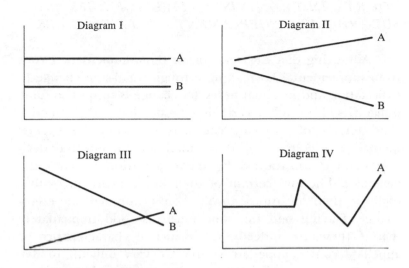

Thus, without denying the importance of judicial attitudes on the outcomes of particular cases, or on the long-run doctrinal drift of the Court, the overall impact of the Supreme Court on other political agencies is largely a matter of the verbal propositions of the law it advances rather than the attitudinal pattern of judges in individual cases. For those propositions not only become part of the governing law that other agencies must at the very least appear to obey, but also determine what kinds of claims the justices themselves will subject to their attitudes in the future. Therefore, expectations about what judges are to do cannot be thwarted by a smoke screen of opinions to cover actual voting. What judges say they are doing in opinions always reflects in large part what they are actually doing, and this is true whether or not the judges wish it to be so.

I have made it, for in fact the judicial attitudes measured are partially a function of the claims handled and thereby of the existing state of the doctrine. To avoid further misunderstanding in an area where too much already exists, let me point out that those pursuing attitudinal studies have not claimed that the only significant aspect of judicial behavior was judicial attitudes.

COURTS AND ADMINISTRATIVE AGENCIES AS SUBORDINATE, SUPPLEMENTARY LAWMAKERS

Admitting that each portion of the argument that runs from supplemental lawmaking through small-step change to expectation and minimal necessary change is subject to some difficulties, I would nevertheless argue that the distinctive characteristic of appellate courts is that they are supplemental lawmakers engaged in small-step incremental decision making constrained by the expectation of both the general public and certain of their key constituencies that each of their decisions involve only minimal, necessary change. Having said this, one must also add immediately that if these are indeed the distinctive characteristics of appellate courts, appellate courts are very difficult to distinguish from the administrative bureaucracy. My position in the remainder of this book will be that the courts and the administrative bureaucracy ought to be considered as two alternative and parallel structures for the administration of government programs.

We have already noted that courts and bureaucracies share a Weberian hierarchical structure. It should also be clear that both are essentially "legal" institutions where the programs to be carried out and the internal relations of the operators are largely defined by statute and supplementary legal regulations such as rules of procedure and civil-service regulations. In both, lower levels can to a certain extent resist higher, and in both the principal sanctions wielded by superiors are not formal disciplinary ones but the reversal of the decisions made or policies adopted by the subordinate. Both tend to operate with a high respect for precedent and written, permanent records. Both tend to develop their own conventional languages so that both place a particularly high premium on the mastery of that language which, while remaining somewhat strange to the public, is supposed to render internal agency communication, and particularly record keeping, more precise.

These, however, are superficial or, rather, secondary similarities which reflect at least one broad identity of function in the two structures. For one basic function of both bureaucracies and appellate courts is to accept general statutes and fill them in with sufficient supplementary and explanatory rules to make them adequate guides to the myriad specific decisions in the individual cases which the "administration" of law requires. Put another way, both the bureaucracy and the appellate courts exist to provide an intermediate level of specificity to which the operating decision makers can look instead of referring directly and unaided to the general statute. For to refer directly to the statute would lead not only to considerable inconsistency but also to great decisional inefficiency as each line decision maker had to work out in each instance the whole chain of reasoning from general command to specific case. This shared judicial and bureaucratic function is clearest in the independent regulatory commissions where all the quasi-this and quasi-that really boils down to the point that either a court structure or an executive agency could do the same job.

Moreover, in doing this job bureaucrats operate just as courts do as supplemental, small-step lawmakers governed by the expectation that they will make only those changes in the statutes necessitated by the internal inadequacy of the statute or its disutility under changing circumstances. Both judges and administrators are much concerned with statutory intent. There is, of course, much talk of administrative discretion, but here again the discretion of the judge and that of the administrator are very much alike. For both, the statute maker fixes the degree of discretion by the precision of the statute. The more precise the statute the less the discretion. For both, the greatest discretion is usually assigned in the areas of greatest technical detail where the agency or court have the most expertise. The remaining enclaves of common law in our now essentially statutory legal system, which seemed at first to contradict the supplementary lawmaking proposition, are really to be understood in this way. They are actually areas in which the statute maker has assigned the court broad discretion to make supplementary laws because the areas require complex and detailed regulation. Typically they are areas like commercial and tort law in which the courts have had very long and successful experience and are more knowledgeable than any other agency of government. Thus common-law remainders are simply the judicial equivalent of the areas of administrative discretion granted to administrative agencies on the basis of the agency's special expertise.

Courts do not have the large research staffs that administrative agencies do. But this is only a superficial difference. Both courts and administrative agencies do and are expected to base their decisions on a proper appreciation of the facts. The courts have developed a whole set of special devices for gaining the facts which are the judicial equivalent of the administrative agency's staff. Among the first of these was the jury which was initially composed of those citizens who knew most about the events at issue. Basically the adversary proceeding is the judicial equivalent of staff, for it is designed to insure that the court gets the product not of one staff but of two, each anxious to present facts or versions of the facts ignored by the other.

Most of the litigants before federal courts who are entangled with federal administrative agencies are either major corporations, units of state government, or labor unions. These litigants usually have relatively extensive staff resources sometimes backed up by the further staffs of various pressure groups who may have an interest in the matter. Thus questions of fact to be decided by courts tend to involve the combined, albeit often conflicting, product of research by two or more large technical staffs—one the government agency's, the other that of its opponent. A glance at the statistic- and chart-laden briefs and records of testimony in antitrust or copyright infringement cases will surely indicate that the bar has been fulfilling this staff role with perhaps excessive zeal.

ADMINISTRATIVE AGENCIES AS PROGRAM OPERATORS

All this is not to argue that administrative agencies are identical to courts. Both the courts and agencies engage in supplementary lawmaking as a necessary intermediate step between the statute and the determination of individual rights and duties under the statute, but the agencies also operate positive programs like building dams and fighting forest fires. Basically, however, this is only to say that while courts and administrative agencies operate with striking similarity within the functional areas they have in common, the agencies also operate in functional areas different from and additional to those they share with the courts.

Nevertheless we have long since become accustomed to the fact that in politics the whole is more than or at least different from the sum of its parts. If the courts and administrative agencies share a common function (and even a basically common mode of operation within that function), but the agencies also have an additional function, it is probable that the two functions of the agency interact in such a way as to affect both. Even the shared function will be performed somewhat differently by an agency than by a court. This is clearest if we now break down our artificial statute maker into its component parts of Congress, President, and bureaucracy. (Or cabinet–parliament and bureaucracy. What I am about to say seems to me to apply generally to parliamentary governments as well.) Since the agencies operate positive programs, they are constantly in need of both authorizing legislation to undertake new programs and appropriations to operate existing or newly authorized ones. Thus they are heavily dependent on the Congress. Moreover, as operators they are subordinated to the President through the process of budgetary discipline within the executive branch. Thus because of their dependence on the cooperation of others in their positive operating programs, administrative agencies are likely to be more thoroughly disciplined by the statute maker than are the courts. It is basically this distinction between the needs and dependencies of positive program operators and courts that gives the notion of an "independent" judiciary real political bite.

THE INDEPENDENCE OF COURTS AND AGENCIES

Yet this distinction between courts and agencies should not be overemphasized. American administrative agencies at least are famous for their ability to play President and Congress off against one another and the ease with which they form agency–congressional committee–pressure-group alliances to protect themselves from outside meddling in their special bailiwicks. It is not always clear whether the agency is dependent on the statute maker or vice versa. More accurately, since the agency is an important component of statute making, the other components are dependent on it as well as it on them. This reciprocity mitigates but does not eliminate agency dependence on the statute maker viewed as a whole.

Both federal judges and agency officials are appointed by the President. While those officials of cabinet and subcabinet rank change with each new President, and indeed even more rapidly, bureau chiefs tend to remain indefinitely. Since the bureaus are in most instances the real working units of the executive branch, in effect both judges and their bureaucratic counterparts serve indefinitely. The average bureau chief lasts just about as long as the average federal judge. Agency officers are not usually concerned with promotion outside their own bureaus, and promotion within the bureau is not much influenced by the Chief Executive or Congress so that both judge and bureau man are relatively independent of the statute maker in terms of career. It should also be noted that judges of the federal district and circuit courts are totally dependent on President and Congress for "promotion" to the next higher court—much more dependent than most agency employees are in the matter of their promotions, although this may not influence judicial behavior greatly. (Note that in the judicial career system of Roman law countries, promotion within the lower ranks is largely an agency matter relatively free from Parliament–Cabinet control. Only at the highest ranks is there likely to be cabinet control similar to that in the United States.) On the other hand, subordinate agency employees are subject to an internal discipline. They will not be promoted to the highest ranks without the goodwill of their superiors. Thus both agency men and judges are relatively independent from Congress and President in matters of career. Bureau chiefs in particular have reached a pinnacle similar in prestige and permanency of tenure to that of federal judges. Lower bureau employees are dependent on their bureau superiors for promotion, but lower federal judges are also in a peculiar way dependent on theirs. While desire for promotion may not cause lower federal court judges to be dependent on higher ones, desire for professional prestige, which motivates most of them to accept judgeships in the first place, does lead them to anticipate the views of their superiors so as to avoid an excessive number of reversals which would reflect on their abilities.

Finally, the President and Congress have almost absolute control over initial appointments to the federal courts. They closely guard the door to judicial power, although admittedly they often open it blindly without knowing what sort of policies the men they admit will pursue in office. But they exercise hardly any of even this limited initial control in the bureaus. Posts of high responsibility in the bureaus are almost invariably filled by promotion from within over which outsiders retain only nominal control.

Thus considering all the pros and cons, one must conclude that in terms of career, as in so many other ways, a disjunction between "independent" judges and "disciplined" bureaucrats would be essentially misleading.

This is clearest of all in the "independent" regulatory commission. To begin with, the commissions rarely run the sorts of positive programs that lead to the dependencies for authorizations and appropriations on the statute maker that we spoke of earlier as being at the heart of whatever distinction can in fact be drawn between dependent and independent political agencies. Commissioners are typically appointed for terms exceeding those of the appointing President and approaching the number of years Supreme Court justices actually serve. There are indeed strong expectations of independence in the commissioners, although these have been frequently challenged,[17] and there has been a strong movement in recent years to subordinate the commissioners to the President—a movement that has so far enjoyed only marginal successes. Commission hearing officers, who play an extremely important part in commission lawmaking, are guaranteed independence of tenure and promotion by statute, although there is little question that their promotion is at least partially dependent on the goodwill of their superiors. Other commission employees are subject to normal bureaucratic restraints, but again these are entirely internal and contribute to the commission's independence from the President rather than tying commission bureaucratics to any hierarchy resting on the President. On the whole, commissions are even more independent of Congress and the President than other administrative agencies and thus even harder to distinguish from courts on this ground.

Of course the ultimate disciplinary power of the statute maker, that of changing the statute, runs against both courts and agencies. It can be argued that whereas the agency cares a great deal about whether its governing statutes are changed, the courts do not, being equally willing to administer any statutory content so long as it is constitutional. But this is to apply one end of a fiction without the other. We must really insist on either the whole fiction or the whole truth. The

---

17. See Landis, *Report on Regulatory Agencies,* Committee Print, Sen. Judiciary Com., 86th Cong. 2d Sess. (1960); 2 Davis, *Administrative Law Treatise* 1-35 (1958)

whole fiction, of course, is that all supplementary lawmakers, courts and agencies alike, faithfully carry out whatever statutory scheme the statute maker institutes, impartially administering whatever law is given them. It is now clear that administrators are not simply political eunuchs guarding the purity of legislative intent, but instead have their own views of the public interest and their own policy goals which they pursue within the constraints imposed by the political system. We know that judges too have policy preferences.[18] Since both agency and court make their supplementary laws on the basis of what they judge the public interest to require, within the limits of frequently vague and broad statutes, it is not at all clear why judges should be any less perturbed than agency bureaucrats when their considered judgments of the good, the beautiful, and the true are upset.

Furthermore, both courts and agencies on occasion administer statutes they don't like, and both can theoretically wash their hands of the moral responsibility for doing so by claiming to be mere servants of the statute maker. Neither, however, are likely to enjoy such a situation, and both are likely to try to find a way out by interpretation or lobbying the statute maker for changes. Courts do in fact frequently lobby legislatures through opinions that point up the difficulties in administering existing provisions or their bad results, or through deliberate and unabashed twisting of previous legislative intent which becomes an invitation to the statute maker either to go along with the courts by inaction or to change the statute itself.

Thus the statute maker has similar degrees of control over both its judicial and bureaucratic supplementers through its power to change the basic statute, and both types of supplementary lawmakers respond by seeking to persuade the statute makers of the correctness of their own policy views. But the attempt to distinguish courts from agencies on the basis of their relative sensitivity to statutory change does, I think, lead us to a distinctive characteristic of courts whose significance has not been sufficiently appreciated.

---

18. See Schubert, *The Judicial Mind* (1965)

GENERALIST COURTS v. SPECIALIZED AGENCIES

Appellate courts have traditionally been courts of general jurisdiction ranging widely through many areas of public policy. Their parallel supplementary lawmakers among the administrative agencies are specialists, each of whom has been granted its lawmaking powers precisely because of its expertise in some narrow area of government action. The judicial lawmaker is thus a generalist, the agency lawmaker a specialist. The general impression that judges are more impartial, less "political," and more obedient to the intent of statute maker than are bureaucrats is less a function of some peculiar quality of the black robe than the routine political phenomenon of contrast between specialist and generalist. The program-operating specialists become excessively wedded to their programs, lose their sense of proportion, and resist outside efforts to coordinate their activities. The cost of introducing expertise into politics and giving it relatively wide discretion is a parochialism in which the more the political actor knows about a given program the less capable he becomes of subordinating it to a more general vision of the public interest.

In this sense the peculiar virtue of the judge is ignorance. He knows relatively little about any of the public policy areas in which he makes his decisions, and thus maintains his perspective toward all. He is not so passionately involved in chicken raising or locomotive inspection or tax collection that he allows any of these government functions to grow out of proportion in his mind to the other functions of government.

If the judge is an expert at anything, it is at law per se —that is to say, at nothing. For the law as lawyers and judges know it is essentially a set of verbal symbols devoid of programmatic content and capable of rearrangement in any way necessary to achieve any specified set of programmatic goals. This is not to deny that there is a legal ideology absorbed in law schools and confirmed by later practice, or that many of the verbal symbols at any given moment have historically defined contents that lawyers mistake for universal, essential, fixed, and "true" meanings. But it means that the study of law does not make a man expert at any substantive, real-world, economic or social problem. He does not teach children, build bridges, or plan cities. His role is essentially that of a facilitator, a go-between and advisor to those who do the things of this world. Thus the lawyer is not likely to make the mistake of believing that chicken raising or educating children alone will save the world or should receive a disproportionate share of social and political concern. At worst he will believe that law will save the world—a relatively harmless romanticism that does not excessively commit him to any particular distortion of public expenditure or to a markedly biased favoring of some social interests over others.

The peculiar value of the judge then is that he is one of the *most political* decision makers in the lawmaking process. He represents the incursion of a layman and a generalist, with roughly the same outlook as the citizenry, into a process increasingly dominated by highly specialized and parochial bureaucrats who claim technical justification for their programs rather than "playing politics." The legislature is sometimes spoken of as institutionalizing the lay mind in government,[19] but with legislatures conducting most of their business through specialized committees and in close conjunction with the appropriate bureaucrats that title belongs more and more to the judge.

It is precisely for this reason that specialized courts, like the Tax Court or the Interstate Commerce Court, look less and less courtlike to us and tend to fade back into the administrative structure from which they were supposed to be partially separated. To the extent that they specialize, they lose the one quality that clearly distinguishes them from administrative lawmakers. Once they lose that quality there seems to be relatively little reason to have two separate specialists, one labeled judge and the other bureaucrat, making policy in the same field.

---

19. I am indebted to Professor Arthur Maass for this notion.

Moreover, it is precisely where the common law or legal tradition seemed to carry inextricably within itself a particular set of policies, so that the legal specialist ceased to be a political generalist and by virtue of his technical skill became overly committed to certain government programs, that judges were felt to be acting unsatisfactorily and were stripped of their power. Thus where the judge allowed himself to believe that his dedication to the common law also dedicated him to becoming an enthusiastic specialist in strikebreaking, he was deprived almost entirely of his jurisdiction over strikes until he regained his sense of proportion and returned to an approach to labor problems not overcommitted to any given line of policy.

ADMINISTRATIVE AND
JUDICIAL IMPARTIALITY

Aside from this general distinction between generalist and specialist, it is extremely difficult to arrive at firm distinctions between courts and administrative agencies as supplementary lawmakers. It is frequently argued that the distinctive feature of courts is that they are impartial. But administrative agencies too are supposed to act impartially. There is no reason to believe the bureaucratic decisions affecting individuals are any more influenced by factors of personal favoritism than those of courts. Impartiality is, in fact, a rather tricky word. Surely courts are not supposed to be impartial between the interests of those who favor and engage in burglary and those who disfavor it and seek to protect their personal property. Impartiality cannot mean an absence of policy preferences in reaching decisions, since those who speak most of impartiality are also likely to speak most of decision according to law, and law embodies a set of policy preferences—for instance, those against burglary. Impartiality must be a norm requiring that any two persons in an equal legal position, with equal claims, be treated alike; that no favoritism be shown to one person over another on grounds of personal like or dislike or hope of personal gain on the part of the decision maker. This norm applies equally to judges and bureaucrats. It is part of the professional standards of each; and, for both, mechanisms of appeal and public surveillance exist to insure its observance.

More than is usually appreciated, impartiality is demanded of all politicians. The notion that public decisions should be made in the public interest is widespread. This notion may mean different things to different people, and may be applied differently in different circumstances, but surely even at the very minimum it means that legislators are not supposed to pass laws to benefit their personal friends simply because they are personal friends. There is now a considerable body of evidence to suggest that many legislators quite consciously cast themselves in the role of impartial arbitrator.[20] Surely congressional behavior reflects a concern for the public interest, and even where a congressman acts to protect the special interests of his constituents he seeks to justify that action by showing that those interests are worthy of protection in the context of all the potential interests at play. Judges simply share in the general political norm that the public business should be conducted to benefit the public interest, and that those who hold a share of public power should not use it for the personal benefit of themselves and their friends.

CLIENTELISM

It is frequently true, however, that some segments of government are captured by particular interests and become "clientele" agencies excessively pushing the claims of those interests. In this sense they might be said to violate the norm of impartiality. The clientele phenomenon is not unknown to courts. The Supreme Court might be said to have exces-

---

20. See Barber, *The Law Makers* (1965); Wahlke, Eulau, Buchanan, and Ferguson, *The Legislative System* (1962); Zisk, Eulau and Prewitt, "City Councilmen and the Group Struggle," 27 *Journal of Politics* 618 (1965)

sively pushed the claims of Negroes at certain times in response to the excessive disregard of those claims by other segments of government. Clientelism is not necessarily a deviation from impartiality when practiced either by courts or other agencies. Instead it may simply be a recognition that certain social claims are not receiving equitable treatment elsewhere and must be especially championed by a particular agency if they are to receive their fair share of recognition in the political system as a whole.

Moreover, to the extent that courts are not as clientele-oriented as other segments of government, the explanation can be found not in some inherent and peculiar quality of courts but in the fact that courts are generalists while administrative agencies, regulatory commissions, and congressional committees are specialists. For clientelism is typically a result of specialization. An agency constantly concerned with a given problem becomes the natural target of private interests and other government agencies concerned with the same problem. The agency is often staffed with expert specialists who have close professional ties with their opposite numbers in the private sector. An agency whose sole concern is a given social or economic function is likely to suffer from the same lack of perspective as the business firms with which it deals and which draw their total income from that function. In short, men who think about airlines all day who work for the government are likely to have certain natural affinities with men who think about airlines all day who work for the airlines. These mutual natural affinities are cultivated by the constant contacts that are bound to occur between government and private executives and technicians working in the same area. And they are not counterbalanced by contacts with others, for the government men who worry about airlines do not see the men, government or otherwise, who worry about trains. The benefits to be derived for their own special area from mutual support soon become apparent to the various experts, public and private, and they join forces at least to the extent of claiming an especially high share of resources for their area. It is often difficult to tell whether the specialized agency has enlisted the appropriate segment of business or profession, or whether the business or profession has enlisted the agency. Usually there is a mutual give-and-take for the common purpose of gaining special attention for the area in which both operate. Courts have typically escaped such clientelism because they do not devote a major share of their time to a single economic or social problem. Most significantly, where they do develop a major specialization, as they had for instance in the area of civil rights during the years when all other government agencies had deserted the field and the only possible avenue of approach for interested groups was constitutional litigation, courts do begin to exhibit symptoms of clientelism.

PREDETERMINED RULES

Another characteristic sometimes suggested as distinguishing courts is that they settle disputes on the basis of predetermined rules, policies, or norms accepted as given. To be sure when the existing state of the statutory law is sufficiently clear, and when the facts are sufficiently clear and fall with sufficient clarity under a particular statutory rule, courts do exactly this. But so do administrative agencies.

All political actors operate within various kinds of constraints. The senator from Wisconsin is theoretically free to vote as he pleases, but in practice he cannot frequently violate the expectation of his farmer constituents by voting no on subsidies. The President may veto any bill he pleases, but because each time he vetos a bill he makes enemies he cannot afford to veto too many bills. There is widespread expectation in American politics that both bureaucrats and judges will obey the existing law. Because of these expectations, existing laws do represent outer boundaries or constraints within which bureaucrats and judges must confine their policy making. Neither may make frontal assaults on existing statutes. Both may make policy within the limits set by existing statutes, and both may sometimes tread into the gray area of violating the will of the statute maker without seeming to do so, as long as they do so with proper caution and after careful calculation of what the reaction of the statute maker is going to be.

FINALITY AND LIMITED SPHERES OF COMPETENCE

It is also frequently said that judicial decision making is peculiarly marked by its finality. Once a judge—or at least the final judge in the chain of appeal—makes his decision it is forever binding on the parties to the litigation, and no one can change it. Certain technical quibbles can be raised against this proposition, but by and large it is correct. It is also irrelevant within the context of administrative and judicial supplementary lawmaking. For what we are concerned with here is not the fate of the individual litigants, but the law that courts create in the process of handing down what purport to be simply judgments in individual cases. These policy judgments are not at all final. They will be modified or even directly opposed by subsequent administrative interpretations. They may be modified or absolutely rejected by future acts of the statute maker. They typically are modified or even reversed by later decisions of the courts themselves. When a judge makes law, his action is no more final than that of any other lawmaker. Our political system is marked by the constant communication, dissolution and recombination of various political forces in the process of continuously adjusting the law to changing social needs and political demands.

One of the most frequent contrasts made between courts and other political agencies is that courts have very limited and severely defined spheres of competence. The jurisdiction of courts is quite rigorously set by statute and by a host of judge-made rules which often seem to take a perverse delight in preventing a judge from intervening even where grave injustice is being done. Here again, however, courts share this characteristic with many other political agencies. All of the regulatory commissions have fixed spheres of jurisdiction. Indeed precisely what problems are within and what problems are outside the jurisdiction of the N.L.R.B. has been one of the major jurisdictional disputes of the last thirty years. Agencies and bureaus within the executive branch also have their jurisdictions set by statute, and interagency quarrels about who has exactly how much authority over what are a commonplace of bureaucratic life.

Moreover, most of the disputes in administrative law over the exact limits of courts' jurisdictions are also disputes over the exact limits of agency jurisdiction, since the crucial issue is often where the authority of the agency leaves off and that of the court begins. It is true that some agencies under some circumstances have a wide-ranging and only very vaguely limited jurisdiction. But this is also true of some courts under certain circumstances—for instance, when a court's equity powers are invoked or under broadly drawn declaratory judgment acts.

As part of the notion of limited judicial jurisdiction it is often noted that courts can act only after the damage has been done, courts act only in "cases and controversies"—that is, where the interests of one person have been damaged by another, and where a conflict already exists which must finally be settled in court. The cases-and-controversies rule, however, is not as clear-cut as it is often made to appear. It has increasingly been the trend of the law that where a genuine difference of legal interpretation exists between two parties, especially if one of the parties is the government, and if this dispute involves grave potential damage to the interests of one of the parties, courts may intervene to settle the dispute without waiting until one of the parties is actually damaged. Declaratory-judgment acts, which are statutes authorizing courts to state what the law is before the need to enforce it arises, recognize this trend.

Thus courts are reacting to a practical social problem and in doing so are growing more and more like other supplementary lawmakers who do not wait to announce what the law is until after someone has supposedly violated it. Even more important, given the complexity and size of our economic and social systems, most litigational situations that reach appellate courts are not unique to the two parties who are in dispute, again especially when one of the parties is the government. Typically many other persons are in roughly the same situation as the parties involved and are awaiting the outcome of the case being fought before they decide whether they should stick to their interpretation of the law or yield to the other side's. In some instances "test cases" involving only a few parties are especially mounted so that a point of law in which whole classes of persons are interested may be judicially clarified. In another sense, however, nearly every case reaching the appellate courts is a test case, since the point of law to be established will subsequently govern the actions of many persons besides the initial litigants. Even under the strictest interpretation of the cases-and-controversies rule, a court in declaring the law for one set of parties after they have come into conflict also declares the law for the future for many parties who are waiting to see how the law is going to turn out before initiating the actions that might lead to a conflict. Here again courts, like other lawmakers, do announce general rules that influence the subsequent conduct of large classes of persons. They do not simply decide after the event who has been legally right and who wrong.

POSITIVE VERSUS NEGATIVE POLICY MAKING

More realistic is the distinction between courts and other agencies based on positive versus negative aspects of policy making. Except in the somewhat anomalous area of constitutional law, courts are rarely responsible for the initiation and operation of positive government programs. Unlike the Department of Health, Education, and Welfare or the Forestry Service, courts cannot give poor children lunches or chop firebreaks through the forests. In general they must await some conflict created by an existing program, and even then they cannot specify how children are to be fed or where firebreaks are to be cut by merely, on a few occasions, indicating that one particular method of feeding or chopping adopted by the operating agency is wrong.

The principal significance of this distinction again can basically be expressed in the contrast between courts as generalists who only occasionally intervene in a given area and certain other agencies tightly focused on one or a few specific programs and staffed by technicians whose working lives revolve around those programs. Agencies do make continuous decisions. Courts do intervene only sporadically. This does lead to certain differences in outlook and expertise that we have already discussed under the rubric generalist versus specialist, but it does not alter the fact that when a court does intervene, it must decide matter X just as the agency must decide matter X. In short, both court and agency must intersect at, and each must achieve, a given policy decision—even though for one the decision is an incident in a continuous stream and for the other it is a relatively isolated occasion.

There are, however, two other important facets of the distinction between positive and negative operations. Agencies operating positive programs are in effect distributing government largesse, each agency to a few particular interest groups. To put the matter most crudely, operating agencies buy political support for themselves with the taxpayers' money. The Corps of Engineers or the Bureau of Public Roads can usually depend on strong political support from those who directly benefit from their services. Since courts do not dispense such largesse, they enjoy far less support from specific groups and are far more dependent on general public sentiment and the general prestige which courts have traditionally enjoyed in Anglo American society. Put another way, courts may be more severely limited by general expectations about how they ought to behave than agencies which have strongly focused support from particular interest groups.

Not too much should be made of this point. After all,

if the operating agencies are less constrained by general expectations they are more constrained by the expectations of
the groups on which they depend for support. The Bureau
of Public Roads would have a hard time indeed if it suddenly became a vocal proponent of rapid transit. Both
specialization and generalization entail submission to the
expectations of extra-agency political forces. Moreover, the
courts' negative services on occasions can and do build them
clienteles who offer political support so long as the judges
meet their expectations. Judicial decisions negating various
government and labor programs deemed inimical to business
at one time created a strong business clientele for courts. Although positive-program operators can deliver more services
faster and more continuously to more groups, those who say
"no" also perform valuable services for some groups. The
distinction is at best one of degree.

This essential similarity between courts and positive-
program operators is perhaps clearest where the same parties
remain continuously as actual or potential litigants. The
American Trucking Association, for instance, constantly
watches I.C.C. decisions on rail rates and forms of service,
ready to challenge any decision deemed to favor railroads at
the expense of truckers. The truckers, the railroads, and the
I.C.C. are thus engaged in an almost uninterrupted bargaining process. Each bargainer continuously maintains the option of appealing to the courts and uses the threat of appeal
as a bargaining tactic. The anticipated result of litigation as
estimated from the courts' previous doctrines and attitudes
is, at any given moment and depending on the exact issues,
a positive resource to some of the bargainers and a negative
one to others. Moreover, from the point of view of both administrators and judges as decision makers, the intermittent
or continuous litigant is in a position to force the decision
of issues that either of them may wish or not wish decided
at any given moment. Thus while the decision makers are
in a position to help or hinder the litigant, the potential
litigant is also in a position to help or hinder the administrator or judge by his choices of when and what to litigate.

Even the litigant may fall into the pattern of mutual influence and interdependence typical of those seeking positive government services.

The other major facet of the positive–negative distinction lies in the area of government planning. Planning has, in the last half-century, become a central concern of government, perhaps less so in this country than in some others, but to a considerable extent here as well. Increasingly this becomes the vital stage. For even though additions, subtractions, and alterations may occur later, planning tends to establish the major alternatives and patterns along which a program will develop.

Even within the broadest limits of the cases-and-controversies rule, courts are unlikely to intervene at the planning stage of new socioeconomic programs. Usually they must await concrete decisions or actions under the plan, and even then they usually must deal with these actions piecemeal. Rarely can a court attack the plan as a whole. On the other hand, courts do choose between alternative policies on the basis of the anticipated short- and long-run consequences of those policies. Moreover, they frequently make clear what steps they are prepared to take in the future as various anticipated stages of the action unleashed by their initial decision occur. Thus courts do engage in a certain amount of planning and, indeed, are frequently more concerned with the pace and continuity of future developments than are agencies enmeshed in day-to-day problems.

An attempt to isolate courts on the basis of their negativism will not carry us very far. It might if we were trying to make distinctions between the "three great branches," but the "branch" approach itself is a very faulty one. At the agency level, many agencies besides the courts carry on only negative functions. The Narcotics Bureau and the F.B.I. do not distribute government largesse to their clients but rather jail sentences. The Internal Revenue Service must be viewed in a similar light by those who come into the most immediate contact with it. Law enforcement and tax collection are positive programs only in the vaguest and most attenuated way—that is, in relation to the public interest taken as a whole but not to the specific groups with which the agencies do business. The Bureau of the Budget, the Comptrollers Office, and other watchdog and auditing agencies are even more purely nay-saying than the courts. More important, most agencies, including courts, participate in statute making—that is, in positive policy formation—to a certain extent and in negative regulation to a certain extent. Here again the question is only one of degree. Certainly many court decisions become the basic seeds of new legislation designed to accomplish positive government function. And in the end the distinction between negative and positive action is difficult to maintain in politics. A planning agency soon becomes aware that certain alternatives are not available to it because they are illegal. Patterns of judicial negatives thus may become a crucial factor in determining what positive alternatives are available. And judicial decisions setting the boundaries of agency jurisdiction may well determine who plans, or indeed whether any sufficiently centralized planning is possible at all. Every practicing politician knows that who plans and how far afield he can plan are decisive questions in the planning process.

Whatever help the positive–negative distinction may be in some grand scheme of constitutional analysis, it is of little help to us here in distinguishing courts from administrative agencies within the realm in which the two interact. This is true precisely because courts interfere relatively little and largely indirectly with government planning and positive programs. Such activity rarely gives rise to litigation. Typically courts review legislative action that is itself regulatory or negative. The independent regulatory commissions, which are the principal administrative agencies with which the federal courts interact, do little planning and operate few programs. For the most part they, just as the courts, act essentially negatively to enforce laws that require or prohibit certain actions on the part of private businesses. Similarly, the administrators within the executive branch with which the court most often deal are agencies like the antitrust divi-

sion of the Department of Justice, the Internal Revenue
Service, and the Patent Office. Typically these agencies do
not operate major positive programs. They are basically concerned with applying existing law to privately initiated and
privately operated economic activities.

If distinctions are to be made between courts and administrative agencies, it is of course most important to make
them in those areas of political behavior where courts and
agencies come in contact. It is in precisely those areas that
the distinction between positive and negative choice or decisions breaks down, for it is in those areas where agencies are
seeking to influence private action by negative sanctions that
courts and agencies meet.

INITIATIVE

It might be argued that at least the agencies can choose
when and when not to apply sanctions—to withdraw or refuse a license, to prosecute, to make an adverse ruling—while
the courts must wait until others have decided to litigate.
But the question of who controls the timing of intervention
is not so clear as it might appear. In the first place, many
legal questions remain relatively constantly before the courts.
Every year there are cases concerning the nature of gifts for
tax purposes, railway abandonment, mergers, public utility
rates, and the like. Courts can choose precisely when in this
constant stream they will decide to enunciate a new doctrine.
Secondly, on many crucial questions of law the circuit courts
of appeals may remain in conflict for indefinite periods. The
Supreme Court, through its powers of certiorari, chooses
when to intervene and when not to. Generally speaking it
takes only the cases it wishes to hear.[21] More generally, ad
ministrative agencies are unlikely to initiate new sanctions

---

21. In certain limited circumstances, defined by statute, the Supreme Court
    is legally required to accept jurisdiction, but such instances compose
    only a small segment of its jurisdiction and even here the justices ap-
    parently exercise considerable discretion. See Hart, "The Time Chart
    of the Justices," 73 *Harvard Law Reviews* 84 (1959)

when they feel the courts are likely to reject them. They act when they sense a hospitable judicial climate. Thus the courts today by their decisions largely control the decisions of the administrators tomorrow on what it is feasible to do next in the realm of prosecution.

On the other side of the fence, agencies rarely have complete control over when they prosecute, either internally or before the courts. There are certain general expectations about the behavior of bureaucrats that set outer limits to their tactical flexibility. A government agency cannot in many instances ignore a major and blatant violation of the statutes it administers. More important, many agencies are largely engaged in maintaining some sort of balance between conflicting interests in the private sector of the economy. If one of those interests seems to be gaining some advantage through an apparent violation of the law, the other interests are likely to put great pressure on the agency to intervene immediately. Where new practices have arisen in violation of an agency's policies, agencies often feel compelled to act at once, although a delay might be tactically desirable; for, although it may often be fair for an agency to nip a new business practice in the bud, it would be quite unfair to make the business abandon the practice after it has invested much time and money in its development.

Finally, administrative agencies frequently find that their flexibility in timing decisions to prosecute is severely limited by the courts themselves. Agencies do not prosecute at random and for the sheer joy of prosecuting. They prosecute selectively and for the purpose of affirming and enforcing their previous policies or announcing new ones. If they have an established policy that is being violated, they must prosecute fairly immediately and continuously lest the policy be eroded by repeated violation. If they wish to use prosecution as the vehicle for changing an old policy, they are confronted by the judicial demand that administrative agencies respect their own long-established policies and do not act capriciously. It is not easy suddenly to begin prosecuting a man for something he has been doing for quite a long time with impunity, for the absence of prosecution tends to establish a presumption of legality. Agencies must frequently move slowly from one policy position to another in order to avoid judicial opposition. This necessity imposes severe restraints on their ability to prosecute whom they please when they please.

At most, then, even in the field of initiating prosecution the distinction between courts and agencies is not very clear. Prosecution is not an autonomous political phenomenon. It is a timing device for the initiation of changes in policy or the maintenance of existing policy. The initiative and flexibility in undertaking prosecutions that lies with the administrative agencies is not so marked as it might appear at first glance, and does not create a decisive difference in the comparative ability of courts and agencies to control the timing and direction of policy change.

JUDICIAL VERSUS ADMINISTRATIVE DECISION MAKING STYLES

Perhaps the most important distinction that has been traditionally drawn between courts and administrative agencies, or indeed all other political agencies, has to do with what is frequently called "the taught tradition" in law.[22] Judges are men trained in the law. They inherit a historically sanctioned method of thought—legal reasoning. They apply this peculiar—and peculiarly well-tested and successful—analytical method to the problems brought before them. Thus they contribute a unique element to political decision making.

It would be extremely difficult to summarize briefly just what this taught style is.[23] That, however, is not to question its existence. Basically it seems to consist of three elements. The first and foremost is really not a logical operation at all but a doctrine of common law, *stare decisis*. No matter how

---

22. See 1 Pound, *Jurisprudence* (1959)
23. See Levi, *An Introduction to Legal Reasoning* (1949)

abstractly the rules of legal reasoning are put, in the end
they reduce themselves to little more than a description of
the way *stare decisis* is *supposed* to work translated from the
lore of common law into the vocabulary of judicial thought.
Perhaps this explains why the rules of "legal reasoning" are
so difficult to summarize briefly. For tremendous floods of
ink have been spilled in attempts to state exactly what *stare
decisis* is and how it ought to be applied in various situations.
There is not space here to follow this tortured path, particularly since I believe it to be basically a false one. What I am
about say may appear only a parody of the debate to those
who still defend *stare decisis*, but it provides a sufficient
starting point for my purposes, and one that can be supported by considerable reasoning and authority should the
need arise.

Stare decisis means that a judge should decide a present
case as a past case was decided. This would be simple if the
facts in the two cases were absolutely identical. But they
rarely are. Thus the judge must decide whether any fact in
the present case is so different and so relevant that this case
should not be decided the same way as the last. To do this
he must discover what the "principle" was upon which the
last case was decided or what *ratio decidendi*—what rationale
of deciding—the last judge used. Let us suppose the principle
was "long-haired men go to jail" or the ratio was "long-
haired men constitute a danger to society—this man has long
hair—this man goes to jail." Then in the present case the
fact that the man has black hair, while in the past case he
had red, makes no difference, and the new case can be decided as was the old. On the other hand, let us suppose that
in the previous case the principle was "men belonging to a
religious sect sworn to murder all unbelievers go to jail,"
and the *ratio* was, "the only men in our society who wear
their hair long and dye it red are those who belong to murder
sects; this man wears his hair long and dyes it red; therefore
he is a member of a murder sect, therefore he goes to jail."
Then the fact that the long-haired man in the present case

has black hair is very relevant and will cause this case to be decided differently from the last one.

Various difficulties, however, arise in discovering the principle or *ratio* of a previous case. First the earlier judge may not have clearly explained what he was doing. He may not have clearly stated which facts he considered relevant and decisive and which he did not, or he may not have set down precisely what logical steps led him from the facts to his decision. Secondly, the judge may have stated a *ratio* which is either patently unsound in logic or one which is so vague and general that it would lead either to the decision he reached or precisely the opposite one. Thirdly, we may discover fifteen previous cases, all with roughly the same facts and all with roughly the same decision. Yet each of the judges in each of the cases may provide a quite different *ratio* than each of the others.

To overcome these difficulties it is necessary to argue that the *ratio* of a previous case is not how the judge said he got from the facts to the decision, but how logically he must have gotten from the facts to the decision. This is where the major element of fantasy enters *stare decisis*. We are no longer concerned with how previous judges actually decided cases, but how they ought to have decided them if they had clearly and correctly followed the rules of *stare decisis*.

Two new problems now arise. The first concerns facts. One determines the *ratio* of a given case by lining up all the facts, choosing the relevant ones, and then looking at the decision. The *ratio* is whatever series of logical stepping-stones will lead you from the relevant facts to the final decision. But you cannot know what facts are relevant until you know the ratio. In our earlier example you cannot know whether hair color is a relevant fact until you know whether the ratio is that long-haired men are dangerous or that religious fanatics who do certain things to their hair are dangerous. Unless you know what facts are relevant you cannot know from where to where the stepping-stones go, and unless you know from where to where the stepping-stones go you do not know what facts are relevant. This chicken-and-egg problem endlessly bedevils those attempting to pin down the single correct *ratio* in a single case. For every different choice of relevant facts a different *ratio* will appear, and for every ratio a different subset of the total facts will appear relevant.

The second problem concerns the *ratio* itself. Even supposing that we could hold the relevant facts fixed, the rules of Aristotelian logic under which lawyers purport to operate do not really demand that there be a single line of stepping-stones from the facts to the decision. In many instances it is quite possible to construct two or more equally plausible lines of logic that will connect a given set of facts and a given result. Which is the true *ratio*?

Because of these difficulties some legal scholars have argued that a *ratio* cannot be found in a single case, but one can be found for a line of cases. If we take a group of cases, all in roughly the same area, we should be able to identify a group of central facts common to all of them, and also some fact elements which, when they vary from case to case, cause the results to vary. These are, then, the relevant facts. Moreover if we take this same group of cases and list all the possible *ratios* in each, we should, by a process like canceling in fractions, be able to find a lowest-common-denominator *ratio* that will work on all of them and allow us to arrive at a single *ratio* summarizing all of these cases.

In fact, grouping cases will not entirely overcome the problems to be found in deriving a *ratio* from an individual case because the same chicken-and-egg problem arises. Unless you know what the criteria of relevance and *ratio* are in each case, you don't know what cases to group together as having enough in common to be considered together, and unless you have a group you cannot discover what criteria of relevance and ratio they have in common. Nevertheless, grouping will give a kind of rough-and-ready result or educated guess about *ratio* which is far better than the results to be obtained from a single case.

The difficulty that now arises is that by grouping different cases you can get different results and that very frequently two or even more lines of precedent came into existence on the same question as cases which do not fit neatly into one group are bunched to create a second. When two or more lines of precedent exist, it is literally impossible to follow the previous case. Moreover, new cases inevitably bring new facts. The identification of the *ratio*, and thus the determination of what is relevant and what is not in previous cases, is always of a rather rough ordering even when only a single line of precedent exists. Thus it is always possible to argue that a given decision either is or is not in line with past precedent in light of the new facts.

Thus the theory of *stare decisis* as an exact and rigorously logical mode of thought resulting in absolutely certain and predictable decisions has broken down, and as the theory has dissolved so has the judge's claim to bringing a unique form of analysis to political problems. For if *stare decisis* does not dictate automatic results, judges would seem to exercise a level of political discretion similar to that of other politicians, and particularly to that of other subordinate lawmakers who are expected to govern themselves at least generally by the existing statutes. It must be stressed that the breakdown in the theory of *stare decisis* does not mean that legal decision making is a form of free play in which every judge can do exactly what he pleases. It is now clear, however, that the judge is not subject to a unique constraint on his thought processes that makes him far different from the rest of us. Instead, like the bureaucrat, he is constrained by the previous state of the law insofar as it is clear. Because it is never entirely clear he always has some discretion. And he is likely to find the law less and less clear and exercise more and more discretion as he finds that old law is giving bad results in new circumstances.

It is precisely in the work of the appellate courts that the old law is least clear, for cases do not get appealed in which the precedents are absolutely clear and commanding. We now have considerable evidence that judges in fact do exercise discretion to support the argument made against stare decisis at the theoretical level. We do not have the space to review this evidence here. It is sufficient to say that a number of eminent judges have testified that appelate-court judging involves, beyond the logical analysis of precedent, both conscious and unconscious considerations of social and political utility, and that a large number of empirical studies prove beyond question that the social and political attitudes of judges are reflected in their opinions.[24]

If then the "taught tradition" is nothing more than *stare decisis* writ large, the judge has no claim to uniqueness. And in the last analysis the tradition turns out to be little more than that. Lawyers are, to be sure, trained in a peculiar form of analogical reasoning so that they seem to be far more comfortable thinking of an automobile as like a wagon or like a ship than simply thinking of it as an automobile. Analogy is a rather primitive logical tool for assimilating new information. It is to be found in large bureaucratic structures and legislative bodies as well as among judges and is indeed typical of much complex decision making. It is only natural to attempt to fit a new problem into the mold of an old one that we have already solved successfully.

Finally the "taught tradition" is much concerned with principles. It may well be that some basic principles of justice and the good life dwell deeply in our legal traditions. Lawyers may imbibe these principles both consciously and unconsciously during their training and later careers to the extent that they learn to accept thinking about certain things in certain ways even without understanding the underlying norms which these thought-ways reflect. It seems unlikely, however, that these principles vary a great deal from the general set of norms which underlie our whole society and which inform the work of bureaucrats and legislators as well as judges. Judges have fundamental notions of right and wrong, but they are surely the same notions that the rest of us have, and no one prefers acting wrongly to acting rightly.

Moreover most administrative agencies are heavily

---

24. See e.g. Cardozo, *The Nature of the Judicial Process* (1921); Hand, *The Spirit of Liberty* (1960); Frankfurter, *op. cit. supra* note 11; Hutcheson, "The Judgment Intuitive," 14 *Cornell Law Quarterly* 274 (1929); Schubert, *op. cit. supra* note 18

staffed with lawyers and the general climate in which they operate is highly legalistic. Even if sound principles of justice somehow hover over the lawyer and judge at their work within the taught tradition, just about the same cloud of the same thickness should be observable over the agencies.

Basically, then, the notion that judges may be distinguished from other politicians through their commitment to the taught tradition boils down to a claim for the uniqueness of *stare decisis* as a tool of logical analysis and the insistence that courts do indeed use that tool almost to the exclusion of all others. Yet we have seen that the theory of *stare decisis* is largely untenable, that judges must exercise policy discretion since *stare decisis* does not automatically and autonomously yield a single result, and that there is strong empirical evidence to support the conclusion that judges not only theoretically must but actually do exercise the same kind of policy discretion as other political actors.

Nevertheless it is undeniably true that when we look at the cases that mark the meeting or clash of courts and administrative agencies there does seem to be, in some areas at least, great concern for precedent, considerable effort to justify positions in terms of the previous state of the law, and generally all the paraphernalia of *stare decisis*. It is possible to dismiss all this as simply a legalistic smoke screen. But it is always naïve and dangerous to suppose that the outward manifestations of political life are only masks for what really goes on somewhere in deep, dark places. Few individuals or institutions have the ability to consciously sustain a masquerade indefinitely. If lawyers and judges still rack their brains and spill their ink over pulling and hauling the precedents, either *stare decisis* or something like it must still be at work somewhere.

INCREMENTAL DECISION MAKING

I think the answer is not *stare decisis*, but indeed something like it—a something, however, that is not unique to courts or to the taught tradition. In the first place much of the concern for the previous state of the law that appears to be a reflection of *stare decisis* at work is simply a function of the fact we have emphasized and re-emphasized—that courts are subordinate lawmakers operating willy-nilly within the limits set down by the statute. Since they are not the only supplementary lawmakers, judges must be sure that their own acts of supplementary lawmaking do not so conflict with previous supplements issued by other courts and agencies that the statute becomes unworkable. All supplementary lawmakers, courts and administrative agencies both, are concerned with the previous state of the law as reflected in the statutes and previous supplements to the statutes in the form of agency and court rules and decisions—not because they are bound by *stare decisis* but because as supplementary lawmakers their duty is to make the law sufficiently coherent to be workable. The use of *stare decisis* does not divide courts from agencies. Instead both share the duties of supplementary lawmakers.

There is, however, an even more fundamental phenomenon linking courts and administrative agencies, indeed linking all political decision makers. This phenomenon tends to exhibit itself in the courts in the language of *stare decisis* although it is essentially the same phenomenon there as elsewhere. It is easiest to perceive this identity between the concern for precedent in courts and the general character of political decision making if we examine the general phenomenon first and then see how it operates in the specific setting of the courts.

This general phenomenon might be labeled incrementalism. It has been described in two recent works, each by a pair of authors, Richard Cyert and James March,[25] and David Braybrooke and Charles Lindblom.[26] Both have recently presented theories of decision making that might apply to both political and economic decisions and particularly to the peculiar mixture of politics and economics that typi-

---

25. *A Behavioral Theory of the Firm* (1963)
26. *Strategy of Decision* (1963); see also Lindblom, *Intelligence of Democracy* (1965)

cally occurs in what we call the "public policy" sphere. Courts are very frequently involved in just such mixed questions of politics and economics. Both sets of authors are seeking to present a method of decision making that proceeds by a series of incremental judgments as opposed to a single judgment made on the basis of rational manipulation of all the ideally relevant considerations.

It is easiest to explain what incrementalism is by way of what it isn't, or rather what it is in reaction against. For a long time the ideal type for decisions in economics or politics was "rational decision making" in which all relevant data were to be considered in the light of all relevant goals, the goals themselves to be precisely weighted according to the decision maker's valuational priorities. The basic sticking point with rational decision-making theories is that real decision makers just did not act this way. The economists found that firms did not act rationally—that is, so as to maximize their profits. The political scientists found that political decision-making bodies, particularly highly bureaucratized ones, tended toward decisions that compromised the conflicting interests of various participants on an ad hoc basis without agreement on either the facts or the priority of goals. This collision of rational decision-making theories with hard facts is marked by the popularity of such notions as "satisficing" rather than maximizing and definitions of public interest in terms of legitimizing processes rather than substantive policies. At this point it might have been said that propositions about how decisions ought to be made were simply at odds with how decisions were in fact made. But then economists began to tell us that the marginal cost involved in gathering every piece of pertinent data and checking it against every available alternative policy in terms of all approved values would frequently itself be irrational in terms of input-output ratios. And students of politics began to urge that the self-preservation of a given political agency and/or the political process as a whole necessitated mediational decisions. It is not quite rational to destroy cherished institutions in the process of making "correct" public policy.

Thus deviations from rational decision-making models not only did occur but ought to occur. Incrementalism is the formal statement of this dissatisfaction with conventional models of decision making.

Let me briefly describe the tactics of incrementalism as presented by Lindblom. Lindblom begins with propositions about "margin-dependent choice." The decision maker starts from the status quo and compares alternatives which are typically marginal variations from the status quo. Formulation and choice among alternatives are derived largely from historical and contemporary experience. It follows that rather than all rationally conceivable alternatives only a restricted number are considered. Moreover, only a restricted number of the consequences of any given alternative are considered. And those that are chosen for consideration are not necessarily the most immediate or important but those that fall most clearly within the formal sphere of competence of the analyst and with which he feels most technically competent to deal.

In the traditional rational model of decision making, means are adjusted to ends, but the incrementalist often adjusts what he wants to the means available. Similarly, he constantly restructures both his data and values. He uses "themes" rather than "rules." That is he does not say "if factor X is present, decision Y must follow," but "factor X is an important consideration." Lindblom's next rubric is "serial analysis and evaluation"—the notion that policy is usually made by following a long series of steps. Rather than attempting to solve the problem in one fell swoop the decision maker whittles away at it. Indeed the analyst is likely to "identify . . . ills from which to move away rather than goals toward which to move."[27] Finally, analysis of a given policy area is likely to be carried on by several different agencies or institutions with constantly differing world views.

Cyert and March working independently of Lindblom and drawing their theory largely from observation of private firms rather than government arrive at startlingly similar

---

27. *op cit supra* note 26 at 102

conclusions. I shall restate their theoretically more elegant but rather cryptic conclusions in more everyday language.

Decisions for large organizations are not made by one man but come about through compromise among the various parts of the organization. Since each part has different goals and values, the organization itself has multiple goals and usually defines the "right" solution not in terms of an abstract best but of a solution which is at least minimally acceptable to each of the parts. In searching for this solution, the organization usually considers only one alternative at a time, and the first one to be discovered that is minimally acceptable to all parts will be adopted. Where the status quo policy is acceptable to all, there is little search for alternatives. But where the existing policy fails, then search will be intensified.

Organizations are not only concerned with finding good or "best" policies. They are also vitally concerned with their interval stability. It is necessary, therefore, to make sure that the process of finding and selecting new alternatives is not conducted with such enthusiasm and preoccupation as to shatter the structure or distract attention from the vital job of maintaining the existing machinery. Just such results are likely to occur if the too vigorous search for alternatives to the status quo were to lead to excessive uncertainty among executives as to what was going to happen next. Thus even organizations very actively engaged in searching for new solutions are likely to stress the following of regular procedures in day-to-day operations. Moreover, to avoid excessive disruption of these operations it is likely to make very small-step changes, waiting for the results of each to become clear before making another. The feedback resulting from each change puts the organization in a much better position to predict exactly what will result from the next. Predicting the future environment and then choosing the major change that ideally suits the prediction might seem rationally best, but it will lead to a tremendous shock to the system if the world does not indeed turn out the way you predicted it would. Making a small change and seeing how it works out before making another may always leave the organization a bit short of ideal adjustment to changing times, but it also reduces losses if the guess was wrong. Moreover the constant feedback or new information that the decision maker gets from observing what happens after each small change helps in producing better guesses in the future.

An organization not only attempts to minimize the uncertainties resulting from decision making—i.e., choice among alternatives; it also seeks to minimize uncertainties within the decisional process itself. "It tends to use standard operating procedures and rules of thumb to make and implement choices. In the short run these procedures dominate the decisions made."[28]

It may be helpful to note some of the correlations between the work of the two pairs of incrementalists. For instance, March's emphasis on organizational goals as multiple rather than unitary and choices as compromises rather than ideal solutions would seem to be a summary statement of the incremental politics which Lindblom says is the foundation of his strategy. For Lindblom's strategy is not an abstract model applicable to all decision making everywhere, but is dependent on roughly the type of pluralistic politics to be found in Western constitutional democracies. No rigorous cause-and-effect relationship need be supposed. But a system containing multiple centers of decision making, all or many of which have to come into agreement in order finally to arrive at and implement a decision, tends toward incremental decision making if for no other reason than that rational decision requires a single set of rationally ordered goals, which is a condition difficult enough for one decision maker to attain and nearly impossible for more than one. The findings of March, and of many others who have studied large organizations, that such organizations, even though theoretically organized on a strictly hierarchical basis, in reality consist of coalitions of decision-making units each with somewhat differing goals, is what makes theories of

28. *op cit supra* note 25 at 113

decision derived from the organizational behavior of private firms applicable to political life.

Cyert and March actually reduce the boundaries of decision even further than does Lindblom. They specify not only the consideration of a restricted number of alternatives but of only one alternative at a time, with the first workable alternative attempted accepted as the preferred solution. Lindblom's general formulation suggests rather continuous decisional activity. Their finding that the search for alternatives begins only when the present policy fails may indicate that Lindblom's point about moving away from ills may apply not only to the direction but also to the initiation and timing of incremental decisions.

Cyert and March's notion of feedback expresses the same thought as Lindblom's reference to historical and contemporary experience and emphasizes a point that Lindblom makes repeatedly. In the face of uncertainty about consequences the best decisional tactic is to take minor steps which will elicit new information and allow one to pull back without excessive loss if the new information indicates unexpected trouble. Finally, they note the use of regular procedures, which also has a damping effect on change. No change at all occurs so long as the regular procedures yield acceptable results. Thus Cyert and March emphasize what is not always clear in Lindblom—that the other side of the coin of incremental change is a limitation and routinization of decision making which produces a relatively slow tempo of new decisions, each of which constitutes a relatively smaller change from the status quo than even the general theory of marginal-dependent choice would require.

Indeed Cyert and March's emphasis on operating procedures and rules of thumb represent an important point for us. Lindblom's preoccupation with "themes" rather than rules seems to me to overrepresent one political style at the expense of another. Certain political decision makers in certain political settings may seek to avoid anything that looks like a hard-and-fast rule, but others, in other settings, may customarily operate through formulating and changing rules, which they take to be binding on themselves as well as others. Cyert and March emphasize that the rules are rules of thumb that are modified on the basis of feedback. In short, policy makers desire several somewhat conflicting conditions for decision to operate simultaneously. They want to be free to change their minds. They also want to be free to concentrate on the most important decisions and so must develop means of handling myriads of routine decisions routinely. Finally, they wish to be free of the constant pressure of those who wish them to alter decisions they have already made. Thus in order to obtain decisional freedom, policy makers will sometimes adopt a thematic approach which, by avoiding rules, gives them maximal flexibility and may expose them to less criticism than a hard-and-fast rule would. Or they may adopt rules of thumb, which will relieve them of future decisions and may serve as a shield against pressure by allowing them to insist that they too are now bound by the rule and so cannot make the decision some outside group desires.

Now it seems to me that if we examine the decisional behavior of courts, where the concern with precedent and the vocabulary of *stare decisis* are ever-present even though the theory has long since broken down, what we find is incrementalism pure and simple dressed up in the peculiar language of the law. Courts are not distinguishable by a peculiar tradition of thinking or decision making. Instead they, along with bureaucrats and business managers, are very central practitioners of incrementalism. Only the technical vocabulary for expressing this incrementalism sets the courts apart.

The key feature of *stare decisis* is, after all, concern for the status quo. Let the previous decision stand unless it fails to adequately meet new conditions. If it fails, search for a new decision. In considering such alternatives, begin by testing those which are closest to the old—i.e., try marginal changes first. Judicial lawmaking is typically accompanied by a great concern for fitting new decisions into older patterns and showing that the changes being made are only minor and compatible variations on the old law. Most of what seems essentially false in judges' opinions—the repeated insistence that they are not changing the law at all when they obviously are—is simply a sort of conventional over-statement of the point that they are choosing that workable alternative closest to the old law.

To some readers it may appear misleading to assign the legal status quo to one of the two contending parties when judicial lawmaking occurs. For in such instances the judge is often confronted with two rival interpretations of a statute which may be said to have no status quo since it is vague enough to admit the rival interpretations. Just how frequently an appellate judge chooses the interpretation that "changes" the statute because that interpretation will yield better results, rather than choosing the interpretation that he believes would maintain the status quo, is a matter for investigation. Yet while we do not know just how often this occurs, we do know that it does occur, for at least the most extreme instances—those in which a court overrules one of its previous decisions—are readily observable.

However, even in the classic instances of rival inter-pretations of an existing statute, each of which is equally plausible in terms of the wording of the statute and its past interpretations, the decisional situation is still basically one of marginal choice based on the status quo. The status quo is the statute's general intention, and counsel for each party argues that his specific interpretation more appropriately relates the statute to the circumstances. In a sense the judge does not face a choice between status quo and change, since if there has been no previous authoritative interpretation of the statute on all fours with the new situation, whatever he decides will be new. Yet neither judge nor counsel is free to propose any interpretation they like. All potential inter-preters are constrained by both technical canons of statutory interpretations and common-sense rules of logic to stay rela-tively close to the statutory language. The status quo here becomes the rather vague one of the very statutory intent that is in dispute. But vague as it is, it remains an anchor around which cluster various marginal choices. While we may argue whether the value of limestone or cement ought to be used in calculating depletion allowances under a statute allowing such calculation on the basis of "the commercially marketable mineral product," no one is going to argue that the value of the bridge eventually made out of the cement should be the basis of calculation.

The constant concern of lawyers and judges to narrow the issues and decide only that issue crucial to the case before them is also typical of incrementalism. If each case is the vehicle for decision on a single issue, and only the narrowest one possible to decide the case, then a major and wide-ranging problem is not considered all at once and in all its facets. Instead it unfolds step by step over time as a series of cases bring up first one aspect of the problem and then another. Thus at any given moment the court considers only a restricted number of alternatives, but the process as a whole constitutes just that serial analysis and evaluation and sequential consideration of alternatives that marks incrementalism.

The great virtue of common law is, after all, alleged to be the case by case development of a solution to a social problem by the gradual inclusion and exclusion of various alternatives. Courts do not make long-range forecasts about social conditions. Instead they attempt to handle each problem as it arises and with a tentative solution. The results of that small step can then be observed and help to inform the court's next decision. This is the much touted flexibility of judicial decision making. Instead of grand solutions that may become grand disasters, courts feel their way, seeking to benefit from accumulated experience with a past step before moving on to the next. Thus the great emphasis in courts on benefiting from historical experience. Here again there is a kind of conventional overexpression in which judges frequently say that they are only the passive utterers of the lessons of past experience embodied in *stare decisis*. But, stripped of the rhetoric, all this seems to boil down to is that judges like other incrementalists prefer the feedback—

small-change–feedback–small-change style of decision making
rather than great leaps forward.

If we run through the rest of the catalog of incrementalism, we shall also find the judge at every point. Judges do
consider only a restricted number of consequences even for
the restricted number of alternatives they handle. Another
of the peculiar virtues of judicial decision making is supposed to be that because judges always decide in the context
of a concrete case, they can see the real and immediate consequences of any given decision rather than making general
decisions on the basis of vague and speculative assessments
of what results are likely to follow. In short, a judge does
not consider all the consequences to all the persons at all the
future times that may follow from a given decision, although
undeniably the decision may have consequences far beyond
those in the given case. The judge trades the rationality that
would come with calculating the probabilities of all future
consequences under all foreseeable circumstances for the ease
and relative certainty of sticking to the probable results in
the immediate case. This point should not be pushed too
far, however. Judges, like other incrementalists, are likely
to look beyond the absolutely immediate consequences, since
they know that their decisions will have more wide-ranging
consequences if for no other reason than that under the traditions of *stare decisis* they will become precedents. The
incrementalist does not rigorously exclude all but immediate
consequences. He simply gives greater weight to those he
is sure about because they are here and now than to those
he is not sure about because they are there and later. The
judge does concern himself with what results the principle
he announces now will have later, but he tends to test the
principle concretely by the results it will achieve now in the
case before him.

Judges also share with other incrementalists a tendency
to consider those consequences that lie within their immediate jurisdiction rather than those that fall in someone else's.
This is precisely why jurisdictional questions are so vital in
administrative law. Debates over jurisdiction are in fact de-

bates about what consequences a judge should concern himself with and which he should leave to others. At least superficially the judge more than any other incremental decision maker cuts himself off from consideration outside his jurisdiction. In reality, of course, there is an interaction between consequences and jurisdiction in which jurisdictional lines are in part drawn on the basis of what consequences are so interrelated that they cannot be considered separately. Nevertheless a judge hearing a slum-clearance case is likely to consider the effect of his decision on the rights of property owners, and on the city's housing program, and perhaps on the future prosperity of the city, but he is unlikely to consider its effect on the gross national product or patterns of migratory bird flight for which his responsibility is minimal.

Cyert and March's emphasis on multiple goals as a characteristic of incrementalism is also confirmed in judicial decision making. Indeed, judges more openly announce that policy decisions inevitably rest on balancing various and conflicting interests or values than do any other group of decision makers. I am speaking here not only of the balancing doctrine in the First Amendment, which in fact frequently covered an inattention to certain important goals, but also of the rather consistent rhetoric of modern court opinions in many areas of both constitutional and administrative law, which acknowledges that many cases involve conflicting goals and that a judge's job is to choose which goal ought to be favored in each particular instance. For instance, in Southern Railroad *v.* North Carolina[29] the Supreme Court argued that one goal of national transportation policy was to maintain the health of the railroads, but another was to move passengers conveniently, that the two might sometimes be in conflict and that in determining when to allow a railroad to abandon a passenger service, railroad revenues and convenience to passengers must both be taken into account.

This sort of approach is so much the stock and trade

---

29. 376 U.S. 93 (1964)

of appellate judging that few lawyers would need to be convinced that judges typically decide on the basis of multiple goals. There is always the risk, however, that the rhetoric of opinions does not accurately reflect the judges actual thought processes. Recent attitudinal data might be naïvely interpreted to suggest that some judges always favor one goal or interest and do not really give any weight to other conflicting goals. In fact these data show, and indeed so those presenting the data have argued, that while a group of judges may be placed at different points along a scale between two conflicting goals, with each judge giving different relative weights to each goal, it is extremely rare to find a judge who favors one of the goals to the total exclusion of the others.[30]

Lindblom speaks of "adjustment of objectives to policies" as one of the key aspects of incrementalism. His basic point here is that considerations of availability of means often and necessarily affect, and indeed partially define, what goals we are going to pursue. This point has, I think, always been evident in many of the more "routine" areas of law. The need to pursue certain legal goals within the context of what the real situation will bear is attested to by such concepts as "the reasonably prudent man," "innocent third-party purchaser," and "last clear chance." All of these concepts represent compromises between certain ideal goals and what can actually be expected of imperfect human beings in an imperfect society. Movements toward and away from absolute warranty, for instance, have always focused on what manufacturing and marketing conditions would bear rather than notions of absolute fairness or responsibility. In these areas judges are quite accustomed to modifying their goals and cutting their losses under the impact of the real world. Indeed, such adaptation of judicial behavior to reality is generally applauded and encouraged.

Another feature of incrementalism which Lindblom calls "reconstruction" also strikes home immediately in the judicial process. "Fact-systems are reconstructed as new ones

---

30. See Schubert, *op cit supra* note 18

are discovered. Policy proposals are redesigned as new views
of the facts are adopted."[31] At the most elementary level,
any experienced reader of cases has many times been struck
by the way in which, in a given case, the facts look so much
different in the majority opinion than in the dissent. The
majority's frightened child, shivering in his cell, cut off
from his loving parents, and confessing in loneliness and
desperation, may become the dissenters' hardened juvenile
delinquent, refusing to see his mother and confessing as a
final gesture of defiance. The poor little Seventh Day Ad-
ventist, who, forbidden by her conscience to work on Satur-
day, is struck off the unemployment compensation rolls,
moves my heart precisely because I almost instinctively think
in terms of an economic system in which there are plenty of
five-day jobs. She moves my heart slightly less when a dissenter
shows that, in the Southern town in which she lives, practically the only employment for women is in the textile mills
which work a six-day week. Thus the lady's religion conveniently allows her to refuse every available job and continue to live off the taxpayers indefinitely.[32] I am not saying
that judges necessarily pick and choose their facts to support
their decisions, but that judges typically decide on the basis
of some model or abstraction from the facts and that the
way they construct this model affects their decisions. As
judges become aware of new facts, they are led to change
the model. For example, the model of free employer and free
employee freely bargaining about wages and working conditions which many judges used to decide early cases involving economic regulation changed under the impact of the
facts about real working conditions in real laundries,
bakeries, and clothing factories. That is precisely why lawyers have in recent years devoted so much space in their
briefs to facts and are likely to emphasize changing conditions
when they wish to obtain changes in the judge-made law.

Another of Lindblom's propositions—that incremental
decisions are remedially oriented—should strike a familiar

---

31. *op cit supra* note 26 at 98
32. See *Schubert v. Verner*, 374 U.S. 398 (1963)

note with those who are acquainted with modern jurisprudential writings. He says "The characteristics of the strategy
. . . encourage the analyst to identify . . . ills from which
to move away rather than goals toward which to move."
Edmond Cahn in his *Sense of Injustice*[33] and *The Moral
Decision*[34] has put forward exactly this proposition to explain
and rationalize the decisions of courts confronted by situations in which the mechanical application of existing law
does not seem to yield just results. Cahn argues that courts do
make decisions based on considerations of justice and moral-
ity in spite of their inability to articulate a rational set of
moral principles or a systematic answer to the question, What
is justice? He shows that courts are sensitized by the injustice
or social failure they see in a given legal situation and move
away from that situation even when they cannot formulate
an abstract, complete, and ideal legal rule to cover the
problem.

The old lawyers saw that "hard cases make bad law"
also comes down to this. Where the old law (the status quo)
yields at least minimally acceptable results, it will be re-
tained. Where a concrete case shows that the old law is
yielding intolerable social results—hard cases where men
seem to be technically in violation of the law but morally
and socially blameless—courts will move from the old law
even if they cannot formulate exactly what the new law
should be. Hard cases make not bad law but new, and therefore frequently incomplete, law.

Courts too typically alternate between themes and rules
of thumb just as other incremental decision makers do. In
many instances the courts do use a rule of thumb which
specifies that, all other things being roughly equal, if X is
present Y follows.

The Supreme Court holds that if violence or the immediate threat of violence is present in a labor-management
dispute, the state may intervene in matters that would otherwise be the sole concern of the National Labor Relations

33. (1949)
34. (1955)

Board—the so-called violence exception to the primary jurisdiction of the N.L.R.B.[35] Where courts must determine
whether a given crime involves moral turpitude, they almost
invariably hold that where fraud was an element in the
offense the crime does involve turpitude.[36]

On the other hand, courts frequently take precisely the
thematic tack Lindblom describes, simply naming various
factors all of which they will consider but none of which
they will bind themselves to treat as decisive. A clear example is the now largely defunct fair-trial rule under which
no given lapse in criminal procedure in and of itself rendered a trial unfair, but the Supreme Court was, in each
instance, to determine whether the trial was fundamentally
fair as a whole.[37] Courts very frequently instruct regulatory
commissions that they must consider a number of factors
and reach a decision representing a balanced appraisal of all
the relevant factors involved. Courts will frequently reverse
agencies on the ground that insufficient weight has been
given to a certain factor even while specifically holding that
that factor alone is not decisive.

In short, courts, like other political decision makers,
sometimes find it convenient to appear to bind themselves
closely by the rules of decision and sometimes wish to emphasize their sensitivity to multiple factors.

Perhaps the most dramatic examples of the alteration
and mixture of rule of thumb and thematic techniques and
the tactical advantages of each to various courts and litigants
are to be found in those areas, particularly labor and antitrust law, where per se rules are much in fashion. In such
areas disputes about whether courts should or should not
adopt per se rules are in effect disputes about whether they
should use the rule or thematic approach. And, of course,
courts have sometimes adopted and sometimes rejected the
per se approach. Per se rules, however, offer an extreme ex-

35. *San Diego Building Trades Council v. Garman* 359 U.S. 236 (1959)
36. See Shapiro, "Morals and the Courts, The Reluctant Crusaders," 45
       Minnesota Law Review 897, 926 (1961)
37. See *Palko v. Conn.*, 302 U.S. 319 (1937); *Betts v. Brady*, 316 U.S. 455
       (1942)

ample. Probably most common is the situation in which a court's doctrine is relatively clear and predictable—in other words, is a rule of thumb or standing operating procedure—but nevertheless is sufficiently imprecise to allow the judge some of the freedom of the thematic approach particularly through his choice of emphasis on particular portions of the relevant law and facts.

On the whole, Cyert and March's emphasis on the use of standard operating procedures and rules of thumb, which in the short run dominate the decisional process, is strikingly applicable to the legal process. The terminology is slightly different in law. But legal doctrines or rules are precisely those standard operating procedures or rules of thumb by which judicial decision makers dispose of most of the cases that come before them. The clear-and-present-danger rule is a familiar example, but it is hardly necessary to belabor the point that, in every field of law, doctrines which fall somewhere between the status of fixed elements in the law and random dicta by individual judges play an important part in the decision of cases. We know that in the short run most decisions are going to be routinely determined by the given state of doctrine. We also know that in the long run the doctrine is going to change. Cyert and March's proposition neatly fits that strange paradox of law in which we can at one and the same time be almost absolutely sure that the case tomorrow will be decided according to doctrine X and that ten years from now doctrine X will have disappeared. The rest of incrementalism explains how and why it disappears.

Finally, Cyert and March's description of organizations as seeking "to avoid uncertainty by following regular procedures," even in the midst of the multiple uncertainties of incremental decision making, is also strikingly applicable to courts. Lawyers have always insisted that regularity of procedure, not substance, was the essential virtue of law and the vital safeguard of individual rights. The enormous concern and acrimonious squabbling over procedure which frequently makes the layman impatient is defended by lawyers and judges precisely because certainty of procedure reduces the degree of uncertainty in a form of decision making marked by a relatively high rate of change and thus uncertainty at the substantive level.

To sum up then: courts, rather than being set apart by a peculiar style of decision making or a unique taught tradition of *stare decisis,* are firmly within the incremental style of decision making generally shared by political and other organizational decision makers.

It is in the end hardly surprising that courts make incremental decisions given the nature of American politics. As we have already noted, incrementalism is intimately associated with the multidecision-maker process which is the central feature of American government and politics, and courts are an integral part of this process. Each court of appeals and the Supreme Court is a multidecision-maker court. With their hierarchy of trial and appellate tribunals, the courts considered by themselves constitute a system of multidecision makers. As subordinate lawmakers the courts considered collectively are one of the multidecision makers in the lawmaking process. Given this integration of individual judge, individual court and whole court system into a process of widely shared decision making, it would indeed by remarkable if courts did not decide incrementally, since none of the decision makers in this process is free to effectuate independent, global decisions fully consistent with his own goals even if his internal rationality were great enough to allow him to make such decisions.

There is a peculiar paradox at work in the traditional separation of courts from other political decision makers on the grounds of their peculiar thought processes. For what is peculiar about courts is that they have always been openly, consciously, and formally incremental, and have even developed a special language and lore of *stare decisis* to express that incrementalism. But this very language and lore has been used to set them apart from other government agencies which, striving at least to appear to satisfy an unrealistic norm of rationality, were not fully conscious of their own incrementalism and certainly not anxious to openly announce it as the courts were doing. In other words, it is precisely because other agencies have always considered themselves to be rational while courts have been stressing incrementalism (reaching right decisions through the case-by-case process of inclusion and exclusion according to the technique of *stare decisis*) as their own peculiar virtue that a gap has appeared to exist. Once it is recognized that other agencies too act incrementally, then the gap disappears.

Courts then are not distinguished by a peculiar taught tradition, style, or technique of decision making. Basically they share the technique of incrementalism just as they share nearly all their characteristics with other political agencies in general and with their fellow subordinate law-makers, the administrative agencies, in particular.

COURTS VERSUS ADMINISTRATIVE AGENCIES— A FALSE VISION

To those who bring a fresh eye to the relations between courts and administrative agencies, all this may seem mildly interesting, but little more. Traditionally, however, the study of administrative law has been burdened with certain visions that have made it difficult to observe courts and agencies in their natural relation. It has generally been assumed that courts were very different from agencies. It followed that the real purpose of judicial review of adminis-trative decisions was to set two essentially different and antagonistic kinds of agencies against one another in some sort of checks-and-balances game or at the very least to allow the courts to improve on the product of the administra-tive agencies by adding their unique virtues to the agency's decisional product.

As a result, administrative law has usually involved a debate between "procourt" and "proagency" forces. Pro-agency forces have usually viewed judicial review as the weapon of those hostile to administrative agencies and the tasks of positive planning and government regulation of private enterprise. Procourt forces have frequently set up the courts as unique sources of fairness and wisdom against the arbitrary, unwise and self-aggrandizing behavior of bureaucrats. Many of these attitudes are historical hangovers from the New Deal and even earlier. Courts, staffed by successful lawyers most of whom had been representing business interests, tended to be hostile to administrative activity. Administrative agencies were, quite naturally, staffed largely by men with a commitment to government programs, and this was particularly true in the first years of a new agency's operation when it was likely to have to litigate most frequently.[38] These phenomena were most marked in the New Deal period when a Democratic administration was creating a host of new agencies and reviving a host of old ones to carry out bold, new government programs, and staffing them with a host of new men of liberal-to-radical persuasion, while the courts were largely staffed with conservative judges and the Supreme Court labored under a conservative majority.

The clashes between courts and agencies that grew out of these phenomena were not, however, a result of the essentially conflicting natures and functions of judicial and administrative agencies but of the essentially conflicting political ideologies of their personnels. The conflicts which an older generation took to be natural and inevitable, because indwelling in the nature of the institutions themselves, were in fact only the historically limited accidents of staffing. Most of the conflict disappeared as the staffs of both courts and agencies came to share the consensus that has built up around the moderate and pragmatic liberalism of the New Deal.

It is extremely important, therefore, not to begin the study of courts and agencies with the traditional assumption of institutional conflict. In fact, courts and agencies are both

---

38. Marver Berstein suggests that regulatory agencies pass through life cycles from vigorous youth to impotent old age. Berstein, *Regulating Business by Independent Commission* (1955)

supplementary lawmakers who perform this task in roughly the same way, in roughly the same political environment and under roughly the same sorts of pressure. In any particular situation differences in the way each functions are likely to be a matter of degree, and these differences of degree are likely to widen or narrow or even reverse themselves from one situation to another. Given these similarities it is more reasonable to assume that a basic harmony will exist between courts and agencies than that they will be in conflict.

POLICY ISSUES IN THE COURTS

Having shown that courts and agencies are both policy-making bodies operating in roughly the same way, it might still be possible clearly to differentiate courts from agencies if the agencies handled one range of policy considerations and the courts quite another. In fact they do not. In many instances—patent-infringement suits and enforcement of N.L.R.B. orders directed against "unfair labor practices" for example—courts must decide precisely the same question put in precisely the same form as must the administrative agency. Where the question for the agency is one of "convenience and necessity," reviewing courts too must ask and answer the same questions about the needs of the real world as must the agency, although they may give the benefit of the doubt to agency answers. Where the issue is the meaning of language in a statute, both the agency and the court look at the language, and both of them must make a decision on what it means on the basis of their policy predilections and those they impute to the statute maker, since there is no other way to make statutory language "mean" anything. Where the problem is filling in the subprovisions of a general or vague statute, or filling in an unanticipated loophole —in short, in the classic case of supplementary subordinate lawmaking—agency and court are both faced with the identical question: What shall the law be? And to the extent that a court wishes to answer this question at all, i.e., to exercise review, it must make the same kind of factual determinations and policy choices as do the agencies. Lawmaking is lawmaking regardless of its author.

Finally in the classic instance that is supposed to separate agencies from courts, the policy questions remain identical. Courts must frequently decide whether an agency had the jurisdiction to do a certain thing. The cases fairly shout that a court that reaches the same policy judgments as the agency is more likely to find that the agency has jurisdiction. Thus the reviewing court goes through the same process of making up its mind on policy as the agency did. And if it reaches the same conclusion, it has gone a long way toward solving the jurisdiction problem.

Perhaps a more important consideration is that questions of agency jurisdiction are not legal puzzles in which a court simply seeks to fit the right piece in the right hole. Typically, jurisdictional questions involve real political issues of whether circumstances justify an agency in pushing its statutory commission outward. What benefits to the public would such an expansion bring? What opposition will it incur? To what extent will it lead to overlap or conflict in jurisdictions? If the agency does not move, will a "no-man's-land" exist where no one is properly regulating what should be regulated? Is this agency or some other best for the job? Will the statute maker react adversely to the expansion? These are the questions the agency must ask of itself before expanding its jurisdiction. They are also precisely the questions a court must ask in deciding whether to approve or require such an expansion.

Often the prototype of judicial review is thought to be the instance in which a court says: It matters not whether the agency's policy is right or wrong; it is clearly illegal and unauthorized by the statutes. Here it would seem that the courts play a noble role isolated from that of the agency. Actually this is not a prototype but one extreme end of a spectrum along which most points concern the much more ambiguous question, What should the statute mean?—a question that is not peculiar to one subordinate lawmaker or the other. But even in the extreme, and thus atypical, instance, the agency must have decided yes before the court decided no. It is not the question, or the way of deciding it, that was different for court and agency. The question was always, What will the statute allow? All that was different was the answer. Two political actors may sometimes arrive at opposite answers, but this occasional opposition should hardly be taken as the definitive aspect of their relation or as proof that they are fundamentally different from one another.

JUDICIAL REVIEW: WHY AND WHEN

If all this is true, the major question may well be why we have judicial review of administrative decisions at all. If we have two large institutional blocs each doing the same jobs in the same way, why should one repeat a task that the other has just completed? If courts are just like agencies, why should a court repeat the same process of decision that the agency has just been through? Given human nature and the difficulty of real-world problems, it may in some instances come up with a different decision, but there is no reason to assume that it will be a better one. Indeed it must be stressed here at the outset that the overwhelmingly typical action of courts exercising review is to refuse to substitute their own decisions for those of the agency, and that only in a handful of the thousands of agency decisions made each year is there even an effort by the adversely affected party to get a second decision from the courts. A leading text on administrative law emphasizes this point by noting that of the 2,000 formal orders issued by the Securities and Exchange Commission in its first ten years of operation only 100 were appealed to the courts, and only three were set aside by judicial decision.[39]

On the other hand, there is no reason to assume that courts will make bad second decisions—at least in the sense of thwarting agency policies. The old conflict-oriented vision

---

39. Gellhorn and Byse, *Administrative Law* 213-14 (1960)

assumed that whatever its benefits in guarding against bureaucratic evils, review entailed very high costs in terms of
policy disruption. Since the courts were so different from
and hostile to the agencies, they would frequently intervene
piecemeal to change agency decisions and thus destroy the
continuity and coordination of administrative policy making.
Given the actual affinities between courts and agencies,
there is no reason to assume that review will be exercised
disruptively.

Nevertheless the time delays and costs of double decision
making, plus the fact that an overworked federal courts
system ought not to do things it need not do, lead to the
general conclusion that courts ought not to review agency
decisions unless, within the particular field of law and within
the particular circumstances at the moment, and considering
the attitudes and policies of the agency, review will yield a
better policy product than nonreview. As we shall see shortly,
this is precisely the rule of review adopted, if not openly
proclaimed, by the Supreme Court. This rule has caused
much distress among practitioners because, not surprisingly,
it is a political rule to handle a political problem, not a
legal rule of the sort to warm the heart of an analytical
jurist. For such a rule does not state clearly, precisely, and
for all time on exactly what legal questions the courts will
substitute their own judgment for that of the administrative
agency. Instead the courts say that while in general they
won't intervene, they will intervene when in a given instance,
all circumstances considered, intervention is politically desirable. And the range of circumstances may be very broad.
An agency may be making a series of mutually contradictory
interpretations of a vague law, choosing in each instance the
one which aids its own position. Congress may have passed
two contradictory laws. The agency's staff may have been
packed with ardent supporters of one of the two interests the
agency is supposed to referee. The agency may be consistently
ignoring real-world conditions that make it impossible to
follow its orders. Two agencies may be involved in a jurisdictional dispute that Congress and the President are unable

to resolve but that must be resolved. In any or all of those circumstances a court may choose to intervene when it feels it can do a better, fairer job. Whether we as political analysts approve the intervention depends upon whether in fact the court can do a better job in the particular instance.

This kind of political rule unfortunately does not resolve itself into a neat series of legal propositions that can be used as paragraph headings in a law textbook. The circumstances justifying intervention are too various and interdependent to permit their reduction to a few simple descriptive statements. Thus many students of administrative law, working desperately to fit the court's behavior into a framework of legal logical rules essentially based on the notion of court-agency antagonism, have become deeply disgruntled at the lack of judicial "consistency." Certain consistencies or at least certain dominant factors are, however, present if the legal materials are viewed from a more realistic angle.

First of all, we have noted that the one major difference between courts and agencies is that courts are generalists and agencies are specialists. It has frequently been found desirable to introduce an element of generalism into policy making to offset the parochialism, lack of perspective, and overvaluing of a few limited goals at the expense of all others that may go with a specialization that quite naturally views the things with which it constantly concerns itself as more important than the rest of us might view them. The Internal Revenue Service provides a simple example. The Service devotes its whole energies to collecting taxes. Increasing the public revenue is its goal, and a good tax collector is surely he who collects all the taxes possible. While no one would doubt that the Service seeks to be fair to all, no one would want the Service to be less than zealous in the interest of the government. Thus there is always the lurking danger that the goals of equity to all taxpayers and tax benefits to some which are part of our overall tax policy may be somewhat subordinated to the goal of maximum tax yield. For after all the I.R.S. is, and is supposed to be, the faithful servant of the Treasury. Put another way, men who spend their lives in a constant struggle to defend the government's coffers against the constant stream of new dodges thought up by tax lawyers, accountants, and wily entrepreneurs are likely to develop a rather peculiar view of the world and one not as favorable to the interests of the taxpayer as might be desirable.

One major organizing concept in examining the relation of courts to agencies is therefore the counterbalancing of specialism by generalism. Where the courts' more general perspective will yield better policy results than the more specialized views of the agency, the process of double decision is justified. The other side of the coin is, of course, that on many questions, only the technically qualified specialist is capable of giving good answers, and on those it would be wrong for courts to challenge agency judgment. This side of the coin has, unfortunately, often been given excessive emphasis and blown up into a general proposition that since agencies are expert, and courts are not, courts should not intervene in agency judgment. There has been much careless language to this effect in Supreme Court opinions. The result is great confusion when the Court does intervene and thus seemingly contradicts its own rationale and breaks its own rule. Once the rule is more carefully stated it will prove useful guidance for both the courts and their critics. Judges do' and should intervene when the decision to be made would benefit from the greater perspective of the generalist. They do not and should not intervene where only the specialist is capable of making the judgment. And they should not intervene where they find that the specialist has maintained sufficient perspective not to need the correction of the generalist. This last point is important. The wastes of double decision should not occur simply because a given question is of the sort that a generalist can understand and handle, but only when the specialist is not handling it well because of excessive parochialism engendered by his specialization. Thus it is not enough to examine the nature of the question. The nature and current attitudes of the agency are also crucial.

This is precisely why judicial review of administrative decision does not fall into neat and eternally fixed categories arranged by legal subject matter. The capacity of any given agency to see things in broad perspective is a crucial factor in determining judicial intervention or withdrawal, and that capacity may change from time to time. Thus courts may quite rightly intervene at one time where they have quite rightly refused to intervene at another.

If the one essential difference between courts and agencies—the contrast between generalist and specialist—provides us with one major category for understanding judicial review of administrative decisions, their major shared characteristic provides us with another. Courts and agencies are both supplementary lawmakers *subordinated* to the statute maker. This shared subordination inevitably determines one facet of their relationship to one another. Where the statute to which they are both subordinated is reasonably precise, the agency is likely to follow it relatively faithfully, and no review is likely to occur. Where the statute is quite vague there may be some quite artificial quarreling over what Congress really meant, when what it really meant was to be vague; but the real question will be, what policy ought to be adopted now that the statute maker by his vagueness has left his subordinates free to choose among several? There is no particular reason for double decisions on such questions, and courts will not usually intervene unless they find that the agency's perspectives are too narrow.

There is, however, a third and frequently recurring situation, in which the statute maker has invited his administrative subordinate to make and continuously alter policy within certain statutory guidelines. These guidelines are theoretically policed by the statute maker himself. Congress, given proper Presidential support or at least neutrality, can pass amendments that in effect chastise agencies and reverse their decisions when they go beyond the guidelines. The theoretical capacities of Congress are, in practice, severely limited by several factors. The first is that of time. The agencies make thousands of decisions concerning hun-

dreds of statutory programs. Given its limited staff and the
pressure of new legislative proposals, Congress cannot actually supervise the agencies very closely. Secondly, an agency
wishing to avoid or eliminate one of the guidelines is not
likely to be so politically inept as to make a direct assault
upon it. Instead it will mount a series of relatively obscure
decisions each of which partially or indirectly encroaches
on the guideline until it is gradually eroded away. Even if
it had the time to examine every decision, Congress has
neither the continuity of review nor the institutional memory
necessary to spot and turn back these covert campaigns.

The courts, however, do have the time, the continuity,
and the institutional memory necessary to identify and
thwart such agency efforts. It was therefore natural for the
statute maker to set its judicial subordinate to watch its
administrative one. Again it must be stressed that this is not
to establish a general and overall, antagonistic relation between two quite different beasts—a sort of tiger–elephant
confrontation. It is precisely because both agencies and
courts are supplementary lawmakers, both decide individual
cases within a legal framework, and each is dependent on the
other as both work at essentially similar tasks that courts
can effectively defend congressional guidelines. For it is only
a court that constantly and intimately confronts roughly the
same problems in roughly the same format as the agency that
will have sufficient sophistication and opportunity to spot
and squelch agency wanderings before they get too far afield.
Here, then, is another special instance in which dual decision
by agencies and courts yields a peculiar advantage and so
justifies review.

What has been said so far assumes relatively clear statutory guidelines within which agencies were intended to
operate. In many instances the statute vests far greater discretion in the agency, allowing it to engage in wide-ranging
policy making of its own. The statute may establish few if
any outer limits to the agency's discretion. In such statutory
schemes it is usually clear that the statute maker did not
intend to leave the agency totally free. But it is typically not

clear what limits were intended, and indeed it must frequently be admitted realistically that no exact limits have been stated precisely because the various participants in statute making could not agree or had not thought about what the limits should be. Such statutes are open invitations to all supplementary lawmakers to make large amounts of law to fill in their meaning. Yet it seems unwise to allow the agency to remain alone in the field, entirely defining its own powers as it goes along and drastically altering its policies whenever it sees fit. Such statutes are in effect announcements by the statute maker that the agency is being granted an exploratory commission to develop a new jurisdiction and new power that will only become clearly defined as the agency explores what limits on its powers and what substantive policies ought to be written into the statute. We return to the problem, however, that neither Congress nor the President is institutionally capable of continuously watching all or indeed any of the explorers it has sent out. Moreover, the reaction time of the statute maker to the new knowledge gained by exploration is inevitably rather slow. What is necessary is a mechanism that will allow the explorer to explore and even undertake important schemes of colonial development, but will prevent him from slaughtering all the natives or diverting the courses of the major rivers at least until those who sent him out can become aware of what he is doing and stop him if they want to.

Here again courts provide a useful surveillance, reporting, and delaying mechanism precisely because as supplementary lawmakers they too are concerned with filling in the statute and so are out and about in the bush themselves. And here too the limited nature of what the courts do must be stressed. Even where the statute is a broadly worded agency commission to explore, dual decision making will be necessary only where the courts feel that the agency is attempting major shifts in policy without giving the statute maker time to react, or is acting so arbitrarily, sporadically, or inconsistently as to thwart the exploratory experiment itself.

Typically where Congress has given a regulatory commission or other administrative agency something of a roving commission, it has not specified very carefully how far the agency is to rove or just what changes in policy should inspire a new look at the whole problem by Congress. On the other hand, it has passed such statute in the context of judicial review and on the assumption that judicial review would operate on the agency. In effect, then, what it has often done is to commission the agency to use its discretion in policy exploration and commission the courts to use their discretion in determining when the problem should be returned to Congress for another look by a court decision saying that the agency has gone further than it legally could under the old statute.

CONCLUSION

Judicial review of administrative decisions is not, then, a constant battle between two great and fundamentally differing institutional antagonists, but a more intimate, cooperative interrelationship between two supplementary lawmakers. In this relationship there is no reason to assign one or the other member special precedence or to finally assign a given weight to either. For the whole advantage of the system is a flexibility which allows either side to intervene to correct the faults of the other. Of course in general administrative decisions ought to stand, not because they are intrinsically better, but because they are usually first in time. All things being equal, there is no need for a second decision maker, no better or worse than the first, to make a decision all over again that has already been made. On the other hand, when all other things are not equal, when agency parochialism or overambition need correction, there is no reason why the courts should not do the correcting. Indeed if the statute maker should choose to vest the courts with initial decision making in certain areas, as it has for instance in antitrust and labor contracts, the courts' decisions will be the only ones unless they appear to be peculiarly un-satisfactory.

Thus it is hardly possible to set down a few, simple iron-clad and legalistic rules that define agency–court relations under all circumstances. It is even less possible to weave all of the courts' past decisions into a complex and logically satisfying pattern of rules that establishes a special rule for each special instance which is compatible with all the other special rules for all the other special instances. Only if one keeps firmly in mind the intimate and essentially political relationship between two essentially similar supplementary lawmakers—one a generalist, one a specialist; one usually vested with first decisions; the other with second; and one charged in certain special instances with watching the ex-plorations of the other—can we hope to make sense out of the actual contacts of courts with administrators recorded in the case books and labeled administrative law.

2

Administrative Law

After an essentially political introduction, we may now turn to the traditional rubric of "administrative law" under which lawyers have treated the relations between courts and agencies. There has been considerable debate about just what "administrative law" means, or more precisely, just what aspects of juristic behavior should be encompassed within its boundaries. This debate is the result of certain historical conflicts about some now largely dead issues and need trouble us only briefly. By the nineteenth century most law in Great Britain and the United States was either statutory law enacted by legislatures or case law (common law) created by judicial decisions and their accompanying opinions. At the very minimum, men could hardly ever be sent to jail or deprived of valuable property or expectations without court action. During the nineteenth century both nations began to proliferate administrative agencies charged with various tasks, such as safety and health regulation, that inevitably entailed supplementary lawmaking and the adjudication of individual claims. This growth of "administrative law"—that is, law made and applied by administrative agencies—was naturally viewed with great disfavor by the adherents of laissez faire and more generally by the champions of courts who quite accurately saw that administrative agencies were displacing courts from many areas of policy making that had previously been left to judges. Much of the thinking that automatically treats courts and agencies as quite different and antagonistic creatures is a hangover from this period in which courts and their defenders fought to prevent the growth of agencies.

As part of this whole polemic it was not uncommon at the beginning of the twentieth century in Anglo-American legal circles to deny that such a thing as "administrative law" existed in English-speaking countries and to claim that it was a purely continental European phenomenon. What was really meant was not that administrative law did not exist, but that some lawyers wished that administrative agencies would not be allowed to make law the way courts did.

Eventually it became impossible for any legal scholar to ignore the existence of administrative law, but the early distaste for it as a foreign, socialistic, antijudicial, and unlawyerly sort of thing continued to cling for many years and in some circles still does today. This continuing distaste had some peculiar results. Those who felt that administrative law should be studied sought ways of making it more palatable to old-line lawyers and thus get it accepted into legal good standing and into law-school curricula. Those who wished it would go away, but knew it was going to stay, wished to make it look as legal and judicial as possible. The two sides reached a mutually satisfactory solution. Administrative law ceased to be the law that administrative agencies made and became instead the rules that governed when, where, and how courts would review agency findings and the rules governing the procedures of agencies.

Defined in this way, "administrative law" directed attention back toward courts and judges not only because it shifted attention from the agencies themselves to the nexus

between courts and agencies but for several other reasons as
well. Since the rules defining judicial review are largely
made by courts and are basically to be found in judicial
opinions, the law student continued his traditional study of
court cases rather than turning to actual agency practice,
and administrative law became simply another pigeonhole
into which court cases could be sorted. Just as before, the
actual lawmaking done by administrative agencies was ignored, perhaps in the hope that it would somehow go away,
and attention remained fully focused on what it had always
been focused upon—lawmaking by judges. Finally, by defining administrative law as the law of procedure the lawyer
kept to ground that was eminently respectable and long
familiar. Lawyers have always felt that procedure was a peculiar and probably the central concern of Anglo-American
law. If administrative law was procedural law then it must
be a good thing worthy of a lawyer's study and creative
efforts. Such a procedural focus tended to leave in some sort
of nonlegal limbo the substantive policies and decisions of
administrative agencies.

    Although this definition of administrative law—and it
is the one most widely accepted today[1]—seems to me to have
grown up from a polemical rather than a scientific base, it
can be defended today as convenient. After all, a definition
is never right or wrong—it can only be convenient or inconvenient. There is a large body of legal materials that bears
on judicial review of administrative action, and a large and
considerably overlapping body of materials on what constitutes proper agency procedure. The two overlap so heavily
precisely because much judicial review of agency action con-

---

1. See 1 Davis, *Administrative Law Treatise* 1-6 (1958). Readers familiar
    with their writings will easily recognize the dependence of portions
    of this chapter on the distinguished work of Professors Davis and
    Jaffe (*Judicial Control of Administrative Action* [1965]). The survey
    of the traditional categories of administrative law presented later in
    the chapter, while hopefully presenting matters in a light peculiarly
    relevant to students of political jurisprudence, relies so heavily on
    these two distinguished scholars as to make no claim to originality.
    I hasten to add, however, that neither author should be held respon-
    sible for my emphases or interpretations.

cerns itself with whether or not the agency has followed proper procedures. It might therefore seem convenient to lump the two together and set them aside as one of the areas of law that lawyers should study, just as it is convenient to set aside an area called torts or one called contract.

Aside from the fact that many of those exposed to administrative law so defined are likely to become confused and think they know all that they need to of agency legal activity, there is another and much more important factor that makes such a definition of administrative law damnably inconvenient. We have already seen that the relationship between courts and agencies is that of two essentially similar supplementary lawmakers subordinated to the same statute maker and that judicial review of administrative decisions is basically a system of double decision. From this it follows that review should occur only when the agency's decision is excessively parochial and would be improved by the intervention of a judicial generalist, or when the agency is essaying major or erratic shifts in policy which seem to go beyond its exploratory commission. Both of these are essentially substantive, not procedural, considerations. In other words when, where, and how a court ought to review an agency decision depends upon the substance of that decision. To be sure, for a number of reasons we shall examine later, courts seek to dress their review in the language of procedure, but review actually rests on the substantive intervention of a generalist against a specialist or of a specially commissioned watchdog against agencies holding vague exploratory commissions. While courts do sometimes intervene to correct poor agency procedures, their procedural objections are more often simply vehicles for their objection to substantive policy decisions. As I have repeatedly pointed out, a court would be wasting governmental resources if it second-guessed agencies on every decision, but under certain limited circumstances double decision is justified, and it is double decision on the substance of policy.

If administrative law is defined to exclude the substantive questions of transportation, communication, labor,

fair trade, antitrust, patent, and other law, which are the
actual subjects of the double decisions, then we are left with
the various procedural vehicles emptied of the real freight
of problems they have been used to haul and which determines when and in what direction they are set in motion.
Moreover courts, with their eye on substance, are frequently
careless of what procedural rule they use, how they phrase
it, and whether today's use is consistent with yesterday's. The
elimination of substantive policy concerns from administrative law reduces it to a formal, verbal, and ritualistic body of
legal rhetoric divorced from the actual political phenomena
which determine court–agency relations. Moreover, since the
whole rationale of review lies at the substantive level of
whether a given administrative policy really does or does not
need a second decision, removal of substantive concerns
leaves administrative law without any fundamental guidelines. Perhaps most important, if courts, their eyes firmly
fixed on substance, seek to make good policy by whatever
procedural tools come to hand, whereas students of administrative law ignore whether the courts are making substantive
sense and concern themselves only with neatness and consistency on matters of procedure, the result will be, and has
been, that administrative lawyers see in the work of courts
great confusion and contradiction. The contradiction may
be there, but it is only at the level of tools—the court may
choose the monkey wrench of "standing" one day and the
screwdriver of "exhaustion of administrative remedies" the
next. Such inconsistency is not unimportant. But it is not
nearly as important as it looks to those who keep their eyes
firmly fixed on the tool kit and never look at the product that
comes off the bench.

In short, when questions of substantive policy are defined out of administrative law, the underlying and unifying
factors in court-agency relations are lost, and what remains
is a clutter of procedural rules which seem to lack coherence precisely because the factors underlying them have
disappeared. And then since the administrative lawyer will
look only at precisely that area of agency–court relations that

is confused, refusing to consider that area from which an underlying coherence might be derived, he inevitably over-emphasizes the disorder and inconsistency of courts in trans-acting their administrative law business.

In proceeding now to a brief outline of what tradition-ally has been called "administrative law" in the narrower sense, it is not my intention to provide a primer or simplified introduction for the beginning student. For such a primer is of little value in a field of law that is so riddled with doc-trinal contradictions, detailed exceptions, and assorted hiat-uses and fluxes. A grasp of the bare general rules will shed little light on the politically crucial cases, for such cases are typically made to turn on some doctrinal ambiguity. For the investigator primarily concerned with the politics of court–agency relations, the best tactic is to master the relevant technical points as they arise in his researches. There is a large corpus of texts, casebooks, and treatises designed to facilitate his efforts in that direction.

It is important, however, to understand that the multi-tudinous and esoteric tags of administrative law, such as ripeness, adequacy of findings, and estoppel, do not exist in a vacuum but are essentially doctrinal reflections of certain fundamental political questions about the capacity and will of courts to intervene in the process of administrative de-cision making. Indeed, a grouping of the doctrinal tags around the fundamental questions, and a frank acknowledge-ment that the cases involve these questions rather than super-ficial and academic quarrels about such things as the precise line between ripeness and exhaustion, yield a kind of general clarity that will escape those overly immersed in the technical details.

PRIMARY JURISDICTION

We might begin at a point where the fundamental ques-tions are most evident, the doctrine of "primary jurisdiction." The word "primary" is an ambiguous one and symbolizes precisely the political question—the question of who does what—that underlies the doctrine. If we say X has primary jurisdiction, we may mean that he handles the matter first. Alternately we may mean that he has the major or overwhelming say in the matter and that others have not second, but secondary, or subordinate, or no jurisdiction.

Within the first of the two senses of the word primary, the argument runs as follows. Where a question of fact arises in the course of litigation that is sufficiently technical to fall squarely within the expertise of an agency but is at the periphery of the court's understanding, then the litigants ought first to go to the agency for a decision on the technical question. The agency's decision will then be of assistance to the court in arriving at its overall decision on the litigation. Judges express this position by opinions which refuse to rule in a case because the matter lies within the primary jurisdiction of an administrative agency. In this sense the doctrine of primary jurisdiction merely establishes a timetable. The agency must hear the matter first. The court will hear it second.

On the other hand, a court may feel that (1) decision of a certain matter has been vested by the statute solely in the agency and is not even within the power of the court to decide (e.g., the reasonableness of a freight rate) or (2) that the matter is so technical that the courts ought, on their own initiative, to refuse to make a decision independently or reverse an agency decision (e.g., the safety of a locomotive), or (3) that the particular matter is so interconnected with other matters in a scheme of regulation requiring uniformity, continuity, and central direction that the court ought not to intervene sporadically but instead leave everything to the agency that is in the business of working out a coordinated program (e.g., the unfairness of a certain labor union practice). Unfortunately the term primary jurisdiction has been used to cover all three of these lines of thought, which really involve quite fundamentally different issues, and in this sense "primary" means not first but exclusive jurisdiction.

When used in this sense the court is not setting a timetable but declaring that the matter is solely for the agency.

Almost inevitably there is also a middle ground where the distinction between these two senses of "primary" becomes confused. A court may say that a given question, which arises as one of several in a given case, ought first to be decided by the agency (timetable). It may, however, mean either that once the agency has decided the question, the court will decide it all over again using the agency decision as an aid (timetable); or that once the agency has decided it, the court will accept the agency's decision absolutely without exercising its own independent judgment (exclusive), or that the court will give "great weight" to the agency's judgment and only reverse the agency if it is absolutely convinced the agency was wrong (timetable but moving a long way toward exclusive). To confuse the matter further, courts frequently invoke "great weight" or similar phrases when they really are using the agency decision only as an aid. And they sometimes speak of the agency as having primary (exclusive) jurisdiction on questions of fact and primary (timetable) jurisdiction on questions of law when, as we shall see shortly, it is impossible to distinguish neatly between questions of fact and law.

As the investigator encounters the primary jurisdiction cases,[2] therefore, he must penetrate deeply enough into the argument to discover what the court wants to do, what it does not want to do at all, what it wants to do only later after the agency has acted, and why it wants to act now, later, or not at all.

---

2. e.g. the *Abilene* case, 204 U.S. 426 (1907); the *American Tie* case, 234 U.S. 138 (1914); the *Great Northern* case, 259 U.S. 285 (1922); *United States v. Western Pacific R. R. and United States v. Chesapeake and Ohio Ry.*, 352 U.S. 59, 77 (1956); *T.I.M.E.*, 359 U.S. 464 (1959); the *Hewitt-Robins* case, 371 U.S. 84 (1962); *San Diego Building Trades v. Garman*, 359 U.S. 236 (1959); *Garner v. Teamster's Local Union*, 346 U.S. 485 (1953); *Smith v. Evening News Assn.* 371 U.S. 195 (1962); *Pan American World Airways v. United States*, 371 U.S. 296 (1963); *United States v. Philadelphia Nat. Bank*, 374 U.S. 321 (1963).

EXHAUSTION

Similar kinds of problems of timing and court withdrawal arise in the confusingly interconnected areas of "exhaustion," "ripeness," and "standing." Hundreds of thousands of words have been expended in distinguishing each from the other, but they persist in coming back together again. The general definitions appear at first glance relatively simple and distinct. A court will not normally admit a litigant unless he has exhausted his administrative remedies —that is, unless he has submitted himself to all the steps in the various agency processes that would gain him what he wanted if the agency were to decide in his favor. When a court deals with exhaustion, it is not concerning itself with the question: "What things should courts do and what things are best left entirely to administrators"? It is asking only: "Has this person done everything he should have to get what he wanted from the agency before coming to us?" After all, why should a court intervene in agency affairs to get something for X, when X with a little more effort and patience might have gotten it from the agency by himself? Moreover, it is to neither the administrator's nor the judge's advantage to allow petitioners to begin proceedings in one place, interrupt them to go to another, and then perhaps bounce back to the first. At this simplified level, exhaustion is simply a category of judicial economy and a guarantee of orderly, one-step and one-place-at-a-time procedures. If you have a dispute with an administrative agency you must seek to resolve it first in the agency and make sure you have done everything possible at the agency level before bothering a court.

While all this makes sense at the superficial level, the realities are much more complex. One of the outstanding authorities in the field describes the real situation succinctly.

The law embodied in the holdings clearly is that sometimes exhaustion is required and sometimes not. No

court requires exhaustion when exhaustion will involve
irreparable injury and when the agency is palpably without
jurisdiction; probably every court requires exhaustion when
the question presented is one within the agency's specialization and when the administrative remedy is as likely as
the judicial remedy to provide the wanted relief. In between these extremes is a vast array of problems on which
judicial action is variable and difficult or impossible to
predict.[3]

It must be added that courts are somewhat less likely to require exhaustion when the constitutionality of a statute is
brought into question, or when some intermediate order of
the agency, which will not be followed by a final order for
some time is likely to severely damage the individual.

Several major problems underlie the confusion in the
exhaustion area, and they are, of course, aggravated by the
ritualistic insistence that courts require exhaustion when the
fact is that courts only sometimes require exhaustion. When
a case is encountered in which the court says that exhaustion
is a firm principle, what it really means is that the court
chooses to require exhaustion in that case.

The first of the major problems is that modern patterns
of administrative authority have become so incredibly complex that it is very frequently difficult to decide whether a
given agency has jurisdiction over a given matter. A very
large share of disputes between individuals and agencies
involves the question of jurisdiction. Now it seems somehow
ridiculous to tell a man who is insisting that an agency has
no jurisdiction over him that he must submit himself to the
agency's jurisdiction for months or years of hearings and
paper-shuffling before he can go to a court which may tell
him he was right and that the agency never should have
bothered him in the first place. On the other hand, precisely
because so many individual–agency disputes involve, or can
be argued to involve, jurisdiction, and the question of jurisdiction is often so intimately entangled with all the other
issues in a case, for courts to say that exhaustion is not re-

---

3. 3 Davis, *Administrative Law Treatise* 56 (1958)

quired where jurisdictional issues are involved would almost totally undercut the exhaustion doctrine and the advantages of economy and order that go with it. As a result courts exercise discretion, allowing exemption from the exhaustion doctrine when it seems fairly clear to them that a serious doubt about jurisdiction exists. Too often, however, instead of simply saying either that the agency does or does not have jurisdiction a court will invoke the exhaustion doctrine when it thinks the agency clearly does have jurisdiction and grant an exemption from the exhaustion doctrine when it thinks the agency clearly does not.

The second major problem involves the very long periods of time, typically several years, that it takes an individual to work his way completely through agency proceedings. For he encounters the paradox that precisely because agency proceedings have become highly judicialized out of fear of excessive administrative discretion the administrator can do him more damage than ever. For instance, where an individual is seeking a license to do business he loses the potential profit from the business while the agency is deciding, and the longer it takes to finally decide the more he loses. And frequently, because of the length of agency proceedings, the agency must issue temporary, intermediate orders, each of which may also damage him. At one time most agency action was negative—that is, it ordered someone to stop doing something, so that the longer it took for the agency to render a final decision the less damage there was to an individual. Increasingly, however, particularly in the regulated industries, the entrepreneur needs government approval before he can do something, and every minute he has to wait for approval costs him foregone opportunity. Thus the time lag in agency decision making pushes every injury up toward irreparability.

The old equity category of irreparable injury was relatively clear. If your neighbor ripped out the rosebushes on the boundary they were gone forever, and so you could get an order prohibiting him from doing so until it was determined whether they were really on your land or his. Meanwhile the roses grew a little bit and the status quo hurt no one. The equity category does not fit modern problems of regulation so well, however. No one can expect the government to grant a license instantaneously. Some waiting is a normal and reasonable cost of doing business, and the loss of the money you might have made if you had been able to start to do something sooner is somehow less tangible and heart-rending than the loss of those rosebushes you already had. On the other hand, a business which is finally told, "Yes, you can begin doing the thing now that would have earned you a million dollars if you had begun doing it a year ago when you wanted to," has lost that million even more irrevocably than the neighbor who has lost his rosebushes. There is no way of replanting a lost million, and the government does not compensate businesses for such losses.

Thus when a court grants an exemption to exhaustion on the grounds of irreparable injury it frequently is exercising its discretion on the question of just how much delay and expense an individual can reasonably be expected to incur waiting around for a final agency decision before going to court. The question then is not one of just what phenomena fall into the ancient pigeonhole "irreparable injury." It is rather a question of degree. Are the costs always imposed on individuals by agency supervision at the point of being aggravated sufficiently by agency time lag to justify immediate judicial intervention?

Finally, and more generally, there is the problem that in many instances any relief the agency might give, even if the individual could convince it, would be insufficient, and the only remedy that could really satisfy him is available solely from courts. It would seem silly to tell the individual that he must spend considerable time and money working his way through an agency that cannot really help him before getting to a court that really can. Therefore exemptions to the exhaustion rule are sometimes granted when the agency remedy appears inadequate or when the individual has no means of compelling the agency to make a decision on whether he is entitled to an adequate remedy. Thus the simple common sense of the exhaustion rule—that you ought not to ask a court to intervene against an agency until you have done everything possible to convince the agency yourself—while compelling, is undercut by some very real problems. The Supreme Court's official position on exhaustion, as enunciated in the leading case of *Myers v. Bethlehem Shipbuilding Corp.*,[4] is probably the most rigid and mechanical of any court in the United States, and yet even it has been forced by the realities of the situation to exercise discretion in granting exemptions from time to time. Exhaustion is not necessarily a lawyer's procedural technicality. It frequently raises fundamental issues as to judicial intervention on behalf of the individual against an agency, and it is not without certain overtones of Kafka.

RIPENESS

Having gone at some length into the real difficulties and areas of judicial discretion that underlie what is the simplest, most mechanical, and most clearly common-sensical rule of administrative law, it may be enough to suggest only broadly the problems of the most metaphysical and esoteric of all those rules, the requirement of "ripeness."

Professor Jaffe introduces his discussion of the subject by saying that

> The requirement of "ripeness" as a condition for judicial review is not so much a definable doctrine as a compendious *portmanteau,* a group of related doctrines arising in diverse but analogically similar situations.[5]

Professor Davis, after describing five major Supreme Court cases that had held one way and three that had held the other, concludes by declaiming in italics

> *If all eight of these key cases had held the opposite on the ripeness question, and if other case law were then logi-*

4. 303 U.S. 41 (1938)
5. Jaffe, *Judicial Control of Administrative Action* 394 (Abridged Ed. 1965)

cally based upon these eight decisions as thus altered, the
body of Supreme Court law on the problem of ripeness
would at least have the virtue of coherence and consistency.[6]

It seems unlikely, therefore, that in a relatively small compass we could succeed in systematically stating the law of
ripeness in a form useful to political analysis. Some suggestions must suffice.

First of all, the question of ripeness goes not, as does
exhaustion, to the procedures of an agency but to the institutional competence of a court. When a judge asks whether a
matter is ripe for adjudication, he is asking, "Is it the sort
of question that the courts are competent to decide?" Ripeness is one of the areas where administrative becomes entangled with constitutional law, for the Supreme Court's
decisions on ripeness, even where no constitutional question
is involved, are much affected by the moods of thought (and
I use the word "moods" deliberately) established in the constitutional sphere.

Because the Supreme Court's power to declare statutes
unconstitutional obviously carries with it the potential for
major political clashes with other branches of government
and major segments of the public, the Court has always
sought doctrinal stances that would allow it to retreat from
such clashes when it wanted to and to insist that it was especially competent, and was compelled by "the law," to decide
those major political questions it wanted to decide rather
than retreat from. Thus the popularity of the cases-and-controversies rule. The Supreme Court has spent much time
and trouble building up the position that it may not decide
questions in the abstract but only those in which a genuine
legal controversy exists between two parties on a concrete
set of facts involving real and immediate damage to one of
the parties. This doctrine kills both birds. It allows the Court
to avoid handling many hot questions by turning away people who just don't like a given law. At the same time it covers
the Court when it does intervene. If a genuine legal contro-

6. Davis, *op cit supra* note 3 at 200

versy exists, the Court can claim that it is compelled to the
intervention, for courts cannot refuse to do what they are
created to do—decide legal disputes between parties—even if
they must declare a law unconstitutional in order to decide
the dispute correctly.

Thus as part of its general constitutional strategy the
Court has placed great emphasis on the point that it will
only decide concrete, immediate, disputes between two interested parties. This emphasis has heavily influenced administrative law because ripeness is the parallel category in
administrative law to cases and controversies in constitutional.

This influence is by and large unfortunate. For while
the Court may need to be especially cautious and self-pro-
tective in the constitutional sphere, it does not follow that
it need be so cautious in administrative matters. Much of
the confusion over ripeness in administrative law arises from
the failure to appreciate that a legal rhetoric which serves
as a useful political weapon in one sphere may yield quite
untoward results in another.

First of all, it simply is not true that somehow in the
very nature of things courts are only capable of handling
controversies between two parties. Nor is it an immutable
command of justice that a court refuse to intervene until
someone can show that if it does not he will forthwith lose
something he has or be fined or imprisoned. Nor is it true
that courts are inherently incapable of deciding a legal question in the abstract without its being imbedded in a concrete and crucial fact situation. Yet the Supreme Court has
said these things so often in connection with its constitutional battles that it finds it difficult to deal with the problem
of ripeness with an open and pragmatic mind.

Let us take a prototypic problem suggested by an actual
Supreme Court case.[7] Let us suppose that the F.C.C. issues
regulations specifying that independent television stations
may buy only a very small proportion of their shows from
the national networks, and announces that it will not en-

7. *Columbia Broadcasting System v. United States*, 316 U.S. 407 (1942)

force these regulations immediately but will take violation by a station into account in deciding whether to renew that station's licenses at some future time. Let us also suppose that as a result of the regulations the networks fear that the stations will reduce their business with the networks, i.e., buy fewer network shows. Note that the regulations apply only to the stations not the network. Thus the only case and controversy that could arise would occur if the station violated the regulation, was consequently denied a renewal of its license by the F.C.C., and then went to court to appeal the agency's denial of its renewal application. The networks and the F.C.C. can never be adverse parties in a case because the F.C.C. rules do not apply to the networks, so the networks cannot break them, and so, in a strict sense, they can never have a legal dispute with the agency.

Now let us suppose that within a reasonable time no station is denied a renewal on the grounds of violating these regulations, either because none of the stations disobey the regulations or none that do are up for renewal for some time. There are then no adverse parties; there is no confirmed damage or punishment to anyone who could be a party; it is a matter of pure speculation whether a dispute between the F.C.C. and the parties regulated ever will arise, and what the concrete fact situation would be if a dispute did arise. In short, there is no case. But the networks do have strong reason to fear that the regulations will damage their businesses substantially. Should they be allowed to go to court now to challenge the validity of the regulations? Should they be told to wait until later when they can concretely show their businesses have been wrecked? Should they be told to wait until a local station gets up the nerve to risk its renewal by breaking the regulation, which may be never?

Aside from this situation there are several others in which an individual or firm may have the strongest need for a present judicial determination without a readily available case and controversy vehicle. An agency regulation or a statute may be ambiguous, the agency may refuse to clarify it, and the individual may be unable to determine whether the course of action he wishes to pursue is legal or not except by undertaking the action and risking criminal punishment or financial disaster. An agency may promulgate a regulation that takes nothing from an individual but renders his future business prospects so dim that he cannot attract investment capital. An agency may classify an enterprise or thing as falling in a certain category. This categorization may effect its business prospects without concretely punishing anyone or depriving anyone of a license. An agency may list criteria on the basis of which it says it will make future legal determinations. To follow these criteria now may seriously hamper an individual's operations, yet he will not know until later just exactly how they will influence agency determinations, or whether they are really valid.

In short, ripeness typically involves two "nows" and a "later." There is some governmental statute, regulation, order, or opinion now. There is an impact on the individual's interests now. There cannot be a case and controversy in the narrow sense until later. In a modern industrial society, more and more economic and social enterprises must plan ahead, and more and more often how they fare now depends on their and other's expectations about how they will fare later. It becomes less and less satisfactory to say, "Wait until the government tries to prosecute you and then challenge the order and see what happens." On the other hand, if judges were to allow anyone to challenge any and all administrative regulations as soon as they appeared, courts would be swamped with business and would be constantly hearing excessively abstract claims devoid of any concrete evidence as to how the regulation was actually going to work out.

The problem is then essentially one of degree and timing, and when a matter is ripe for adjudication will vary on pragmatic grounds from area to area. This has been recognized by Congress in the Declaratory Judgments Act, which directs the courts to settle certain kinds of legal questions more or less in the abstract, in the provisions of various statutes specifying what agency orders are "final" and/or "reviewable" and which are not subject to judicial review, and finally in the courts' own ripeness doctrines.

A court speaking of ripeness today is probably balancing the desirability of two sets of factors. Should it intervene only after the individual and the agency have come to final loggerheads, when the issues and facts are full, firm and concrete, the injury certain not speculative, and thus when the problem is clearly and unavoidably judicial? Or should it step in to mitigate the very real damage to the interests of individuals and businesses that delay may cause in certain instances?

Because of its constitutional concerns the Supreme Court has probably erred on the side of overripeness. Certainly it has not carved out a clear and general policy, and the investigator encountering a ripeness problem in any given area must juggle the precedents on an ad hoc basis. Any court must in the end decide how much of a price in uncertainty and delay it is willing to make the litigants pay for the neat, concrete and final litigational situation it prefers to handle.

STANDING

The problem of "standing" is intimately connected with that of ripeness. In the example we used earlier, ripeness was the question of "when." Can someone go to court now to challenge the F.C.C. regulations or must he wait till later when a renewal is denied? Standing is the question of "who." Since the regulations are directed against the local stations and they alone can be punished by the F.C.C. for violation, can the networks go into court (do they have standing) to challenge the regulations? There are basically two answers to this question. The first is that anyone whose interests are damaged in fact by an agency action has standing to challenge the action in court. Under this answer the networks have standing, for their business is in fact being damaged. The second answer is that only he whose legal rights are infringed has standing. Under this answer the networks may not have standing, since they do not have a legally guaranteed right to do any particular level of business with the local stations.

In comparing these two answers a certain philosophical queasiness occurs. Many modern legal theorists would define a "right" as a legally protected interest.[8] If a court decides that a party has standing, it has said that the court will protect his interest and thus in a sense has endowed him with a legal right. Thus when a judge is asked whether X has standing, he is being asked whether he is willing to make X's interest a right. How can he say, "I will give him a right [i.e., grant him standing] if he has a legally protected interest [right]," when whether or not he has a right (i.e., has standing) is what the judge is being asked?

Would it not be better then to say that any man who has actually been hurt has standing? The tendency of courts, including the Supreme Court and the commentators, has certainly been in this direction. The leading Supreme Court decision is F.C.C. *v.* Sanders Brothers Radio Station,[9] in which an existing radio station sought to challenge the grant of a license to a new station on the ground that there were insufficient resources in the community to support two stations. Surely Sanders had no legal right to be free of competition, and freedom from competition was the only interest it had in a proceeding between the F.C.C. and some other party entirely. The Court specifically acknowledged this and nevertheless found Sanders to have standing.

While *Sanders* has been a very influential case its impact remains ambiguous, and the Supreme Court still retains much of the legal-right approach. So far we have treated standing as if there were one general rule for all situations. While there is a kind of general federal common law of standing, many federal laws have specific and varying provisions as to who has standing under the particular act. *Sanders* arose under the standing provisions of the licensing

---

8. See Ch. III, "The Supreme Court and the Patent Office," pp. 153-55.
9. 309 U.S. 470 (1940)

portion of the Federal Communications Act. The Court's specific argument was that if an existing station could not challenge a new license no one could, and Congress had not intended that new license decisions be unchallengeable in court. Thus the *Sanders* ruling can be narrowly read as applying only to F.C.C. licensing or, even if it is read as influencing the common law of standing, courts can and do frequently find that the specific wording of the standing clauses of other federal statutes demand a lot more than simple financial interest. To add to the confusion, the standing provisions of the Administrative Procedures Act, which establish the general rules to be used if a particular statute does not have its own peculiar standing requirements, are not clear—or at least the courts say they are not clear—as to whether Congress meant to follow the legal-right or adversely-affected-in-fact doctrine.

Why have courts failed to move completely to the adversely-affected-in-fact position which seems far more just than quibbling and circular argument about legal rights? The problem is that in a complex, modern society an incredibly large number of persons and firms can claim to be adversely affected by many government decisions. Even in a simple situation like *Sanders* for instance not only the existing radio station in the town, but stations in surrounding towns, newspapers, billboard owners, theaters, small businesses that cannot afford advertising, stores that sell and repair radios—in short, anyone who sells or buys advertising or entertainment or radio-connected services—might be affected. Think of the thousands of parties affected by an I.C.C. decision on whether two major railroads can merge.

While standing to challenge an administrative order in court does not legally and automatically carry with it standing to participate in agency hearings preceding the order, there is a strong tendency for a legal system to extend hearing participation along with court standing. It does not seem to make very good sense to say that a man may challenge an order in court after it has been made, but may not seek to convince the agency it is wrong before it is made.

The administrative, particularly the regulatory, agencies are already overcome by interminable hearings, with too many parties and far too many arguments and too much evidence to reach quick and efficient decisions. The courts are reluctant to add further to their burdens by adding still more parties with still more arguments and evidence.

Another judicial concern has been that in broadening standing, the floodgates of litigation would be open to every crank with an ax to grind, and that agency decisions compromising the differences between the major parties would then be challenged by individuals with only a peripheral or abstract interest. Allowing Sanders to challenge is one thing, but should every potential listener to the new station be allowed to challenge as well if he feels it should be required to devote itself entirely to health food information or poultry-raising tips?

Nevertheless there has been a marked current of opinion toward greater and greater scope for standing. Strong suggestions have been made that the federal government, like many of the states, grant standing to taxpayers to challenge any public order involving the spending of tax dollars. Of more immediate interest is the broad feeling, to be found particularly on the 2nd Circuit, and reflected in the *Sanders* decision itself, that where administrative orders ought to be challengeable in court to insure that the public interest is protected—and no one is in a position to challenge them under a narrow concept of standing—the concept of standing ought to be broadened. In this connection one can speak of "private attorneys-general," that is, individual citizens allowed to come into court to challenge administrative orders that they believe to be invalid and detrimental to the government or the public, even though they cannot demonstrate peculiar damage to themselves personally.

The law of standing is currently in flux, and the issues raised primarily revolve around the extent to which courts ought to accept responsibility for reviewing all administrative actions that may be legally invalid or limit themselves to those where a major party to the question can assert concrete injury.

UNREVIEWABLE ORDERS

While exhaustion, ripeness, and standing basically concern who may seek review when, courts must also concern themselves with what administrative orders they may review. We have already seen that the invocation of the primary jurisdiction doctrine sometimes means that the court is excluding itself entirely from review and that ripeness may also concern the total unreviewability of certain administrative decisions. In addition some statutes provide that certain agency orders and decisions be excluded from review. Courts generally, but not always, faithfully obey these specific statutory exclusions. More difficult are situations in which the statute's words seem to grant some but not complete judicial review, or where the statute seems to grant administrative discretion unbounded by explicit legal rules, or where the area of administration seems to inherently require such discretion (e.g., foreign affairs). These are all situations in which review is not explicitly excluded but in which either the will of the legislature or the nature of the world suggest that something less than complete review is required. For instance, if an administrator has been given discretion to either do or not do something with no provision in the statute as to when or why he should or should not do it, a court reviewing his decision would simply be substituting its discretion for his. There is frequently no special excuse for such a substitution. When courts argue about nonreviewability in these areas they are usually working out ad hoc judgments that are not reducible to a single neat rule, and the investigator must simply make his own ad hoc judgments to accompany theirs. Again using discretion as an example, most courts will rule that matters assigned by statute to administrative discretion are not subject to review except for "abuse of discretion." This apparently means that a court will not intervene if the administrator is good or bad but will if he is horrid. And of course if the administrator in exercising his discretion makes an error of substantive or procedural law—that is, breaks any concrete statutory rule that does happen to be around—that error is subject to judicial correction.

Courts have generally exercised a fairly strong presumption in favor of review, and this presumption is reinforced by the Administrative Procedures Act, but both the Court's tradition and the exception clauses in the Act sometimes leave judges in doubt about whether certain agency decisions are reviewable.

FINDINGS OF LAW AND FINDINGS OF FACT

Much more troublesome even than the questions of who can get review and of what orders are the questions of how much of a given administrative decision may be reviewed. The briefest summary answer is that courts may review an agency's findings of law but not its findings of fact. This answer, however, carries with it some of the most recondite mysteries of administrative law. What is a question of law and what is a question of fact, and what is a question in which law and fact are too mixed to separate (and thus reviewable), and what is a question of jurisdictional or constitutional fact (and thus reviewable because the answer to this fact question determines whether the agency had any right at all to decide the other fact questions involved)? Courts and scholars have devoted thousands of pages to these questions without totally clearing them up.

Understanding certain basic distinctions and modes of legal thought, however, will help guide the political observer through the morass. The first of these is a distinction between first- and second-order facts that courts themselves frequently fail to make. If we ask did A in fact move from point X to point Z through point Y, we are asking about first-order facts. In other words, we are simply asking about what physically happened. Courts will not normally review agency findings of first-order facts. If, however, we ask did A in fact cross the street from point X to point Z, we are asking quite a different question because we are asking not only what physically happened but also whether Y is a street or not. We are asking for something more than for raw facts. Let us say that points X and Z are on cement objects commonly known as curbs, and Y consists of the space in between and is filled with a mixture of dirt and gravel and water two feet deep. If Y is a street, then A in fact crossed the street. If Y is not a street then he in fact did not cross one. Now at first glance it may also seem a question of simple fact whether Y is a street or not. Either it is or isn't. But whether Y is a street within the meaning of a statute that forbids drunkenness in the street is also a question of law— that is, what is the legal definition of street, and does Y meet that definition? It is the duty of courts to say what words in statutes mean, whether they do or do not refer to any given phenomenon. Perhaps in a legal sense Y is not a street, but a private driveway, an abandoned easement, public property formerly but not now a thoroughfare open to public use, etc., etc. In other words, whether Y is a street is a question of second-order fact. It requires establishment of some first-order physical facts, but also interpretation of these facts to decide whether they fit into a certain legal category.

Did A in fact swing his arm and did his fist in fact contact B's jaw? is a question of first-order facts. Presumably all observers could agree on their answers no matter what their knowledge or lack of knowledge of law. Did A in fact assault B? is a question of second-order fact. An answer to it depends on what you and the law mean by assault. My answer might be "No, all A did was give B a friendly tap on the chin." Your answer might be "Yes, true it was only a tap but to me any kind of blow is an assault." Courts sometimes review findings of second-order fact and sometimes they do not. Generally speaking, the more interpretation of the first-order facts is necessary to reach a conclusion on second-order facts, the more likely they are to review.

The second major distinction is that between appellate courts and fact finders. Much of the relation between agency and reviewing court was built up by analogy to the relation between trial court and reviewing court. An appellate court generally prefers not to alter a trial court's findings of first-order facts because the trial court has heard the witnesses, seen the physical evidence, and is generally much closer in time and space to the physical happenings involved than is an appellate court which sees only a printed record. Reviewing courts tend to treat administrative agencies in the same way because it was the administrative agency that held the actual hearings to discover the facts. Unlike trial courts, however, most administrative agencies deal largely in documentary evidence that an appeals court could evaluate just as well as the original evaluators. On the other hand, a hearing usually involves such volumes of documentary evidence that appeals courts would not have the time to work through it all. These two considerations thus balance one another and leave the trial-court analogy dominant.

As to second-order facts, reviewing courts have always been more willing to intervene against trial courts, but this willingness is counterbalanced by the consideration that the trial judge too is a judge and presumably shares the appellate judge's expertise in matching facts to legal categories. The hearing agency is not, of course, staffed with judges and so appellate courts might be more willing to review its second-order fact-finding.

This consideration is in turn counterbalanced by judicial appreciation that agencies typically make second-order fact-findings peculiarly within their own area of expertise, and frequently in areas where their expertise is far greater than the reviewing court can bring to bear. Let us take a safety question. The first-order facts are those concerning the thickness of the boiler plate, the failure of the steam valve to open at 2,000 pounds pressure, and the crack in the window glass. The second-order question is: Given these facts, is the locomotive in fact safe? "Safe" is the word used in the statute. It requires interpretation of the word and comparison of the first-order facts with the legal category to make a correct decision. After all, nothing that moves is entirely safe, and the question is one of the degree of safety intended by the statute maker. Nevertheless few courts would want to substitute their judgment as to whether Old 64 is safe for that of the I.C.C. safety inspectors who have spent their whole working lives around locomotives.

In summary, then, courts are quite unaccustomed and unwilling to challenge an agency's findings of first-order facts and relatively willing to challenge its findings of law —that is, its findings as to what legal rule or doctrine properly carries out the intent of the statute. Judicial feelings are mixed on findings of second-order facts. The larger the proportion of legal interpretation, the less the agency's special expertise and the greater the suspicion that the agency is twisting the evidence to fit some preconceived result, the more tempted the court is to intervene. If it decides not to intervene, it will label the challenged finding one of fact and thus nonreviewable. If it wishes to intervene, it will label the finding one of law or one of mixed law and fact and will review it.

THE CLEARLY ERRONEOUS AND SUBSTANTIAL EVIDENCE RULES

Of course a reviewing court is not totally debarred from reversing even a finding of fact. In the federal courts, a higher court can reverse a lower court's finding if it is "clearly erroneous." Reviewing courts, operating under the Administrative Procedures Act and the specific provisions of other acts, will invalidate agency findings not supported by "substantial evidence" on the whole record.[10]

It has never been quite clear whether these two tests are the same. It appears, however, that the federal courts will actually do less review of agency decisions than of lower

10. See *Universal Camera Corp. v. N.L.R.B.*, 340 U.S. 474 (1951)

court decisions. Whenever a reviewing judge feels that a lower court finding is "clearly erroneous"—i.e., is certain it is wrong—he will reverse. The substantial evidence requirement typically leads to somewhat different results for agencies. There is usually a substantial amount of evidence on both sides of a disputed fact-finding. Even when a judge feels that an agency finding of fact was clearly wrong, he will usually uphold it because typically there will be substantial evidence on the agency's side as well as on the other.

The requirement that his judgment be on the whole record complicates things however. Does this mean that the judge does not simply look to see that the agency has some solid evidence on its side but instead balances everything in the record to see which side is more substantial? If so, then the judge is really deciding for himself not deferring to the agency. On the other hand, if the judge confines himself to looking at just the evidence on the agency's side he must nearly always find substantiality, for nearly anything looks substantial if you don't look at the evidence on the other side.

The federal rule today can only be stated as follows. Courts will look at more than the evidence favorable to the agency finding in evaluating whether the evidence favorable to that finding is substantial, but once they have done this they stop short of weighing the record as a whole to see whether the evidence on one side is more substantial than the evidence on the other. It must also be noted that even when a court holds an agency finding of fact not supported by substantial evidence, it does not substitute its own finding of fact but simply refers the matter back to the agency.

A final complication to be added is that just as federal courts do not entirely refuse to review findings of fact, they do not always review findings of law. If both courts and agencies are indeed subordinate lawmakers working under the statute maker, courts when called upon to review agency findings of law are frequently being asked simply to make a different supplementary law than the agency has just made. The courts' answer, along the lines suggested in the Introduction, will frequently be: "Why should we go through the whole process of lawmaking all over again that the agency has just been through, when the agency is as competent, or more competent than we are?" Thus, unless the agency's opponent can satisfy the court that there is some special reason for its intervention, the court is likely to say that the finding is committed by the statute to the agency's discretion, and discretion is not reviewable. What it frequently means, of course, is that so long as the agency's supplementary lawmaking appears reasonably fair and within the terms of the statute, the judges see no reason to do the job all over again.

In short, while it is possible to make and necessary to understand the various analytical arguments about fact, law, and discretion, from the point of view of behavioral analysis, it may be clearest to say that whatever findings of an agency courts do not wish to review are matters of fact and/or discretion, and whatever they do wish to review are questions of law. Certainly it would be impossible to understand the decisions of the Supreme Court without employing this mode of analysis.

FINDINGS

From what has been said so far it must be fairly obvious that in order to review adequately, courts need relatively detailed indications from agencies as to precisely what decisions they made, and what rules of law and findings of fact they relied upon in reaching those decisions. The general rule is that the agency must provide, in the form of its "findings, reasons, and opinions," sufficient information to allow the courts to make the review decisions entrusted to them. The Supreme Court has been quite consistent in this demand. In view of this degree of certainty it is somewhat surprising that in a fairly large number of instances reviewing courts find it necessary to remand cases to the agencies for further findings of fact and/or law. There are basically

three reasons for this phenomenon. First, the issues surrounding agency decisions, particularly in the field of business
regulation, are frequently very complex. The agencies are
very busy and somewhat understaffed. In constructing their
case records they sometimes simply make very human errors
of omission that the courts subsequently discover. Second,
in many agencies opinion-writing is done by one section
after the actual decisions that the opinions are supposed to
explain have been made by another. When the opinions are
too blatantly or carelessly rationalizations of decisions that
appear to have been reached on other and unstated grounds,
courts may register their protests by returning the decisions
for further findings. Third, an agency's findings and opinion
will have been shaped to support its policy preferences. For
this reason a court that wishes to pursue a different policy
may not find in the record the raw materials for defending
any policy other than that of the agency. Its remand to the
agency may be less a statement that the findings are inadequate to support the decision the agency has made than that
the court wishes the agency would reach a different decision.

REMAND

Perhaps this is a good point to introduce the question of
what good it is for a court to remand a case for further decision by the agency as it does when the findings are inadequate, or when there is a lack of substantial evidence, or
where the agency has made or applied the wrong legal rule
—although in the last instance the court need not remand
but may itself apply the right rule of law. The court may
actually want the agency to tidy up the record. But frequently courts remand not so much because there are loose
ends as because they disagree with the policy embodied in
the decision. In such instances the agency can if it wishes
simply present the court with the same (but now tidied up)
policy on the second go-round. Remand is then an exercise
in futility because having ducked a final decision once by

remanding, the court will now face the same decision again. Remand is, however, useful because it allows for a more subtle and flexible mode of communication between courts and agencies than would otherwise be available. Instead of having to say either, we approve of what you are doing, or you can't do what you are doing, a court can say, "We disapprove, but if you think it over, taking our views into account, and still insist on doing it, we will not stop you." This is one of the most commonly used and valuable messages in politics. Remand makes it available to judges as well as bureaucrats and legislators.

ESTOPPEL, STARE DECISIS AND RES JUDICATA

We now turn very briefly to a covey of the greatest mysteries of the law, indeed mysteries so great that they are still expressed in archaic words—estoppel, *stare decisis,* and *res judicata.* The doctrine of equitable estoppel commands that if one has made a promise or said that something was true, and another has relied upon such a representation, then the first may not act in violation of his promise or deny that what he said was true if his action will harm the person who has depended upon his word. In short, the rule is simply fair play. There is, however, an old tradition that the government does not have to play fair, and most courts under most circumstances rule that the government cannot be estopped. Nevertheless, there has been a strong movement toward the notion that the government should be treated like anyone else, and the Supreme Court no longer says that the government can never be estopped. The decisions will undoubtedly remain mixed for some time to come as the courts work on a new solution to an old problem.

Whether an agency can change a past ruling and apply the new one retroactively against someone who has been relying on the old presents a more difficult problem. It would seem unfair to punish conduct that was in accord with the old rule just because it violates the new. Yet if the courts forced agencies to always follow their old rules they would be saying that an agency could never correct its past mistakes in its new decisions. The major problem arises when the old state of the law was vague, an individual has chosen the interpretation of it most advantageous to himself, and the agency then issues new rules or decisions making the old law clearer. Under the clarification it now appears that what the individual had been doing was wrong. Should he be punished for doing something that might or might not have been illegal when he did it? Should he be excused, thus rewarding him for having used his legal skill to milk maximum advantage to himself out of a vague law? The court decisions are mixed, and the present position of the Supreme Court seems to be that while an agency cannot normally retroactively apply a new rule to old conduct, the more vague the previous state of the law, and the more the individual manipulated the vagueness to his own advantage, the more likely the Court is to allow the agency to make new and clearer law to cover the situation and in the process bring the individual to book for his past maneuverings.[11]

The rule of *res judicata* as developed for courts is that once a court has reached a final decision the same parties may not litigate the same issues again in another court. This works relatively easily in courts because a trial is a distinct and discrete act with carefully labeled parties and specifically delimited issues. Administrative agencies, however, employ all sorts of consultations, and informal and formal hearings, in and out of which drift various participants and issues. Moreover they reach all sorts of unofficial, informal, intermediate, semipermanent decisions. It is very frequently unclear whether the agency decision was intended to be final and permanent, what issues it settled and what left open, or even who the parties were. For instance, when the F.C.C. decides to renew a radio station license, are the other stations that might have appeared at hearings to dispute the renewal (but in fact did not) parties to the decision and thus unable

---

11. See *S.E.C. v. Chenery Corp.,* 332 U.S. 194 (1947)

to open the question again in the sense that Smith and Jones in the case of *Smith v. Jones* are parties? While the doctrine and policy of *res judicata* are relatively clear, courts are frequently faced with very difficult judgments of degree in deciding whether one intersection of an individual with some particular agency proceeding is sufficiently like *Smith v. Jones* to warrant refusing to allow the individual to challenge the agency subsequently.

HEARINGS

Most of what has been said so far assumes that the party in conflict with the agency has been engaged in a proceeding before it. But when a party does or does not have a right to a hearing is also a crucial question of administrative law. In general the courts hold that the due process clause of the Fifth Amendment entitles an individual to a full-scale adversary proceeding when facts relating particularly to him are at issue. This constitutional right is limited in three ways. First, if the facts involved are general or "legislative" facts— that is, facts about the state of the world in general, not about what the party has done or what has been done to him in particular—the right disappears. Thus if the question is, Did X send trucks over the mountain?, he is entitled to a trial-type hearing. If the question is, Can trucks go over mountains?, he is not. The right also disappears if the facts at issue bear only on a "privilege" rather than a "right" of the individual. The theory is that if the government is only deciding whether to do or not to do something which it is free to do or not do no matter what the facts, it need not hold a hearing. If it is legally bound to hold one way if the facts are one way and decide another if the facts are another, then the party has a right to a trial-type hearing to discover the facts. There has been some judicial whittling away at the privilege doctrine. Thirdly, in some instances the government can claim that secrecy is required for national security in order to avoid the hearing requirement.

Where facts peculiar to the individual are not involved, he is not constitutionally entitled to a hearing (or at least the Supreme Court has never firmly said he is), but many statutes governing various types of agency decisions guarantee him one. Where the issue is not one of fact, "hearing" is usually taken to mean not a trial-type adversary proceeding with right to call witnesses and cross-examine, but an "argument" in which the party is entitled to state his views fully to the agency. In many instances there are disputes about whether the hearing guaranteed by a given statute is a trial-type hearing or an argument, and if an argument, whether the statute guarantees the opportunity for oral argument or only the submission of written materials. Since these are matters of interpreting particular statutes, decisions vary from case to case, but the word "hearing" as used in most statutes is so vague that the courts have considerable policy leeway, and the underlying issue is obviously just how much judicialization of agency procedures is desirable.

Once a requirement of hearing has been established there are, of course, many, many questions of the proper procedures for conducting the hearing. These rules of procedure are established by the agencies and vary enormously in detail. The Supreme Court has not been inclined to force the agencies into aping courtroom rules. The general task of the courts is to insure that the agency has followed its own rules —in short, that the proceedings have been fair.

BIAS

Courts must also consider charges of bias against agency decision makers. In fact, however, the private party dealing with an agency gets almost no judicial protection from decisions made by officials who have prejudged all the relevant issues of policy and even of fact. Administrative agencies were established to do supplementary lawmaking, that is to gather and evaluate facts and establish policy positions. They were also intended to judge individual cases. Inevitably this combination means that the men doing the judging are the inventors and proponents of the very policy, and the compilers of the very facts, challenged by the individual in proceedings before the agency. The courts have recognized that this was the inevitable and intended effect of establishing a system of administrative regulation and have confined the notion of bias largely to personal financial interest in the outcome of a proceeding on the part of the decision maker.

HEARING OFFICERS

However, as it has become clear that agencies must deviate substantially from the detached traditions of courts, considerable concern has been shown for giving the individual some protection in a situation where the agency acts as both protagonist and judge. The Administrative Procedures Act seeks to insure that the prosecuting and advocating functions of an agency will be somewhat separated from its judging functions by creating and setting apart a corps of hearing officers or examiners who are partially insulated from the rest of the agency. Such separation always presents very subtle questions of degree. The very purpose of the agencies was to make decisions on the basis of their special expertise and to gain further expertise from their continuous involvement with real-world problems. If those who reach decisions in the actual cases coming before the agency were completely cut off from the rest of the agency, they would be cut off from the expertise which is supposed to make their decisions better than those of the courts. The tremendous fund of knowledge and insight they gain in hearings on concrete problems would also be cut off from the rest of the agency, thus depriving it of a principal source of its expertise. In view of this fact both the A.P.A. and the interpretations of it by the Supreme Court have called for only a very partial structural separation of hearing officers from the remainder of their agencies. The Supreme Court is likely to follow the broad intent of the statute in insisting that those agency personnel who were directly concerned in the preparation and prosecution of a complaint not be among those making the agency's final disposition of the case, but it is unlikely to insist on rigid separation.

While the courts are likely to insist on a separation between agency prosecutors and hearing officers, they have generally left both hearing officers—that is, those who make initial findings and decisions in litigation before the agency— and the agency heads who render final decisions free to consult with the staff of the agency so that the agency's total institutional expertise can be brought to bear on the decisions before it. On the other hand, hearing officers typically conduct adversary hearings in which the agency prosecutor presents his version of the facts and law and the other party has an opportunity to fully rebut that version. If the hearing officer is free not only to listen to his own agency's case as presented by its prosecuting staff, but also to consult with his agency's experts—who after all have prepared the prosecutor's case—in a way he gets twice as much of one side of the case as the other, and the outside party gets no opportunity to even know let alone rebut the added advice given him by the agency personnel.

The A.P.A. therefore provides that no examiner (hearing officer) "shall consult any person or party on any fact in issue unless upon notice and opportunity for all parties to participate." Taken literally, this would deprive examiners of all contact with the staff resources of their agency. There is strong reason to believe that the agencies are not reading the statute literally. The Supreme Court has not yet made a decisive pronouncement on the question. Agency heads, who make the final decisions, may consult with any of their staff except those directly involved in prosecuting. Indeed, they may make final decisions on the basis of such consultation without themselves personally having mastered the evidence and arguments presented at the hearings on the question. Given the huge work loads and complex masses of evidence before modern administrative agencies, it would be impossible for their heads to do otherwise.

ADMISSIBILITY OF EVIDENCE AND OFFICIAL NOTICE

A similar permissive tendency is evident in the Supreme Court's supervision of what evidence may or may not be considered by an administrative agency. In general, administrative agencies are not bound by the rather strict rules as to admissibility of evidence to be found in courts. They may, in the words of Learned Hand, rely upon any "evidence on which responsible persons are accustomed to rely in serious matters."[12] The A.P.A., while authorizing agencies to hear any sort of evidence, is not entirely clear as to whether decisions must be supported with some modicum of evidence that courts under their stricter rules would admit. Thus questions of the quality of evidence still sometimes arise in judicial review of administrative proceedings, but the Supreme Court is likely to give the agency the broadest possible leeway.

A similar range of problems is involved in the notion of "official notice." If an agency were required to make decisions solely on the basis of the facts presented at hearings, it would either be deprived of the use of the huge body of expert knowledge it has acquired over the years, or hearings would have to be stretched out interminably as the agency introduced everything it knew into evidence. On the other hand, if, once a hearing has closed, an agency can rest its decision on (take notice of) facts not presented at the hearing, the other party may find that he has spent his whole time at the hearing talking about one set of facts only to have the agency decide on the basis of another set, on which he has not had the opportunity to comment. The Supreme Court has sought to strike a rough balance between these two considerations. The Court will generally allow an agency to notice, without introducing into hearing evidence, "legislative facts," that is, general facts about broad categories of phenomena (steam locomotives have pressure gauges). But it

12. *N.L.R.B. v. Remington Rand Corp.,* 94 F.2d 862, 873 (2d Cir. 1938)

is likely to insist that agencies enter into the record, and thus allow opportunity for explanation and rebuttal of "adjudicative facts" relating to particular things and events (the pressure gauge on locomotive 66 was not functioning on October 22). Moreover the court is likely to be far more liberal toward agency notice when the agency has told the adversely affected party what facts it intends to or has noticed and allowed him an opportunity to present contrary evidence.[13] There have been attempts to state these tendencies as firm rules, but it seems more realistic to admit that the Court is engaging in rough-and-ready judgments in each case as to whether a party has really been denied a chance to present his side of whatever facts the agency relies upon in its decision.

RULES, RULE MAKING, AND DELEGATION

We might end this rather rough orientation to administrative law by a brief discussion of rules and rule making. In certain instances a statute may delegate to an agency the power to make law in a given area. Where this has occurred, the agency is in effect exercising the lawmaking authority of Congress, and courts will allow the agency wide leeway, checking only to insure that it is operating within the scope of the power delegated to it by Congress, is following proper procedures, and is not acting with patent unreasonableness. In other instances a statute may authorize an agency to make rules interpreting and rendering more specific the general terms of the statute. It is these sorts of rules that are subject to the greatest judicial scrutiny. For here the agencies and courts are acting as rival or complementary subordinate lawmakers. It is in this area that the Supreme Court weights its policy differences with the agency, balances agency expertise

---

13. See *Ohio Bell Telephone Co. v. Public Utilities Commission,* 301 U.S. 292 (1937); *United States v. Pierce Auto Freight Lines, Inc.,* 327 U.S. 515 (1946); *N.L.R.B. v. Seven-Up Bottling Co.,* 344 U.S. 344 (1953); *American Trucking Association v. Frisco Transportation Co.,* 358 U.S. 133 (1958).

against parochialism, checks congressional intent against agency practice, and invokes or fails to invoke the long-standing practice and/or reenactment doctrines, depending upon whether it believes that there is or is not some special reason for double decision making.

In short, in the realm of delegated legislation or "legislative" rule making, the Court exercises minimum power. In the realm of adjudicative or interpretive rule making, it exercises maximum power. But in reality these are not two distinct and mutually exclusive categories, but two ends of a continuum running from least to greatest statutory specificity. Congress never delegates in the sense of saying to an agency, "Make any law you please." The delegating statute nearly always states some purpose, goal, standard, or general policy aim toward which the delegated power is to be directed. Any agency rule made under such a statute is an interpreting and further specifying of the statute's provisions, not a completely independent act of lawmaking. All "legislative" rules are, therefore, interpretative, and quite obviously all adjudicatory rules are legislative in the sense of creating some more law or new law. Thus while the distinction between legislative and adjudicatory or interpretative rule making may be analytically useful, it must be kept in mind that a clear line cannot be drawn between the two, and that court action runs from complete nonintervention in agency policy making to complete substitution of judicial for administrative judgment.

The subtleties of the distinction between legislative and interpretive rule making should not, however, be allowed to obscure the fact that frequently the crucial issue for the Court is just how much decisional power Congress did give to the agency. In the narrowest form this is the question of "delegation" which was once one of the most energetically argued of administrative law. How much of its power could Congress delegate? Did it have to provide standards to guide the agency in its use of delegated power? How clear and definite did these standards have to be? Today the Supreme Court is unlikely to object to even very broad and ill-defined congressional mandates, so that the delegation issue in the narrowest sense rarely arises any longer.

CONCLUSION

The broader question of whether the agency is using the powers given it in the way Congress intended, or whether it is legally authorized to do what it is doing, usually resolves itself into a series of issues about the policies embodied in a given transportation, or antitrust or labor statute and the meaning of the words used to express them. As we have seen earlier, while these questions are central to judicial review of administrative decision making, they fall outside of the more narrowly conceived category of administrative law that we have been examing in this chapter. Curiously enough then, what is typically a central issue in judicial–administrative relations plays little part in our examination of administrative law. But the problem of congressional mandate will appear repeatedly in the remainder of the book.

This discussion of the major categories of problems that have traditionally been encompassed in the category "administrative law" has been designed to give the observer sufficient familiarity with the vocabulary and the issues of policy and power that lie behind them so that, in examining the relations behind the Supreme Court and administrative agencies, he can follow the game. It is a kind of scorecard presented with the caution that simply knowing the crude names and numbers is only the beginning, that the reality lies in the subtle details of the movements on the field, in the human judgment and skill reflected in the patterns of play, and most crucially in who gains and loses advantages. And the game, after all, is not about administrative law but about the substantive law of labor, transportation, antitrust, communications, and the like—in short, about the areas of law in which the real issues of public policy lie. We now turn from the scorecard to one such game which we shall replay in some detail.

3

The Supreme Court
and the Patent Office

In recent years social scientists have produced a large number of "case studies," relatively detailed analyses of a relatively small segment of the political process—for instance, just how the decision was made by the government to sell some of its surplus property or how a particular piece of legislation was passed by Congress. As a technique for marshaling social science evidence, and particularly for "proving" anything, the case-study approach is subject to serious methodological shortcomings. The study of the relations between the Patent Office and the Supreme Court offered here does not purport to prove general laws of Supreme Court behavior. It will, I hope, provide illustrations of some of the generalizations made earlier and, by offering concrete examples, help the student of law and administration to grasp the rather complex and subtle style of politics practiced by courts and administrators in their dealings with one another. In the long run, of course, the examination of this particular aspect of the Supreme Court's work should be combined with the study of all other segments of the Court's jurisdiction to build up a general and complete picture of the Court's role in the political process.

In the meantime, the Court–Patent Office area provides a particularly useful introduction to the concrete workings of judicial involvement in administrative decision making for a number of reasons. First of all, patent law presents an intimate commingling of "constitutional" and "statutory" questions. The distinction between judicial review as the testing of a law or administrative action to see whether it is in accord with the Constitution and judicial review as the testing of an administrative regulation or action to see whether it is in accord with a statute passed by the legislature is an analytically useful one. Nevertheless, this distinction, frequently so essential in following the legal logic and rhetoric of a given case, is often misleading politically. Excessive preoccupation with the Supreme Court's power of constitutional judicial review has led American scholarship to concentrate unduly on the grand and sporadic confrontations between Court and statute maker that characterize the constitutional sphere and to relatively neglect the Court's intimate and continuous involvement with the everyday affairs of government through its interpretation of the statutes under which administrators operate.

Perhaps more important, too much emphasis on nice logical distinctions between constitutional and statutory review tends to obscure the fact that in the real world it often makes little difference to the government agency or the private litigant whether the courts have said yes or no for constitutional or statutory reasons. It may be the yes or no that counts. For the observer of Washington politics, the quantity and quality of judicial intervention in administrative decision making may be far more important than whether the nominal basis for that intervention was Article I Section 2 or Paragraph 64(a)(3) of a statute passed by Congress last year. This is not to deny that whether the Court can find, or chooses to employ, a constitutional as opposed to a statutory ground for intervention may be tactically important in determining how to blunt or facilitate or change or eliminate the Court's intervention. It is the substance of the Court's intervention, however—just exactly what it requires agency or citizen to do or refrain from doing—that is the real crux of the matter.

Thus in the patent field the Supreme Court's announcement in 1966 that the standard of invention is a constitutional rather than purely a statutory one has some tactical significance in strengthening the Court's hand. But by that time the judiciary had been intervening in Patent Office decisions for over a hundred years without it having been decided whether their review was constitutional or statutory. The decision that it was one and not the other does not promise to bring about any striking change in the tempo or substance of judicial intervention. In short, patent officials, inventors, patent lawyers, and judges were able to negotiate and indeed battle with one another intimately and sometimes furiously for all those years without knowing the answer to the seemingly essential preliminary question of whether they were fighting over the Constitution or a patent statute, and they will go on acting in roughly the same way now that the earthshaking question has been answered. Indeed they would have gone on in essentially the same way if the question had been answered in just the opposite way or not at all.

A second characteristic of the patent field peculiarly useful for my purposes here is the clarity with which it shows courts and agencies deciding precisely the same question. The inventor files a set of papers consisting of a description of his invention and what it accomplishes. Is the invention new, is it useful, and is it sufficiently different from what we have known all along to warrant giving the inventor certain legal rights that he otherwise would not enjoy? These are the questions that the Patent Office must answer. These are precisely the questions that the judges must answer all over again if the patent is litigated. Both the judge and the Patent Office official are influenced in their answers by precisely the same set of policy considerations, considerations that we shall get to shortly. The history of American patent law clearly shows this identity of judicial and administrative concerns. The power to issue patents was first vested in a board of administrators, but courts from the beginning made independent decisions on the validity of patents. Then the Patent Act of 1793 vested all powers of patent examination in the courts. Subsequently the Act of 1836 created an administrative agency, the Patent Office, to make initial patent decisions, but the courts never ceased their labor. Finally in 1949 a statute added to the courts' traditional duty (to decide patent questions when the validity of an issued patent was subsequently raised in litigation) a new procedure for appeal from Patent Office decisions directly to the courts at the time the office grants or refuses a patent.[1]

Thirdly, while the Patent Office directly determines private economic rights, and its policies have a direct impact on American business, it is not a regulatory commission like the Interstate Commerce Commission or the Civil Aeronautics Board. Study in the patent area thus allows us to get at some of the major problems of administrative–judicial relations in a somewhat simpler political matrix; that is, without the special complexities created by the commission form of organization, the general failure of the regulatory commissions to live up to advance expectations, and the peculiar ideological and economic problems of government regulation of rates and business practices in an officially free-enterprise system.

Finally the Patent Office and the Supreme Court appear to have had major policy differences, extending over a considerable period of time, and involving at one time or another the lower courts, Congress and major private interest groups. The patent jurisdiction of the Supreme Court thus introduces many of the characters who play recurring parts in the process of creating policy through administrative–judicial interaction.

---

1. 35 U.S.C. Sec. 145 (1958)

PROPERTY IN IDEAS

Before turning to the policy dispute, however, it is necessary to canvass the issues that underlie patent policy in the United States. These issues cluster around a series of paradoxes which suggest that there may be better or worse patent policies from various points of view but hardly correct and incorrect ones in any general sense. The first of these paradoxes, and one rarely treated openly by the participants but underlying much of their thought, is the notion of intangible property. The Anglo-American law is equipped to deal with property in a thing; the ownership of a piece of land, an automobile, or a kitchen chair. A thing generally can be put in the possession of one person at a time and the law can establish rules governing its physical transfer from one person to another and its physical use. The law can say that if I sell you the chair, you may take it away with you and I may not stop you, you may sit on it and prevent me from sitting on it, and you may in turn sell it to someone else, in which case he may take it away so that neither of us can sit on it.

Property in an idea is a much more difficult legal problem. An idea is very different from a chair. If I sell you an idea, you can take it away, but I will also still have it. You can use it, but your possession and use of it does not prevent me from possessing it and using it. Moreover ideas do not have hard edges. The fundamental existential factor underlying the law of property is that each thing is distinct from every other thing. Land can be surveyed and the exact boundaries of each parcel established. One automobile is quite distinct and separate from every other, and if they are not, we call it a collision not a brilliant synthesis. Kitchen chair *A* is physically separate from kitchen chair *B* and there is no chair *A/B* that is a combination of the two. Each of us can take one of the chairs away and neither of us takes anything of the other's, and nothing is left over.

Ideas, on the other hand, tend to form a seamless web.

It is never clear where one idea leaves off and another begins because both are typically recombinations of certain older ideas, and both do their recombination according to certain logical principles common to both. A wholly new idea is almost, in two senses, unthinkable, and partially new ideas, unlike kitchen chairs, cannot be neatly separated from their predecessors and consequently from one another. Ideas are also considerably larger than kitchen chairs. While the law can make one person the exclusive owner of a chair or even a steel mill with only a relatively small risk that it has deprived the rest of society of something it cannot get along without, giving the exclusive possession of certain ideas—for instance, major scientific principles or theories—to one man might well cripple society.

Patent law seeks to create private-property rights in ideas and thus must deal with these problems. It does so essentially by saying that the creator of a new idea may have the exclusive right to its use for a certain number of years. The law cannot, of course, prevent other persons from thinking the idea. It hurries back into a more familiar area and says that others may not produce, sell, or use things—machines for instance—that embody the idea. Only the "owner" of the idea may produce, sell, or use such machines or license others to do so.

At this most fundamental point, patent law runs into its first major problem. In effect the only way it can find to create and protect intangible property rights is by creating a monopoly. Now in a sense all property is monopoly. If I own a chair, I enjoy a "monopoly" in the use of the chair since no one else may use it, buy it, or sell it. But my monopoly in chair *A* does not prevent others from making, using, buying, and selling chairs *B, C,* or *D.* If, however, I owned the idea of a chair, and others could not make, use, buy, or sell anything embodying that idea, the whole society would be left standing until I chose to sell them chairs on my terms. Monopolies in ideas have a far broader and more serious impact than the kind of monopoly created when the law says I own a certain distinct thing.

Patent law is thus inevitably in potential conflict with antitrust policy in the United States. The basic device it employs is the governmental grant of monopoly, and that very government, in the person of several of its agencies outside the Patent Office, is busy discouraging monopoly and punishing monopolizers. Yet if we want to create and protect property in ideas, it is difficult to see how else we could do so.[2]

The second major problem of creating property in ideas lies in the indivisibility of ideas. There are two aspects to the problem. First is the terrifying extent of monopoly that would be granted if we created property in really big ideas like scientific principles. Patent law seeks to avoid this problem by saying that principles cannot be patented. In doing so patent-policy makers are faced with the almost impossible task of specifying just how big an idea has to be before it is unpatentable. Moreover, for this reason patent law creates the curious paradox that government and society use patents to magnificently reward the tinkerer who comes up with an idea for a better mousetrap while denying any such reward to the scientific genius whose ideas may improve the lot of all mankind for generations to come.

The other aspect of the problem of attempting to create property in the indivisible realm of ideas is that patent law must differentiate between ideas in the way that other property law differentiates between chair *A* and chair *B*. For we surely cannot give a man a patent protecting an idea for which we have already given a patent to someone else. Nor do we wish to give one man property in an idea which is not original to him but has already been thought of by many

---

2. It is sometimes argued that copyright law provides an alternative in that the production of copyrighted materials by others without the author's permission is forbidden, but not their use. Anyone is free to read a book once it has been printed, and anyone is then free to use the ideas in the book any way he pleases. The situations are not, however, comparable if for no other reason than that the copyright prohibition on reproduction alone is sufficient to protect the economic interests of authors while a similar prohibition in the area of patents would not be sufficient to protect the economic interests of inventors.

other men and is, so to speak, the common property of all, like the air we breathe. When men think, they inevitably use other men's ideas as building blocks, combining and recombining them. In this thought process just what quantity or quality of recombination is sufficient for us to find that X had a "new" or "original," and thus patentable, idea rather than just saying a little differently what has been said in a hundred ways before? The man who thought of the wheel had a "new" idea, but has there truly been a new idea since? (Come to think of it, the man who invented the wheel had probably seen somebody else using logs as rollers, so maybe his idea wasn't so new either.)

Even if we could satisfy ourselves as to just what constituted an original idea in a given instance, how could we express our agreement *in general words* applicable to all instances, how could we define originality of thought? Because it is necessary to do so in order to legally vest property rights in ideas as opposed to things, patent law is doomed to the endless attempt to define the undefinable.

WHY CREATE PROPERTY RIGHTS IN IDEAS?

Patent law thus creates one major set of problems because it seeks to create property rights in intangibles. But why do we wish to create such property rights? The second major set of problems in patent law revolves around this question.

The origins of the patent institution do not lie in notions of individual private property but rather in the realm of public policy. In Europe letters patent, granting monopolies or other special privileges, were given by the crown to encourage "adventurers" to undertake some task that the crown wanted performed for the public good but was unable or unwilling to do itself. Thus someone who undertook to introduce a new technique, such as the weaving of silk, into a nation where such activity had previously been unknown, and so benefit the economy, might be granted a monopoly for such manufacture by the king of his own country. The origin of patents as royal incentives in exchange for the performance of a public service means that a patent has traditionally been considered the result of bargaining between the individual and the state. Patent laws do not acknowledge and protect a "natural," individual "right." They only establish the terms of a bargain between the state and an individual by which the state grants the individual some privileges in return for some service to the state performed by the individual. In modern American patent law the bargain is essentially one in which the government grants an inventor a monopoly of manufacture, sale, and use of his invention for a limited time (17 years), in return for which the inventor gives the government a complete description of his invention and how to use it so that after the 17 years is up anyone can produce and operate it. In short, what the inventor gives up is his idea, which he might otherwise keep secret.

Because patents are essentially bargains, there can be and is considerable disagreement over just how much the state should give up in return for what it is getting. Many of the quarrels over the legal standard of patentability of invention are in reality quarrels over whether the government is or is not making a good bargain. Naturally opinions are likely to differ widely on this question from case to case, and there is frequently no way of determining how much the patent grant is "costing" the public in terms of discouraging other producers or higher prices, or how much the idea is "worth."

More important, because a patent is a set of privileges granted by the government as an incentive to having and exploiting new ideas, one's enthusiasm for patent law depends on the extent one thinks it is possible to stimulate new ideas by the promise of a limited monopoly. To what extent does the patent system inspire new ideas? To what extent does it thwart intellectual progress by turning ideas into personal property? For instance, do established entrepreneurs buy up and then refuse to use new patents (new ideas) that otherwise would threaten their old ways of doing things? Would the simple spur of competition force companies to come up with new ideas to keep one step ahead of their competitors even if their competitors could use them as soon as they could discover them, and does the monopoly inherent in the patent system actually thwart this competitive force? If there were no patent system would inventors keep their ideas secret, and, on the other hand, could you keep a secret in a fast-moving technology for more than 17 years anyway? If not, the patent system does not result in more technological knowledge for the public. We simply do not know exactly what forms of governmental intervention in the world of ideas stimulate ideas and which retard intellectual progress. Who knows what makes a man think of a better mousetrap. Many of the proponents of patent law simply assume that the more economic reward you promise the thinker the more he will think, and many simplistic arguments seek to directly link the rate of invention or number of inventors with the degree of reward promised by the patent system. It is improbable, however, that the incredibly complex phenomena of creative thought and technical innovation can be fully explained by this nickel-in-the-slot theory. A whole host of economic, historical, ideological, political, and other factors undoubtedly interact to establish various intellectual climates favorable or unfavorable to new thoughts and their practical application.

It might be argued that all these questions were settled in favor of the patent as an incentive to thought by the founding fathers when they inserted a patent clause in the Constitution, and by the various Congresses which have enacted patent statutes. Nevertheless the guesses of administrators and judges about the answers to these fundamental questions of incentive undoubtedly are a major determinant of their attitudes toward patent policy, and more specifically toward whether the patent system should grant the fewest possible or the most possible patents. As we shall see shortly, neither the Constitution nor the Patent Act contain many specific commands on the liberality with which the government should bargain and, therefore, basic beliefs about whether patents encourage or discourage intellectual and economic progress can lead the various administrative and judicial recipients of those commands to widely varying interpretations of them.

RIGHTS VERSUS PRIVILEGES

There is, then, considerable doubt as to whether creating property rights in ideas does in fact encourage intellectual progress. Behind this doubt lies still another problem of patent law. Those readers versed in legal philosophy will have already noted carefully that I have spoken of "creating property rights" and at the same time of patents as "privileges" granted by the government. The basic jurisprudential position reflected by this language is that property rights are not "natural," that is, things inherently possessed by individuals, but are legal claims created by the society, for its members, usually through the instrument of government. To say that an individual "owns" or has property in an object means only that the community has established procedures through which he may claim the return of or compensation for the object if it is taken by someone else and the expectation that his claims will be satisfied. To say one has a property right in a piece of land does not mean that he somehow has an absolute or God-given or moral right to it, but that he has been designated by society as the person who may go into court to claim the aid of the government in ejecting other persons from that land if he is satisfying the conditions the government imposes for possession and use of the land by him.

Under this view of "right" there is no essential distinction between rights and privileges. Whether we say that the patent provisions of the Constitution and statutes acknowledge the inventor's property right in ideas or are the grant of restricted monopoly privileges to an inventor, we are making identical statements, namely that the government authorizes a claim by the inventor or creates a legal interest for the inventor so that the inventor may call upon the force of government to restrain other individuals from doing or not doing certain things about a certain idea or device.

In this sense too a right is not something the government *must* always protect and a privilege something that government may give when it pleases and take away when it pleases. Instead, politically organized societies create the legal claims or interests of individuals, and in doing so acknowledge that such claims or interests may not be arbitrarily or invidiously withdrawn but may only be altered by proper procedures themselves specified by law. Patent "rights" or property in ideas provide a clear example of this view of law, for we can point to the exact time in history when they were created in various societies. No one could argue that patent rights have existed from time immemorial or are part of the Divine scheme of things.

Nevertheless, given the strongly laissez-faire, natural-rights bent of American ideology, once the patent system was created it became natural to speak of patents in terms of patent rights, and patent monopolies as the protection of the inventor's property in his ideas. And once this transposition was made it was even more natural to invoke the whole logic and rhetoric of the natural-rights theory of property; that is, that property rights are inherent or indwelling in the individual personality and come into existence through the personal efforts of the individual, only being acknowledged and protected, not created, by the law. Under this view the patent system ceases to be simply a government policy designed to stimulate intellectual and economic progress, to be judged pragmatically by its actual results in achieving this purpose. It becomes instead the legal protection of the inventor's natural or God-given "rights" to the fruits of his labor, i.e., his ideas, to be judged by whether it does give the full fruits of the ideas to the man who has a right to them.

It would be difficult to hold this latter position with full logical consistency, for it ignores the historical origins of patents as state-granted, monopolistic privileges in specific instances rather than general acknowledgments of universal or ancient rights, and if argued consistently would require patents not of 17 years but of unlimited duration, just as property rights in land and objects are of unlimited duration. No one is willing to go that far. Nevertheless the whole ideology of private property rights has become deeply entangled in patent policy and is surely an important factor in determining the attitudes of many policy makers.

Thus the general jurisprudential debate over artificial legal claims and interests v. natural rights—a debate that has been going on for centuries and shows no signs of abating—tends to further confuse the already confused problems of patent law. The whole tone and approach to questions of patent policy, what one instinctively favors or disfavors and then constructs arguments to affirm or condemn, stems partially from this issue of legal philosophy which enters the minds of the participants in patent policy making in various confused and muddled ways but which few of them consciously bring to the surface and subject to logical analysis.

BASIC ISSUES AND STANDARDS

I have spoken at length, but in very general terms, about various problems, paradoxes, and contradictions underlying patent law, all the time running the risk that the reader is mumbling to himself, "All right, cut the philosophy and get on to what's really happening." It would be a great mistake, however, to approach any serious problem of administrative–judicial relations totally within the narrow framework of the specific issues raised in litigation, or to believe that if only an agency would adopt a slightly different rule or a judge employ a somewhat different verbal formula our problems would be solved. It is quite common to find judges, administrators, and practitioners agreeing that the major difficulty lies in defining a certain word that somehow seems to elude definition, the word "obscene," for instance, or "invention" in patent law itself. Endless tinkering then goes on to arrive at better definitions, and everyone, including the scholarly observer, is likely to get so entranced with the details of the game that they fail to see that the reason the participants cannot find a mutually satisfactory definition, even when they all agree that one is necessary, is that they are in unconscious or only half-conscious disagreement about the underlying philosophical and policy premises upon which the definition is to rest.

More generally it should be clear that a judge who visualizes himself to be a government agent bargaining with an inventor over how much an idea is worth in terms of monopoly privilege is likely to act differently from a judge who views himself as the guardian of the intellectual property rights of the individual. And the differing guesses of administrators and Supreme Court justices over whether liberal issuance of patents on balance encourages or discourages technological development may be more significant than learned discourses on congressional intent.

To realistically analyze the relations of judges to administrators, relations that are frequently carried on in the language of legislative intent and legal definition, it is necessary constantly to bear in mind the fundamental issues that underlie the fancy legal footwork. Otherwise judicial review of administrative decision making appears to be a rather elaborate verbal game rather than the serious attempt to solve major policy problems that it very frequently is.

Judicial–administrative relations in the patent area revolve about the "standard" of patentability. Whenever it is discovered that a given area of judicial review is concerned with standards, the observer should anticipate that the statute giver has been general or abstract in his language and more importantly that the general language covers an unresolved policy dispute. For the word "standard" is generally invoked in law when subordinate lawmakers are struggling to pour some real content into statutory provisions. A legislature bans "obscenity," but precisely what did it mean by obscenity? Just which books did it want burned and which saved? Administrators and judges could simply judge each and every book in the world, one at a time, but both wish to reduce their work load by announcing in advance some rules of thumb or themes of the sort we examined in the Introduction whose routine application will be sufficient to allow their subordinates to sort most of the books and leave the top decision makers free to concentrate on the few difficult decisions. The better constructed the "standards" the fewer decisions have to go to the top. Thus courts continue to struggle manfully with standards of obscenity.

The continued difficulty in establishing obscenity standards also illustrates the second major phenomenon associated with such concerns. Where there is relative unanimity, or at least a clear policy preference stated by the statute maker, on the basic policy underlying a generally worded statute, administrators and judges will have relatively little difficulty in agreeing upon standards. Law in such areas may be heavily laden with standards, but they will not provide the major issues in the bulk of the litigation that serves as the vehicle for judicial review. In such areas standards come to be well settled and administrative–judicial conflict, if it exists at all, will be carried on in terms of procedural questions such as fair hearing. But where the statute maker has used certain legislative language precisely because it did not know what it wanted, but only that it wanted to do something good, then administrators and judges must devote the major share of their energies to hammering out what that something is. It is precisely because Americans cannot agree about what kinds of books are good and what kinds evil, that the legislative gesture of banning evil books results in constant quarrels over the standards of obscenity.

Conflict over standards of patentability is the central feature of modern American patent law as it manifests itself in judicial review of Patent Office decisions. Indeed, as we shall see shortly, the battle rages almost entirely in terms of whether the courts have "raised" the standards of patentability or maintained the "established" ones. There is even an elaborate sort of meaningless scholastic dispute about whether the standard is stricter or the standard is the same but the application of the standard is stricter, or the standard and the application are the same but nonlegal factors make the results stricter.

We have already seen that the essential reason for this continued dispute over standards is that there can be and are major and genuine differences of opinion about patent policy and that those differences are not easily resolvable. A brief examination of the basic patent law will show that the statute makers did indeed gloss over these differences in writing the statutes so that the continued dispute over standards is quite natural and not due to some curious perversity on the part of some judges or administrators.

THE LAW OF PATENTS: NOVELTY, UTILITY, AND INVENTION

The initial statute makers, the founding fathers, wrote that

> The Congress shall have power . . . to promote the Progress of Science and the useful arts, by securing for limited Times to Authors and Inventors the exclusive Right to their respective Writings and Discoveries. . . .

There has been some dispute about how this sentence should be parsed, but about all that can really be said is that the founders did believe that some sort of limited monopoly grant by government would sometimes and somehow encourage intellectual and economic development.

Shortly thereafter Congress passed the first of what became a series of statutes, and there is rather wide agreement that these statutes consistently establish two requirements for a patent—novelty and utility. Neither of these terms are totally self-explanatory or self-applying. If the problem of "standards" arose whenever a general or vague word was used, we should expect considerable legal debate over standards of novelty and utility. In fact, except in one very narrow and atypical area (chemical process patents), no such debate has arisen because no serious ambivalence about policy lies behind those two words. Whatever one's views about patent policy, everyone can agree that usefulness and newness are necessary conditions to patentability. Underlying policy differences come to the fore over the question of whether these are sufficient conditions, and it is for precisely this reason that the standards debate rages not around utility or newness but over standards of a third requirement, "invention."

Congress seems to have been the statute maker for the requirements of novelty and utility. The Supreme Court itself, in a major piece of judicial legislation, added "invention" to the statutory requirements. Something like it flits through the early cases and is to be found in the writings of Thomas Jefferson, our first scholarly commentator on patents and our first administrative decision maker in patent matters.[3] A full enunciation of the requirement occurs in *Hotchkiss v. Greenwood*.[4]

> For unless more ingenuity and skill in applying the old method . . . were required . . . than were possessed by an ordinary mechanic acquainted with the business, there was an absence of that degree of skill and ingenuity which constitute essential elements of every invention. In other words, the improvement is the work of the skilled mechanic, not that of the inventor.

In another leading case, *Pearce v. Mulford*, this was put in terms of patentability involving "something more than what is obvious to persons skilled in the art to which it relates.[5] The requirement of invention has been an integral, indeed a commanding, part of our patent law since it was first given legal force by the Supreme Court, although it was not to be found in a patent statute until 1952.

In writing invention into the law it is clear that the

---

3. Jefferson, as Secretary of State, was one of the initial group of Patent Commissioners.
4. 52 U.S. 248, 267 (1850). For a more complex reading of the cases than presented here, one essentially designed to persuade the Supreme Court to move in new policy directions, see Kitch, "*Graham v. John Deere Co.*: New Standards for Patents," 1966 *Supreme Court Review* 293.
5. 102 U. S. 112, 118 (1880)

Supreme Court was giving expression to an almost unanimous view that the government would not be getting a good bargain if it traded monopoly privileges for the disclosure of any and every thing that was new and useful. For many things that are new and useful are trivial, and many others can be stumbled upon by any fool, with no creative thought involved at all. What we want to bargain for is some real intellectual effort, not just the little elaboration or frill that anyone could have immediately seen for himself and six other persons immediately would have seen if one hadn't rushed off to the Patent Office first.

It has often been argued that the debate over standards of invention, which we shall shortly trace, represents one of those not infrequent instances where we all know what we mean, but we can't put it into words. Again the parallel to obscenity law is striking. Many a judge and commentator has said: "We all know a dirty book when we see one—it's just that we can't express our knowledge in a neat verbal formula." Similarly, it might be argued that we all intend that to qualify for a patent a device has to show that certain extra something that makes it an invention rather than a gimmick or a simple variation or elaboration of existing knowledge, but we can't quite put that into a one sentence definition of invention.

For both "invention" and "obscenity" this position proves quite false at the proof of the pudding stage. If there existed substantial agreement about invention and obscenity at the phenomenal level, then administrators and judges would almost always agree as to what devices were inventions and what books were dirty. If they almost always agreed, then we wouldn't need any standards—that is, verbal directions from some of them to others as to what decisions they should make—and our verbal infelicities might exist forever without producing even a ripple on the calm surface of the law. If standards of invention and obscenity make waves, it is because we don't know inventions and dirty books when we see them. It is precisely because one man's dirty book is another man's daring masterpiece, and one man's gimmick is another man's invention, not because of some inherent incapacities of the English language, that quarrels over standards continue.

More specifically, the real question in patent law is how hard a bargain should the government drive, and this is the question upon which substantial agreement has never been reached. Since the government can pay only one price, 17 years monopoly, the bargaining issue becomes: What is the least worthy device for which the government should pay that price? That, in more than a word unfortunately, is what the debate over standards comes down to. Now just how hard a patent bargain each individual wants his government to drive for him is going to depend upon a whole host of factors we have already discussed. The more one believes that patents actually do encourage technical innovation and that men have a natural right to the creations of their intellects, and the less one is concerned about economic monopoly and the difference in rewards for scientific geniuses and mere tinkerers, the more generous one will wish the government to be in its bargaining.

In essence, then, patents present the age-old political question "Who gets what" from the government. The "what" has been set at 17 years monopoly. The remainder of this chapter will be devoted to the endless political struggle over the "who."

SUBTESTS OF INVENTION

By the very injection of an invention requirement the Supreme Court had partially answered the "who" question in the sense of replying: Not everyone who does something new and useful. The patent applicant must have something more to strike a bargain. Subsequent to *Hotchkiss*, new cases reached the Supreme Court from time to time in which it rephrased the invention requirement, but whatever the phrasing the requirement remained very general and vague. As is the wont of lawyers there were also attempts by both judges and Patent Office officials to work out a series of more specific "subtests" of invention. These subtests were designed to make the law more stable and certain, an urge of course felt by the Patent Office as well as the courts, for the Office must reach thousands of patent decisions each year. Both negative and positive subtests emerged. Patents would not issue to protect:

1. A new use for an old device.
2. Change in material in an otherwise old device.
3. A change in form which did not change the actual mode of operations of an old device.
4. Mere rearrangement, omission, duplication or multiplication of elements or superior workmanship.
5. Mere arrangements of elements that do not cooperate with one another in a new way (the rule against aggregations).

On the other hand, patents might be held valid if:

6. The device achieved new results.
7. There was a history of long and unsuccessful attempts by others to achieve the results the device was now achieving.
8. The device was a commercial success after being patented (this test is closely allied with the notion that a beneficial and widespread industrial result supports the validity of a patent).[6]

If the reader will recall the discussion of incremental decision making in Chapter 1, he will quickly identify the subtests as basically a thematic approach to decision. Each subtest presents an element to be weighed, but few of them represent rules of thumb in the sense that if X is present or absent Y must follow. Even some of those that seem most definite do not turn out to be so in application. The rule against aggregations (5), for instance, comes into play in the area of combination patents where all the elements are admitted to be old, but when they are supposedly put together

---

6. Prager, "Standards of Patentable Invention from 1474 to 1952," 20 *U. Chicago Law Review* 69 (1952)

to form something new (e.g., the internal-combustion engine). Whether we decide such a device is an aggregation or combination really depends on whether we think anyone could have thrown these things together, or whether throwing them together is really an out-of-the-ordinary new contribution—and we are back where we started with the notion of "invention."

The positive subtests have always been acknowledged to be themes, not rules; that is, a new result (6) was to be taken into account but was not decisive. This is a good example of how thematic statements, if each is taken as an absolute, are often contradictory. Compare subtests (1) and (6). Taken together they really mean that the newness of the result is to be considered along with the nature of the device, and if the results are new enough, a device that is not so different from the old state of the art may still get its patent. In a sense too many of the subtests are not guides to decision making but legal tags to hang on the decisions made. The crux of many patent decisions is whether or not a new use, and/or change in material and/or change in form, does indeed represent a real advance over the former way of doing things. Almost invariably there is some change from the old way, and if that change is coupled with an idea that the Patent Office or court wishes to reward, it will provide a sufficient base on which to rest a favorable finding. If Patent Office or court is not so attracted, it invokes subtests (1), (2), and/or (3), but really as a summary of its conclusion of noninvention rather than as a black-and-white test of whether invention was present.

I go into the subtests in some detail here because a curiously comforting myth has grown up about the good old days of patent law that is an important factor in the modern political struggle. It seems to have been widely believed among patent lawyers that from about 1880 up to about 1930 the *Hotchkiss-Pearce* test of nonobviousness plus the subtests insured a high level of certainty and stability, and a law that was not too hot, not too cold, but just right. Obviousness and the negative subtests, so the romanticizing runs, provided the government a decent bargain, but were very favorable to the flourishing of the patent system, i.e., the reward of the inventor. As we have seen, however, a thematic approach is not designed to yield high levels of certainty from instance to instance. Quite the contrary, it is calculated to free the discretion of the decision maker from limitations imposed by his previous decisions while allowing him to inform others of what factors he wants brought to his attention in making decisions. The themes of patent law allow for either "pro" or "anti" patent decisions. Moreover there is nothing peculiarly specific or favorable to the aspiring inventor in the *Hotchkiss-Pearce* statements of the invention requirement, nor is there anything in the Supreme Court's rhetoric or action in the 1880s that suggests an especially high level of certainty, let alone uniformly favorable treatment of inventors.[7] Nevertheless the yearning to get back to the "old" law manifests itself repeatedly in the struggles of the 1940s, 1950s, and 1960s.

SUPREME COURT AND PATENT OFFICE

It would seem natural that the uncertainties of the invention standard and the unresolved policy questions lying behind it would generate conflicts between the various decision makers involved in the patent process. Such conflicts have always been evident between the Patent Office, which initially issues patents, and the Supreme Court, which is the ultimate judge of the validity of the patents issued. Even in what the propatent forces consider the good old days, the rate of invalidation of patents considered by the Supreme Court was

1880-99	69%
1900-09	24
1910-19	62
1920-29	50

7. Allyn, "Supreme Court Patent Cases 1875 to 81 v. 1935 to 41," 25 *Journal of the Patent Office Society* 27 (1943)

Not too much should be made of these figures, for the Court takes so few patent cases that different decisions in two or three cases every ten years would have caused very large percentage changes. Nevertheless they do indicate that the inventor, firmly grasping his Patent Office certificate of "invention," was quite likely to find that the Court and the Patent Office were in disagreement.

In the 1930s, however, the percentage of invalidation jumped to 80, and between 1934 and 1939 the Supreme Court did not sustain a single patent. Indeed from this period until the 1966 term it held only two patents valid on their merits.[8] Perhaps even more important, between 1935 and 1965 the Supreme Court did not reverse a single lower-court finding of invalidity.

Something seemed to be happening. To understand what, it is necessary to introduce the full cast of participants and procedures. An inventor seeking a patent files an application with the Patent Office. The application consists essentially of specifications describing the structure and operations of the device and "claims" in which the applicant claims what his invention can do that others cannot, thus staking out the boundaries of the monopoly he wishes the government to grant him. His claims are considered by an Examiner in the Patent Office, which then decides whether or not to issue a patent. Its decision can be appealed first to the Patent Appeals Board within the Patent Office and then to either the Court of Customs and Patent Appeals or to the Federal District Court for the District of Columbia. Appeal from these courts to the Supreme Court can be taken on writ of certiorari—that is, the appellant petitions the Supreme Court to hear the case and the Supreme Court can either do so or refuse to grant a further hearing, in which case the lower court decision stands. Of course the inventor who is granted a patent by the Patent Office will not appeal its

8. See Prager, *op cit supra* note 6 at 77; Note, "1966 Patent Cases, Creation of a Constitutional Standard," 54 *Georgetown Law Journal* 1320, 1330 (1966)

decision, and so Patent Office actions favorable to the applicant will not find their way into court by this route. The successful applicant may find himself traveling into the courts by a far different route, however, and it is by this latter route that nearly all the patent cases decided by the Supreme Court reach it.

A patent in itself does nothing more than establish the right of the holder to go into a federal court to request it to prevent some other person from manufacturing, selling, or using the device upon which the patent has been issued, or to force the other person to pay damages to the patent holder for past manufacture, sale, or use detrimental to the patent holder. In short, it is the infringement suit that protects the monopoly granted the inventor in his patent. The second party in such a suit may assert as a defense the invalidity of the patent held by the party suing. Obviously if he does not hold a valid patent, no legal right of his has been infringed. Infringement suits are initiated in the federal district courts, may be appealed by either party to the federal courts of appeal, and may then go on writ of certiorari to the Supreme Court. Those accused of infringing a given patent will almost always claim the patent is invalid. A patent to be valid must show "invention," so the finding of presence or absence of invention is typically a central feature of the infringement suits that are the usual vehicle for judicial policy making in the patent field.

One final note about infringement suits to avoid confusion for the beginner. Where a court finds the patent invalid, there is, of course, no infringement because there is nothing to infringe. But even where a court finds the patent valid, it may find that no infringement has occurred, that is that the device being made, sold, or used by *B* is not the same as the one on which *A* holds a patent. *A* must get from the court both a finding that his patent is valid, and that it has been infringed by *B*, before he can enforce his monopoly by forcing *B* out of the field through an infringement suit. Thus a court which is dubious about the bargain struck for the government by the Patent Office can nullify or at least reduce the value of what the government has given either by a declaration that the patent is invalid or by narrowing the boundaries of the patent and holding that rival devices do not infringe it.

THE COURTS OF APPEAL

So far in speaking of invention we have dealt entirely with the Supreme Court and its doctrines. At the purely doctrinal level this is appropriate because the Court does have the last word, when it chooses to use it, in the construction of formal judicial doctrine. It should now be clear, however, that the circuit courts of appeal play a crucial role in the making of patent policy. If the major vehicle for review of Patent Office decisions is the infringement suit, and the Supreme Court seldom grants certiorari in such cases (it rarely decides more than three patent cases on their merits per year) the courts of appeals are where most infringement suit appeals stop and thus where much of the judicial policy is made. Thus even if we wish to focus on the relations between the Supreme Court and the Patent Office, a crucial factor is the behavior of the circuits, for it is their responsiveness or lack of responsiveness to Supreme Court direction that will determine the extent to which Supreme Court policy decisions are actually enforced upon the Patent Office through the medium of the infringement suit. If the circuits were finding every patent that came before them valid and infringed, the Patent Office would, from its point of view, be enjoying an almost perfect relationship with the courts, no matter what doctrinal pronouncements the Supreme Court were making.[9]

The crucial position of the circuits is not peculiar to

---

9. This argument assumes that the district courts invariably obey the circuits. While this assumption remains to be tested, there are certain mechanisms built into the district–circuit relation that enforce a far higher level of loyalty by the districts to the circuits than necessarily exists, except on a voluntary basis, between the circuits and the Supreme Court.

patent law but is to be found in the complex of relationships existing between the Supreme Court and most of the administrative agencies of the federal government. Occasionally it is interrupted by peculiar circumstances such as direct appeal from the district courts to the Supreme Court in review of Interstate Commerce Commission decisions, or the propensity of the Supreme Court to grant certiorari in a large number of crucial antitrust cases. Generally, however, the combination of a right of appeal from the agency up to the circuit courts, so that the circuits must take a great many cases, combined with the availability of only certiorari from the circuits to the Supreme Court, so that the Supreme Court only takes the cases it wants to, and thus takes proportionally few, means that in administrative–judicial relations the circuits almost invariably play a crucial role.

This may be clearer if put in communications terms. If the Supreme Court is not managing to communicate its policy position clearly to the circuits, and insuring that the circuits obey that communication, then the Supreme Court will be deprived of its major channel of communications with the agencies, and of its principal means of enforcing its position on the agencies. For the inescapable institutional limitations on a nine-man court dealing with a huge governmental apparatus mean that if the justices do not receive adequate support from their "subordinates" in the judicial hierarchy they simply cannot intervene extensively or intensely enough in the administrative process to be politically effective.

At this point, then, our question becomes: When the Supreme Court's rate of invalidation jumped in the 1930s, did the Court manage to communicate its attitudes toward patents to the circuits, and did the circuits respond? The late Judge Learned Hand, for many years one of the most outstanding members of the circuit court bench, and, as we shall see presently, a leading figure in the disputes over patent policy, indicated that his circuit (the 2nd Circuit, sitting in New York City and invariably one of the most important) did discern and respond to a shift in the Supreme

Court's decisions as early as 1931.[10] Up to 1940, however, there seems to have been no major shift in the behavior of the circuits,[11] and no formal announcement by the circuits that they were following new policies. By 1940 the patent bar—that is the body of lawyers who specialize in patent matters—had an uneasy feeling that something was going on. A goodly number of them were saying openly that the Supreme Court was taking an "antipatent" position, that is, raising the standard of invention, or trying to get better bargains for the government. At the crucial level of the circuits, however, the position seems to have been one in which the judges had been alerted and were hesitantly preparing to make, but had not yet made, a major movement.

JUDICIAL REALISM

At this point it is necessary to break into the narrative again to deal with another problem that is relevant to the development of our patent policy but is also of very great general importance in the field of administrative–judicial relations. During the 1930s a school of jurisprudential theory became popular in this country that has been labeled judicial realism. In brief, and in badly oversimplified form, the realists argued that it was what judges did, not what they said, that counted. The law was what the courts decided, not the elaborate verbal formulas that the judges used to rationalize their decisions. And what the courts decided was not the result of logical interpolation and extension of what they had previously said—i.e., the arguments from precedent and the logical search for analogy which are the stock-in-trade of legal discourse—but of the judges' attitudes toward the issues of public policy raised in the cases.

This kind of thought had immediate and striking relevance in the field of patent law. If the Supreme Court kept

---

10. Hearings on H.R. 3760 Before Subcommittee No. 3 of the House Committee on the Judiciary, 82d Cong., 1st Sess., ser. 9 at 327 (1951)
11. See Evans, "Disposition of Patent Cases by the Courts," 24 *Journal of the Patent Office Society* 19 (1942)

saying that it was following the standard of the 1880s, but what it was really doing was striking down nearly every patent that came before it, was the law that the circuits were to follow what the Court said or what the Court did? Should the circuit judges in deciding new patent cases reason logically from the traditional verbal formulas still employed by the Supreme Court, or should they be guided by the new policy attitudes that seemed to lie below the verbal surface of the recent Supreme Court opinions?

This situation in patent law in the late 1930s neatly illustrates, I think, the oversimplification of most either-or arguments. The problem is not one of deciding that law in the operative sense is either words or deeds. The problem is one of the relative effectiveness of various modes of communication to various recipients. For Judge Hand, who maintained an especially delicate sense of judicial propriety that included loyal obedience to the Supreme Court, a few rather vaguely worded opinions were sufficient to change his behavior even before the new pattern of what the Court was doing emerged. For other less acute or less loyal judges, clearer messages were necessary.

The great weakness of judicial realism as a theory of law is that it is only true if you believe it is true. If the circuit court judges had uniformly believed that what the Supreme Court did, not what it said, was the law, then the Court's record of antipatent decisions might have been sufficient. For better or worse, however, many of the judicial subordinates of the Supreme Court then and now cling to the traditional belief that, if the Supreme Court wishes to tell them something, it must tell them in the language of English, not statistics, and in the course of an opinion clearly setting out the doctrine to be followed, not in the pattern of who won and lost in the last twenty cases. In terms of the Court's political role, it is neither here nor there whether these judges are behind the jurisprudential times. Their attitude is a fact which the Court must take into account if it is to communicate effectively.

Secondly, the loyalty of the Court's judicial subordinates

is not to be automatically assumed. In many instances circuit judges may have very different policy views than the Supreme Court majority, and some of them may be willing to resist the Court. The less clear and direct the policy communication from the Supreme Court, the more likely are the resisting circuit judges to "misunderstand" it and continue along their own path. Since the traditional position that doctrine is the law remains available, Supreme Court communications in the form of changing patterns of results while doctrine remains constant are relatively easy for circuit judges who do not like the new results to misunderstand. The circuit judge can only misunderstand a clearly stated doctrinal change at a high cost to himself in terms of violation of the organizational ethics of the judiciary and the professional ethics of the bar. He may sometimes be willing to incur these costs if he values his policy preferences highly enough, but again the question is one of degree. The clearer the message the higher the cost in ignoring or misunderstanding it; the higher the cost of resistance, the less resistance there is likely to be.

Finally, the notion that a court's deeds are the law assumes a kind of archetypal relationship between courts that is not typically present in the relations between the Supreme Court and the circuits. If an appeals court always does X while saying Y, the subordinate trial court will eventually stop doing Y, even though it likes Y better and can still make a good doctrinal case for doing Y, if the appellate court consistently reverses the trial court on appeal. Here again organizational and professional ethics are at play. A judge who is constantly reversed loses status as a judge and as a lawyer. Besides few men wish to take regular exercise in political futility, and if every time you decide Y your superior forces you to do X, you will soon do X without being told. This pattern of behavior presupposes, however, that the subordinate court will actually be reversed most or all of the time. Only then is the decisional behavior of the appellate court the law. If both courts profess the same doctrine, and the appellate court only takes and reverses one in twenty of the lower court's decisions, then the lower court can persist indefinitely in doing Y, and get a result of $20Y - 1X$ at a very low cost to itself in reversals. The more firmly attached the lower court is to its policy preferences, of course, the higher costs it may be willing to bear. Put another way, the more resistant the lower court is to the higher, and the fewer cases the higher court takes from the lower, the less legally effective are the deeds as opposed to the words of the higher court.

The Supreme Court is invariably in the position of taking very few cases on any given question from any given circuit over any given period of time. It handles problems over which there are typically honest and major differences of opinion within the political system that are likely to inspire major resistance from some of its judicial subordinates no matter what position it takes. Thus its archetypical situation is precisely the reverse of that upon which the deeds-not-doctrine notion is predicated.

DEEDS AND DOCTRINES

Why then do not courts generally, and the Supreme Court in the patent cases in particular, always fashion clear doctrinal communications to accompany their deeds? In many instances the judges themselves are not aware that their changing policy attitudes have caused them to put new effective meaning into the old verbal formulas. Themselves unaware of the discrepancy between their deeds and doctrines, they do not develop new doctrines to end the discrepancy. It is precisely in such instances that sensitive and loyal subordinate judges will follow the deeds, not the words. In many instances, however, courts, and particularly the Supreme Court, are involved in problems of dual or multiple communication that are typical of all politics. There are many instances in which a politician wishes to deliver one message to some of his constituents, superiors, allies, and/or subordinates, and quite a different message to others. For

one of the principal social functions of politicians is to
mitigate intergroup conflict, and one of the principal devices
for maintaining a tactical position from which to perform
this function is to tell different groups different things.
Courts, like other political institutions, may wish to deliver
several messages simultaneously. They sometimes do so by
vaguely worded doctrines that can be interpreted in several
ways. At other times they may deliver one message with their
deeds and another with their doctrines. As with all other
politicians, however, there must be some core of commonal-
ity between the various messages, and the content of the
various messages cannot diverge excessively or indefinitely.
The politician succeeds at multiple messaging only when
the relationship between the messages is relatively subtle
and dynamic.

Courts will frequently allow a certain discrepancy between deeds and doctrines, but if that discrepancy becomes
static and sterile they will have to suffer the political consequences of loss of prestige and frustration of policy preferences. We should expect then not an analytically pure world
of deed or doctrine, but an interplay between the two to
achieve the Court's goals. To the extent that we find a static
discrepancy between deed and doctrine, we have not so much
found a clear illustration of the position of the judicial
realists as discovered a clear illustration of a politically inept
court.

THE NEW MOOD

After the deeds of the 1930s, therefore, some new words
from the Supreme Court were to be anticipated. They came
in a cluster of cases beginning in the early 1940s. The most
important was probably *Cuno Eng'r. Corp. v. Automatic Devices Corp.*,[12] and it is *Cuno* that many circuit opinions subsequently cite as the message they received to tighten their
standards of invention. The second was *Jungersen v. Ostby*

12. 314 U.S. 84 (1941)

& Barton Co.,[13] and the third *Great Atlantic and Pacific Tea Co. v. Supermarket Equip. Corp.*[14] The general impression left with the patent bar and with lower-court judges was that these three cases announced in official doctrine the new position of the Supreme Court which previously could only have been guessed at or sensed by particularly discerning observers.

This reaction is in a way curious and illustrates the subtle interplay of deeds and words in judicial communication. For viewed in the coldly analytical way that judges and lawyers are supposed to treat cases, none of the three individually, nor all three collectively, actually make the slightest change in the existing state of the legal doctrine. In *Cuno* the Court did nothing but invoke the traditional subtest against aggregations and hold, as it has always held, that where an applicant is seeking a combination patent—that is, one where he claims nothing new except the way he has combined already known elements—such applications must be given especially careful scrutiny to distinguish patentable combinations from unpatentable aggregations. The essential conservatism of the actual holding can be seen when the applicant's principal legal argument is examined. The combination involved was so obviously lacking in invention by any standard that the applicant was forced into centering his case on the argument that the standard of invention itself was unconstitutional and that only novelty and utility could be required. In short, the application was so weak that the applicant had to demand that the Court overthrow *Hotchkiss v. Greenwood,* the leading case for almost sixty years, before he could have had a chance of getting his patent declared valid. The actual holding in *Cuno* is that *Hotchkiss,* the case that the propatent forces have always enshrined, was still good law.

Justice Douglas wrote the opinion in *Cuno* and in it coined the phrase "flash of genius" as what was necessary to meet the invention requirement. In a sense these were the

13. 335 U.S. 560 (1949)
14. 340 U.S. 147 (1950)

new words to match the deeds, for the phrase was caught up by the newspapers, the patent bar and the lower courts and repeatedly used by them to express the new Supreme Court attitudes. The Supreme Court, however, never subsequently used the phrase. And again viewed in the way lawyers are supposed to view the words of our highest court —that is, in a way far more carefully analytical than the layman glancing at a newspaper headline—"flash of genius" was not a new doctrine at all. What Douglas actually said was "the flash of creative genius, not merely the skill of the calling." The older Supreme Court cases he cited in support of his words had said "something akin to genius, as distinguished from mere mechanical skill" and referred to a "flash of thought." "Flash of genius" was not a new doctrine but merely a kind of digest of a whole series of phrases that the Supreme Court had long used in seeking to verbalize the invention requirement.[15]

The *Jungersen* case was not a particularly close one and, viewed on its merits, the patent was one that there is a very good chance that the Court would have struck down in 1890 or 1920 as well as 1949. It was chiefly notable for Justice Jackson's dissent:

> It would not be difficult to cite many instances of patents that have been granted, improperly I think, and without adequate tests of invention by the Patent Office. But I doubt that the remedy for such Patent Office passion for granting patents is an equally strong passion in this Court for striking them down so that the only patent that is valid is one which this Court has not been able to get its hands on.[16]

Here then finally was a verbal acknowledgment in a Supreme Court opinion of the feud between the Patent Office and the Court which had been simmering at the level of deed

---

15. See *Rechendorfer v. Faber*, 92 U.S. 347, 357 (1876), *Densmore v. Scofield*, 102 U.S. 375, 378 (1880), *Smith v. Whitman Saddle Co.*, 148 U.S. 674, 681 (1893), *Potts v. Creager*, 155 U.S. 597, 607 (1895), *Concrete Appliances Co. v. Gomery*, 269 U.S. 177, 185 (1925), *Mantle Lamp Co. v. Aluminum Products Co.*, 301 U.S. 544, 546 (1937)
16. 335 U.S. 560, 572 (1949)

for some time. But a dissenting editorial is not a Supreme Court enunciation of doctrine and, under the canons of case law, is not a command to anyone or legally binding in any way.

The third case, *A & P*, struck down a combination patent that was clearly a borderline case. The invalidation may be viewed as another deed to add to those of the 1930s, but the language of the majority opinion was quite standard and traditional. No one could have read it as a new doctrinal message. Indeed the opinion was written by Justice Jackson, who obviously was thinking of the decision not as a part of the Court's alleged new crusade against the Patent Office but as a sober application of the traditional law to a marginal instance. It was a concurrence by Justice Douglas condemning the Patent Office for issuing patents to "gadgets," and offering a large number of particularly glaring examples, that got most of the play in legal circles. Again, however, the editorial concurrence of a single justice does not a legal doctrine make or change an existing one.

Nevertheless throughout the 1940s and 1950s these three cases were a constant litany of citations chanted by courts and commentators to show that the Supreme Court had changed the level of invention, and it was obviously these cases which moved many of the circuits in the 1940s and 1950s to follow the trend of deeds established by the Supreme Court in the 1930s. Yet the cases themselves are ambiguous. They do not clearly announce a new doctrine. Indeed they officially, even if only superficially, proclaim the old. What the words of the justices do, *when taken in conjunction with the deeds of the 1930s,* is to create a *mood* which is conveyed to the lower courts. The deeds taken by themselves are ambiguous, since they are accompanied by the repetition of the old doctrine. The *Cuno, Jungersen,* and *A & P* opinions taken by themselves are ambiguous by lawyers' lights. The ambiguous deeds and ambiguous words taken together, however, even if they merely create something so vague it can only be called a mood, do constitute a clear enough message to be openly received and acknowledged by a great many circuit-court judges. That this sort of messaging is the stock-in-trade of the judicial process should not be obscured either by judicial realisms' emphasis on "who won" each case or by excessive preoccupation with the rules of "correct" judicial communication as dictated by the traditional notions of *stare decisis, ratio decedendi* and the general lore of the lawyer's craft.

CONFLICT AMONG THE CIRCUITS

The situation in the 1940s and 1950s was not exactly a model of judicial propriety. The Supreme Court was invalidating nearly every patent on which its opinion was asked. And its opinions seemed to transmit a mood of disapproval of the Patent Office's standards. Yet the Court purported to be applying the traditional standards, and those were certainly the standards the Patent Office claimed to be employing. Faced with a continued stream of Patent Office issuances on the one hand and a continued stream of Supreme Court invalidations on the other, the intermediate courts were in something of a dilemma.

Different courts solved their problems in different ways. Some of the circuits, most notably the 2nd on which Learned Hand sat, openly acknowledged "a pronounced new doctrinal trend"[17] in the Supreme Court and announced that they were applying a stricter standard of invention than they had a few years earlier. This position eventually led some courts to specifically acknowledge the policy differences between the Patent Office and the Supreme Court and denounce the Patent Office for not obeying its legal superior.[18] Other circuits while running to very high rates of invalidation did not admit that any change in the standard had occurred, and still others were quite vague as to whether they were or were not marching to a new Supreme Court

---

17. *Picard v. United Aircraft Corp.*, 128 F. 2d 632, 636 (2d Cir. 1942)
18. See Ladd, "Business Aggression Under the Patent System," 26 *U. Chicago Law Review* 353 (1959). See also *Packwood v. Briggs and Stratton Corp.*, 195 F. 2d 971 (3d Cir 1952)

cadence. One circuit, the 5th, staunchly insisted that nothing at all had happened and generally supported the Patent Office's decisions.

A glance at the percentages of patents held valid by the circuits in the period 1945–49 will suggest the extent of disagreement among the circuits as to what the law was.[19]

Current Court	Per Cent	Current Court	Per Cent
1st	38	6th	24
2nd	7	7th	17
3rd	17	8th	6
4th	25	9th	43
5th	77	10th	14

This kind of disagreement among the circuits should not, however, be taken as peculiar to patent law, and now that this data has been introduced perhaps another general aside is warranted. It is quite typical in the legal areas in which the Supreme Court reviews administrative decisions to find conflicts among the circuits, and not at all unusual to find massive conflicts in which roughly half the circuits line up on each side of a quite specific and narrowly defined legal issue. Such conflicts frequently last for four or five years or longer.

Theoretically, of course, such conflicts should not last very long. It is not at all disturbing that they initially occur. After all, courts of appeal exist to deal with difficult legal questions whose answers are not immediately self-evident. It is precisely such questions that merit appeal from the decision of the agencies and the lower courts. Naturally enough then the circuits themselves may disagree on questions about which other lawyers and policy makers have already disagreed. On the other hand, surely the federal law ought at any given moment to be the same in Houston as in New York, and the legal rights of litigants should not vary according to which circuit hears their case. Theoretically, this problem is resolved by the structure of the federal court system

19. See Note, "Enforcement of Rights Against Patent Infringers," 72 *Harvard Law Review* 328 (1958)

in which the Supreme Court is in a position to identify conflicts between the circuits and, using its discretionary power of certiorari, to take cases that embody the legal issues in question. Again in theory, once the Supreme Court has decided the issue, the circuit conflict is resolved because thereafter all of the circuits are bound to accept the Supreme Court's solution.

What is theoretically true does in fact happen, but not necessarily completely or immediately. The Supreme Court's potential to resolve circuit conflicts only sets some outer limits to their extent and duration. But why doesn't the Supreme Court act immediately to settle any conflict that arises, thus maintaining the ordered neatness of legal doctrine? In the first place, there is so much federal law and so many circuits that hundreds of conflicts necessarily arise. The Supreme Court, given all its other business, could not possibly handle all of them immediately. Secondly, a delay by the Supreme Court gives the circuits time to settle conflicts among themselves thus markedly reducing the amount of work the Supreme Court must ultimately do. Thirdly, the circuit courts are generally of quite high judicial calibre. If conflicts on points of law arise between them, it is usually because the point is really a very difficult one.

Supreme Court justices must often feel that they are no more able to resolve the difficulty than are the circuits. For the Supreme Court to act might be to impose one firm and final, and wrong, solution on a problem, in the place of two tentative and evolving, and partly right, solutions. The gain in uniformity may well be outweighed by the cost of freezing a wrong answer into judicial doctrine. Two wrongs don't make a right, but two wrongs in unsettled conflict may be better than one settled wrong. For if nothing else, the long continuance of conflict on the circuits eventually gives the Supreme Court the benefit of the vast amount of hard thought the circuits have invested in evolving and defending their conflicting positions. Indeed, as is not unusual in human affairs, frequently in the course of the conflict new facts are discovered and new alternatives evolved that lead to a far better solution than could have been achieved if the conflict had been resolved immediately by the imposition of one of the alternatives initially suggested.

In short, the Supreme Court tends to handle circuit conflict over administrative action the way most political decision makers handle policy conflict—by the maxim that only fools rush in. For instance when Congress becomes aware of new policy demands, it rarely rushes to embody them in a statute immediately. Instead it proceeds tentatively, introducing a draft bill here, holding a hearing there, and only over the course of several sessions or several years finally getting around to a major statutory decision. In the course of committee hearings, parliamentary maneuvers, marking up bills, killing bills, reintroducing bills, proposing amendments, and so on, Congress educates itself on the facts and the issues of policy, discovers what groups want what and how much they want it, and allows the various groups time and opportunity to bargain with one another and with Congress. The final legislation that results will fully reflect the facts, the available alternatives and the constellation of political forces both within and without the Congress. Protracted conflict on the circuits tends to serve the same function for the Supreme Court that the prolonged ritual of considering and passing a bill serves for Congress.

Put another way, prolonged circuit conflict tends to enhance the incremental quality of Supreme Court decision making. Over a period of prolonged conflict the circuits will themselves attempt a great many small-step changes. Even if these do not succeed, and the conflict resolve itself, in the process the circuits will have acted to consider and reject one alternative after another. Through the handling of hundreds of individual units of litigation they will eventually have worked their way down to isolating a few relevant facts and alternatives on which an authoritative decision can be reached. The Supreme Court need not then consider the whole universe but only those things that the repeated trial-and-error experiments of the circuits have demonstrated to be crucial.

In the patent field, of course, the conflict was not limited to the circuits. If the Court had indeed raised the standard of invention, then it was the Patent Office and the Court which were in direct conflict, for the Office professed to see no change in the standard, and there was no observable tendency on the part of patent examiners to be less liberal in their treatment of patents. The unofficial voice of the Office, and its allies among the patent lawyers, took a decidedly hostile tone toward the *Cuno* decision. While this sort of confrontation between Supreme Court and administrative agency is not typical, or at least is present in patent law to an unusual extent, it is typical that circuit conflict does not exist in a vacuum. In the area of review of administrative decision making, conflict on the circuits usually exists because some circuits have backed the agency stance on a certain question and others have opposed it. In patent law, of course, the disagreement between the circuits was not so much expressed in doctrinally phrased dispute over the word "invention" as in differing rates of acceptance of actual Patent Office decisions. Because circuit courts do not consider policy issues in the abstract, but only through the medium of litigational challenges to administrative decisions already made, it is almost inevitable that conflict occurs in terms of proagency versus antiagency circuits.

In the patent area one additional court can enter the fray, the Court of Customs and Patent Appeals, which is in one sense less a court than the highest appeals board within the patent system. While this court cannot be viewed as simply a faithful follower of the Patent Office,[20] on the question of invention it has stood four-square with the Patent Office even to the extent of acknowledging a new doctrinal trend in the Supreme Court and openly setting itself against the trend.[21] The District Court for the District of Columbia, which serves as an alternate route for reviewing decisions of

---

20. See for example the dispute over pharmaceutical patents described in Note, "Utility Requirements in the Patent Law," 53 *Georgetown Law Journal* 154 (1964)

21. See *In re Shortell*, 142 F.2d 292 (1944)

the Patent Office Board of Appeals, also took a position far more favorable to the Patent Office than did most of the circuits. Obviously the applicant who was appealing the refusal of the Patent Office to issue a patent under the seemingly loose Office standard would have had almost no chance of winning an appeal under the apparently stricter standards of the Supreme Court and most of the circuits. Thus the positions of the Court of Customs and Patent Appeal and the District Court left the initially unsuccessful applicant some hope of winning an appeal. They offered no particular hope, however, for the successful applicant trying to defend his monopoly through an infringement suit, for infringement suits are handled through the regular federal district and circuit courts.

So far I have emphasized the advantages of protracted conflict on the circuits. Such emphasis is necessary because of the almost instinctive reaction of both lawyers and laymen that such conflict is per se wrong or bad. This reaction, of course, stems from a basic vision of law as uniform, logically consistent, and substantively complete that is fundamental to much of Western legal philosophy—so fundamental that it has become an integral part of our folk beliefs or ideology. In order properly to understand the role of courts in politics, however, it is necessary to shake off this excessively static vision and appreciate that much of what we call law is not a set of things to be logically ordered but a process by which decisions are made. Inconsistencies at certain points in the process are not bad, or good, in and of themselves. The question must always be, Do the inconsistencies further the on-going of the process, do they aid the participants in the process, do they contribute to getting a better policy product from the process? Circuit conflicts are not to be condemned abstractly but evaluated politically.

All this is not to say, however, that prolonged conflicts do not involve important costs. The principal cost is forum shopping. Frequently in the area of review of administrative decisions, one or the other of the litigants may choose which court he wishes to use. For instance, at any given time lawyers and accountants in at least twenty major cities in the country are likely to discover the latest tax loophole almost simultaneously. Let us say that the Internal Revenue Service has decided it wishes to have this loophole problem adjudicated by the 1st Circuit, which serves New England. It will simply allow the new deduction to go unchallenged when taxpayers take it in every state but Maine. It will challenge the deduction in Maine. The Maine taxpayer will go into the federal courts serving New England.[22] So while superficially it was the taxpayer, not the Service, who chose to go to court, it was actually the Service that chose what court to go to. Now let us say that the 1st Circuit rules adversely to the Service. The Service can then stop challenging the deduction in New England, and so avoid any further unfavorable judgments by the 1st Circuit, since taxpayers will not go to court to get the Service reversed when the Service says yes to them. It then can start challenging the deduction when made by far-Western taxpayers. The taxpayers, encouraged by what the 1st Circuit has done for their east coast compatriots, will then go to court, and now cases involving this particular issue will pop up on the 9th Circuit, again at the taxpayers initiative but the Service's choice. Note that the Service not only can initially choose the circuit it thinks most favorable, but it can also actually seek to create or avoid conflict among the circuits by the geographic sequence of challenges it makes. For instance if conflict suits the Service's purposes, as it will for instance when the Service wants to force the Supreme Court into committing itself, then the Service can challenge the taxpayers of two geographic areas, one served by a "protax" circuit, the other by a "protaxpayer" circuit.

Few agencies of the federal government have quite the flexibility of the Internal Revenue Service in conducting litigational campaigns, but most administrative agencies and

---

22. I have put the matter this way to simplify it. Technically it is often the Service that goes into court to compel the taxpayer to pay his taxes. But the taxpayer, by choosing to pay or not to pay, chooses whether to give in to the Service or end up in court.

regulatory commissions have it to one degree or another. The Patent Office does not, for the Patent Office is not a party. to the infringement suits which provide the major means of judicial review of the Office's decisions. Infringement suits occur between two private parties, and the Office cannot control who sues whom where. The litigants, however, may be able to forum-shop. The patent grant prohibits manufacture, sale, or use by another of the item patented. Even if it is only being manufactured by one rival in one location, it is probably being sold or used in many places. Often then the patent holder can initiate his infringement suit against a seller or user who is geographically located in such a way as to bring the case into the circuit court that he feels will be most "propatent." The infringing manufacturer will then frequently join in the defense of the suit no matter where it is in order to try and prevent a judicial finding of invalidity. For, once one circuit has invalidated a patent, it is almost impossible to get any other to uphold its validity. Thus even when the infringing manufacturer is located in a "safe" circuit's jurisdiction he may be lured into a dangerous circuit by suits against his customers.

It should also be noted that while the Patent Office has no direct control over choice of forum, the patent holder acts in behalf of the Patent Office in getting its decisions on to favorable circuits. The patent holder after all has a decision from the Patent Office which he is trying to defend. His interests are therefore identical to those of the Patent Office. In choosing the circuit on which he is most likely to win his infringement suit, he is choosing the circuit that is most likely to agree with the Patent Office, which is presumably exactly the one the Patent Office too would use if it were choosing. What the Revenue Service does for itself, the Patent Office's clients do for it. The *Journal of the Patent Office Society,* which is both the unofficial voice of the Patent Office and the main house organ of the patent bar, has published a series of articles comparing the batting averages of the various circuits and pointing out, as if that were necessary, which circuits were the best bet in an infringement suit.[23]

THE CONFLICT BETWEEN THE
SUPREME COURT AND THE PATENT OFFICE

Having now outlined a policy dispute that seems to involve a major conflict between the courts and the Patent Office, and between some courts and others, it is time to admit that it is an odd war. For a good part of the debate in the judicial opinions and the professional journals, which is itself a major symptom of the war, is about whether there is really a war going on at all.

While few disinterested observers could come away with any other impression than one of a feud between the Patent Office and the Supreme Court, each with attendant allies among the lower courts,[24] it is quite difficult to provide concrete support for the impression. The Supreme Court handles so few patent cases that even major fluctuations in its percentage of invalidation for various years or decades reflects only a handful of actual decisions and are not statistically significant, or persuasive of fluctuations in the Court's standard of invention. In short, we cannot prove from their actions that the Patent Office has stuck to the old standard of invention while the Court has switched brands.

Even the continually high gross rate of invalidations by

---

23. It is not possible, however, to prove statistically that forum shopping is prevalent. The 5th Circuit, which has been most favorably inclined toward patents, has not handled a markedly higher patent case load than the others. But the fact that the 5th is well known to be propatent would cause many more alleged infringers in that geographic area to settle infringement suits before they reach the circuit level than would normally do so. Conversely on antipatent circuits far more alleged infringers than normal would carry their cases up to the circuit. There is thus a kind of equilibrium effect which tends to equalize the case loads of propatent and antipatent circuits even where forum shopping takes place. A number of other factors, such as the geographical clusterings of industry, corporation headquarters, and major law firms, also muddy the statistical waters.

24. See Frank, "The United States Supreme Court: 1948-49," 17 *U. Chicago Law Review* 1, 19-20 (1949)

the Supreme Court cannot "prove" that Court and Office are using different standards. The Court does not review every patent the Office issues, but only those that become involved in infringement suits. Few firms will take the risk of infringing obviously valid patents. Those firms that do are likely to settle infringement suits before they come to trial and certainly long before appeal to the Supreme Court. The infringer will make the long fight when he has a strong argument for the invalidity of the patent. Thus the tactics of patent litigation pretty well insure that generally only the most questionable of all the patents issued by the Office reach the Supreme Court. Therefore the percentage of Supreme Court invalidations would always be very high even if it and the Patent Office were using exactly the same standard. This phenomenon is frequently encountered in judicial review of administration. The clearly correct agency decisions are not appealed to the courts. The judges only get those that the agency itself thought of as on the borderline, but was forced to make one way or the other. Getting only the shaky decisions, the court's percentage of agency reversals climbs far above what it would be if the courts got all the decisions to review. The figures then tend to exaggerate the extent of disagreement between court and agency.

Aside from this general phenomenon, certain peculiarities of the patent process lead to high rates of judicial reversal of agency decisions even if no major policy difference exists between court and agency. First of all, when in doubt the Patent Office issues a patent. In some fields of governmental supervision it is clear that doubt should be resolved against the private party. When in doubt about whether the locomotive will blow up, you don't issue the safety certificate. But a good case can be made for Patent Office resolution of doubt in favor of the applicant in terms of incentive to inventors, advantage to the public of the disclosure of technical information which would remain secret if the patent were not granted, and the irreparable injury that would follow if the Office said no mistakenly. For if a patent is once refused, and the device is subsequently used or reinvented by others, the original inventor cannot subsequently get a patent because the device will by then have become part of the prior knowledge or state of the art and thus be unpatentable. Nevertheless by following the policy of issuing when in doubt the Patent Office produces many more chances of court invalidation than it otherwise would. This situation is reflected in the fact that while the courts themselves long ago created the presumption that patents issued by the Office were valid (i.e., the burden of proof was on the litigant claiming invalidity), they have in practice largely abandoned that presumption.

Secondly, there is the problem of prior art and prior use itself. A patent is not, of course, issuable for something that has been known about or used by others previously, but only for something new. The Patent Office searches the "prior art" by going through its own files to determine whether the new application duplicates patents issued earlier. However, the Patents Office budget granted to it by Congress is inadequate to do this job thoroughly. Each of the patent examiners has far too heavy a work load to do a really complete search. And the office really has no facilities at all for checking on "previous use." It must confine itself largely to searching its own records generated by previous patent requests. If a device has been used previously but no patent application made on it, there is no way of the Office discovering such use.

All this changes when the defendant in an infringement suit challenges the validity of a patent. The stakes in such suits are often high, and the defendants are frequently business firms with considerable resources. They can afford to support weeks of research in the prior art on which the Patent Office can afford no more than a day. They can send men into the field to discover actual previous use and conduct extensive correspondence and interviewing. In short, an infringement suit provides both the incentive and the resources for a really thorough search of the prior art that cannot be found in the Patent Office. As a result the courts typically know far more about the prior art in reviewing a patent than the Patent Office did when issuing it and consequently discover far more invalidating duplications of the prior art than the Patent Office does. There is no question that in a large number of instances in which the courts invalidate a patent, thus reversing the Patent Office's decision, the Patent Office itself would have come to the opposite decision if it had known as much about the prior art as the court did. Thus at least part of the statistical rate of judicial invalidation is less indicative of a disagreement about policy between the Supreme Court and the Patent Office than of the greater ability of the courts to discover invalidating duplications of prior art.

A second difference in the information position of courts and office, although one having a more ambiguous impact on the statistics of invalidation, concerns the element of commercial success. As we shall see later, the mere fact of commercial success is not enough to warrant the issuance of a patent. Nevertheless if a new device is widely and enthusiastically adopted, particularly by industry, which is at least more cost and efficiency conscious and less subject to high pressure advertising than the consumer, that in itself is some indication of its novelty and of the quality of invention. If the thing had been old or obvious and had been badly needed all along (as proved by its wide sale when it did appear) presumably all the people who bought it now would have been using it all along and had no need to buy now. Thus commercial success is likely to favorably influence a judgment on patentability.

The Patent Office typically must make its judgment just as an item is being commercially introduced and so cannot await commercial results. Infringement suits come later and so such data are frequently available to courts. One might then expect this factor to work against high rates of judicial invalidation as commercial success came along to bolster some of the Office's marginal guesses, and make such patents even more clearly valid to the courts than they were to the Office. Commercial failures are not likely to inspire copying and subsequent infringement suits, so that commercial failure will rarely come along at the court stage to make patents less clearly valid than they were at the Office stage. On the other hand, being unable to predict the future, the Patent Office is likely to give the benefit of the doubt to the applicant lest it inadvertently block the wheels of progress, while the courts have a picture of what has actually happened before them and need not resolve doubts in favor of the applicant as insurance against cloudy crystal balls. In any event, the different access of courts and Office to the actual worth of a device as demonstrated by its commercial success would probably lead to somewhat different rates of invalidation even if the same standard were being used.

CLAIMS BARGAINING

A third factor involves the wonderful world of claims. It is interesting that when patents were proved, as they initially were in Europe, by the deposit of models, there was little litigation and indeed little check on patent issuance. Obviously neither the lawyers nor the royal bureaucrats could understand the models well enough to argue that the screw channel on one was really the same as the beveled cam on another. As the deposit of models was replaced by the deposit of working drawings and specifications, and supplemented by "claims," which are purely verbal descriptions of what the device can accomplish, lawyers get more and more involved. For now they get away from the alien field of technology and onto their home ground of comparing the words in various documents to see whether they are alike or different, engaging in the verbal manipulations that are the lifeblood of law.

It is now a truism among patent lawyers that if you sit around the Patent Office long enough, and change your claims often enough, you will eventually get some kind of a patent on almost anything. Patent examiners and the lawyers representing applicants constantly bargain with one another. The broader the set of claims, the more likely they are to overlap a previous patent and thus be unpatentable. But a too narrow set will mean that the inventor gets such a narrowly drawn patent that a would-be infringer, by making a few small modifications, can take his device outside of the scope of the granted patent. The patent examiner is a man frantically trying to empty his in-basket into his out-basket. The only sure way to get an application out of his in-basket once and for all is to approve it, for every time he disapproves, the persistent patent lawyer will change a few claims and throw it back in again. The examiner is desperate to save time. The lawyer has time but is anxious not to repeatedly whittle away his client's claims until the monopoly he gets is too narrow to be valuable. The result is usually a compromise in which the inventor gets his patent, but on less than he wished to claim, and the examiner gets on to the next file piled on his desk.

The patented claims, however, are in words, and words can invariably be expanded or contracted in meaning and coverage. While negotiating with the Patent Office, the patent lawyer accepted the narrower scope; when trying to bring the infringer to heel in court, he naturally takes the broader. Indeed the whole art of writing patent claims is to find words that look narrow enough to the Patent Office to get them to grant you a monopoly and can subsequently be made to look broad enough to make the monopoly worthwhile. Thus while the Patent Office and the court may be looking at the same patent number, they may quite literally be looking at different patents in terms of the claims that define the real legal and economic impact of the patent. And just as the patent lawyer may have narrowed his claims too much at the Patent Office in order to get the patent, he may broaden them too much in court in order to get the infringer. For the broader his claims the more likely they are to overlap the prior art. Thus the lawyer hell-bent on proving infringement may very well prove that his client's patent is invalid. Since the courts see far broader claims on the same patent than does the Patent Office, the courts would quite naturally be invalidating far more of them than would the Patent

Office, and this would account for part of the high rate of judicial reversal of Office decisions even if their standards of invention were identical.

THE BENEFITS OF DOUBLE DECISION

I have not spent all this time on the various factors that differentiate the Patent Office's from the court's decisional environment just to show that invalidation statistics do not "prove" that a policy conflict exists between the Supreme Court and the Patent Office. These factors also provide a very concrete and specific example of how the double-decision process implied in judicial review of administrative decisions works, and why—although it may seem wasteful in general—it may be extremely valuable in certain circum stances.

The special reason justifying active judicial review in the patent field is that the courts' institutional capabilities differ widely from those of the Patent Office and complement them in such a way as to yield a far better decisional product than the Office could produce by itself. The key to this phenomenon is the relation between the ex parte proceedings of the Office and the adversary proceedings of the courts. When a private individual applies for a patent, there is no way for other private individuals to challenge the validity of his application before the Patent Office.[25] The Patent Office must make its decision solely on the basis of the arguments presented by one party (ex parte), the party that favors issuing the patent—namely the applicant. I am not arguing that ex parte proceedings are deficient per se, but combined with the limited budget of the Office, they insure that the decision maker has an incomplete picture of the prior art and practically no picture of prior use. When a Patent Office decision is reviewed by the courts in an infringement suit, however, the very form of the proceedings produces someone

---

25. "Intervention" proceedings are only available as between two applicants, both of whose applications are pending, and concern only the chron-ological priority of invention.

with the money and the incentive to perform a search of the prior art and use of which the Patent Office is institutionally incapable—namely the alleged infringer. The court in effect enlists the alleged infringer into a more thorough search of the prior art and use than the Patent Office is willing or able to undertake. Since finding a prior invention is the surest way of winning his case, the infringer is likely to do a good job.

It might be argued that the same results could be gained by introducing adversary proceedings or the budget for thorough search, or both, into the Patent Office itself. To do so, however, would endlessly delay the granting of applications, thus markedly reducing whatever incentive the patent system presently provides. As things stand we get rapid but not very well-researched decisions on all new applications and slower but very well-researched decisions on some patents. Moreover the adversary system, and the whole format of legal suits, insure that the some that get the more thorough research before the courts are generally those that need it. For the infringer is likely to settle before they get to court suits where the Patent Office has committed no oversight, because his chances of losing these are fairly high. He will fight on into the courts those in which he thinks more research will support a different result than the Patent Office's.

The adversary nature of court proceedings also complements the Office's work in another way. You will recall that patents are essentially a matter of bargaining between the government and the inventor. This bargaining is now carried on through the process of filing and amending "claims." The applicant can nearly always get a patent if he will narrow his claims enough, and will generally attempt to make his claims appear narrower to the Patent Office than they really are. The Patent Office has no check on this tendency of applicants to make what in effect are bad faith bargains except the skill and patience of its examiners, the latter of which at least is severely limited. When we add the courts we get a semiautomatic mechanism for protecting the integrity of the bargain. For in an infringement suit before the courts, the patent holder must broaden his claims to what he really wanted and thinks he got from the Patent Office in order to insure that his patent is actually broad enough to block the kind of infringement he was seeking to protect himself from all along by getting the patent. Then when he states his true claims in court, the court can match them against the prior art fully researched by the alleged infringer. If the patent holder stated his claims too narrowly to the Patent Office in order to avoid appearing to overlap prior art, he gets caught at this point by the courts.

The Patent Office system standing alone tells the applicant: State your claims narrowly but ambiguously. The Patent Office and the courts together say: If you state your claims too narrowly, you will get by the Patent Office, but your patent will not be broad enough to protect you from infringers. If you state your claims too broadly after you get by the Office, the courts will catch you and invalidate your patent as overlapping prior art. Therefore you must state your real claim, and then the patent system as a whole will protect your intellectual property if it really is your property, that is if someone else didn't think of it first.[26]

I hope I may be excused for emphasizing once again that because it is basically a process of double decision, judicial review should operate actively only when there are special reasons for it in particular areas of governmental decision making. The factors described above indicate the basic framework of special reasons that justify active review in the patent area. There are some other reasons as well. Essentially they revolve about the institutional interests of the Patent Office. In theory the Office has two functions. One is to provide incentives to the private inventor. The other is to protect the government's interests. In short, the Patent Office

---

26. The doctrines of equivalents and file wrapper estoppel, which I do not have space enough here to deal with adequately, reinforce this pressure on the inventor to make proper claims rather than narrowing or broadening them at various points to suit his tactical needs.

stands at the fulcrum of the bargain between inventor and government. It must insure that a device which is of sufficient merit to warrant a patent gets one, and that the government does not pay the high price of monopoly for inventions not worth that price. The Patent Office, however, tends almost inevitably to shift over to the individual's and away from the government's side in this bargaining. Its ex parte proceedings mean that it only hears the individual's arguments and evidence for the merits of the device and none against, and the general rule is to accept such evidence at face value. The Office's search of prior art is limited and doubts on invention as well as novelty and utility are resolved in favor of the applicant. Added to all this is the fact that the persistent applicant, patiently drawing and redrawing his claims, must be rewarded and sent away if the examiners are to keep their heads above their work loads.

Perhaps even more important than these specific factors, and partially causing them, is the natural identification of the Patent Office with the patent system. The Patent Office naturally wants the patent system to work well. That is its job, and a job well done is both personally satisfying and rewarding to the institution's prestige. That the patent system work well is in the public interest, and the Patent Office pursues the public interest by making the patent system work well. Unfortunately, as we saw earlier, there is no way of actually measuring how well the patent system is working, of gauging exactly how much technological progress it is independently responsible for. Where it is impossible to determine results, organizations quite typically resort to some other factor which is measurable even though it may be irrelevant or misleading as an indication of organizational success in accomplishing its goals. Thus a bombing force that for some reason cannot assess target damage is likely to measure organizational performance in terms of number of tons of bombs dropped or number of sorties flown. The Patent Office is likely to identify its success with the number of patents issued. If no patents were issued after all, there would be no Patent Office.

In this way we get in the patent area a phenomenon quite typical of administrative behavior, the identification of the public interest with the institutional interest of the agency, and the pursuit of the public interest in terms of the single-minded pursuit by the agency of its own particular function and those of its clients without a balanced regard for other interests. The parochialism of the Patent Office is understandable and not very undesirable, but that parochialism provides yet another reason for judicial review. The federal courts are courts of general jurisdiction. They can put patents in the perspective that their other work provides. (It is interesting that the one totally specialized court that hears patent cases, the Court of Customs and Patent Appeals, has sided with the Office against the Supreme Court.) They fully develop evidence and argument on both sides of the validity question. Infringement suits bring the whole history of commercial practice into courts, so that judges are in a far better position than patent examiners to see the negative as well as the positive effects of a given patent issuance on the actual workings of the economy. Perhaps most important, the courts are in a position to balance the public interest in the limited monopoly called patent against the public interest against monopoly in general expressed in the antitrust laws. If we could afford the space, a long digression on the treatment of patents under antitrust law would be appropriate here. Suffice it to say that the federal judge, who by virtue of his office constantly sees the interconnection of patent and antitrust matters, is in a position to do something the Patent Office is not—decide the validity of any given patent and frame general patent standards in the light of the interrelated needs of patent and antitrust law. Given their institutional positions, it would be unnatural to expect the Patent Office and the Antitrust Division of the Justice Department to do this. Given his position, it is almost impossible for the federal judge not to think about both, and reasonable to expect that judicial review will in this instance yield a better coordinated set of policies than those adopted by the Patent Office alone.

BACK TO THE CONFLICT
BETWEEN COURT AND OFFICE

This part of our story, however, is basically supposed to be about how the war between the Patent Office and the Supreme Court is rather an odd one, since most of the fighting is about whether there is really a war. We began, you will remember, by showing that the statistics could not prove a war but might be, and often have been, read as simply reflecting the differing and complementary institutional capabilities of the two decision makers. When we move from statistics to doctrine, a similar phenomenon is to be observed, and it is easy to collect endless commentary saying that the Court had or had not changed the standard.

In the first place, during the 1930s and 1940s the Supreme Court resolutely continued to cite as precedent the old cases setting out the "old" standard of invention. It did not overrule them; it did not cast doubt upon them. Indeed, each time it enunciated the standard of invention it either quoted directly from them or used them as footnotes which is the judicial way of saying: We are saying the same thing here as we did there. The *Cuno* case, which is often hailed as the great departure from the old standard, specifically says that it is applying the *Hotchkiss* standard. That standard is precisely the one that all the propatent forces, singing about the good old days, are always insisting that the court ought to go back to. Justice Douglas echoing *Hotchkiss* spoke of "more ingenuity . . . than the work of a mechanic skilled in the art." The "flash of genius" language may from one point of view set a new tone, but doctrinally speaking it was simply a digest or compacting of a number of verbal formulas used in the older cases. It was sometimes argued that the apparent tightening of the standard of invention was not a new development by the Supreme Court but a return, after lapses in the 1920s, to the old standard which had always been very high.[27] Certainly comparing the substance of the decisions of the 1880s with those of the 1940s yield no great

---

27. See e.g. Smith, "Recent Developments in Patent Law," 44 *Michigan Law Review* 899 (1946)

discrepancy.[28] In 1949 the Supreme Court did unanimously hold a challenged patent valid again citing the old cases as authority.[29]

Lawyers began to talk of the standard of invention remaining the same but of the strictness of administration or enforcement varying; the quarrel perhaps was not over the standard but over whether it should be strictly or loosely applied to each given set of facts. In certain instances, for certain purposes, the distinction between the strictness of a standard and the strictness of the application of a standard may be useful and enlightening. But very frequently it is a theoretical distinction without a practical difference. Only a scholastic could tell us why it would make any difference whether the Patent Office were using a looser standard of invention than the Court or were applying the same standard more loosely.

Yet for all the debate and evasion, two of the circuits were openly saying that the Supreme Court had so changed the standard that their own pre-1936 decisions were no longer law.[30] The Court of Customs and Patent Appeals, seconded more circumspectly by several of the circuits, was saying that the Supreme Court had changed the standard, and that it would fight the change to the bitter end.

If all this sounds curiouser and curiouser, it is not at all atypical of what frequently happens in the realm of court–agency relations. In the midst of much lawyerlike precision about rules and statutes, with much talk of paragraph 172b, sub 2 at 14 U.S.C. 732, a great vagueness often hovers. Partly this is due to the fact that courts and agencies typically deal with one another in the context of statutes that lack specificity and partly to the genuine difficulty of precisely phrasing difficult policy problems. Patent law exhibits both of these factors. But partly it is due to the fact that some or all of the participants can sometimes gain great tactical advantage from being vague. Patent law exhibits this phenomenon

---

28. cf. Prager, *op cit supra* note 6
29. *Graver Mfg. Co. v. Linde Co.,* 336 U.S. 271 (1949)
30. See *Foxboro Co. v. Taylor Instrument Co.,* 157 F. 2d. 226 (2d Cir. 1946); *Alemite Co. v. Jiffy Lubricator Co.,* 176 F. 2d 444 (4th Cir. 1949)

as well. Much of this has to do with the problem of multiple communication that we examined earlier. The President, for instance, frequently would like to deliver one message to the American people about foreign policy and quite another to those abroad. At home he might wish to outline various alternatives and show why he chose one rather than another. Abroad he might wish to show that the United States was united behind a single policy which was unarguably the best for it and the world. Yet his presentation of alternatives and reasons at home, and the arguments and criticisms that followed, might be taken by foreigners as meaning that the United States had not really made up its mind and that other policies might soon be introduced. The President cannot seal off his two audiences from one another and insure that the home audience gets one message and the foreign audience another. Nor can the city councilman who wishes to tell the federal government how badly his city needs federal aid and his constituents how much things have improved during his time in office—though both messages may be true.

While there is no complete solution to this problem, politicians have developed a set of techniques for mitigating its effects upon them. Among these techniques is the framing of messages in such a way that they will have one meaning to one audience and quite a different meaning to another. A second technique is to deliver two separate messages each of which is in a form that is likely to be picked up by one audience and not the other. A third is to simply issue very vague communications that serve as a screen for action but have no message. The cost of all these techniques, however, is the risk that the messages will in fact interfere with one another, will not be understood, or can be manipulated by their recipients in ways unfavorable to the communicator.

Various combinations of these techniques and costs can be seen in the patent field and account for the curious situation that a conflict does exist but is expressed as a debate over whether a conflict exists. The Supreme Court did indeed want to toughen its stand against excessively liberal patent policies, and it wished to convey that message to the lower courts and the Patent Office. At the same time it wished to say that it was simply following the traditional law and precedents, for given the general ideology of the Anglo-American legal system, such a message strengthens the Court's institutional prestige with various audiences including the bar and the general public. Therefore, it sought to convey its change of policy by a change in the tone of its opinions while technically maintaining their doctrinal continuity with the old cases. The Patent Office, on the other hand, wished to continue its policies, which presumably the old cases permitted, so it too argued that the old cases were still good law while at the same time suggesting that the Court was moving away from them improperly. Conversely, the Patent Office could not say that the Court had officially changed the doctrine, for to do so would have been to admit that the Office was disobeying the law. Thus the Patent Office by its issuance practices and through unofficial spokesmen was saying that the Office would issue patents that the Supreme Court thought invalid, and the Court was saying that it would invalidate many of the patents the Office issued; but both had resolutely to continue saying that the legal doctrine had not changed and the old cases were good law. Caught in the midst of these messages some courts received the Court's new tone and ignored the doctrinal message, thus tightening their patent policies; other did the reverse. Thus one of the major costs to the Supreme Court of these multiple-communications techniques was that, absent a single clear command, those of its subordinates who wished to disobey could do so by accepting the doctrinal message meant for outside consumption and screening out the tone that had actually been intended as an order to them.

THE SITUATION IN 1952

In 1952 Congress chose to enter the fray and it is, therefore, worth summing up what things looked like at that point. The Patent Office together with its ally, the Court of Customs and Patent Appeal, continued to insist that the standard of invention had not changed and continued its policy of very liberal patent issuance. The Supreme Court by deed and obliquely by word continued to insist that the Patent Office policy was wrong but also continued to say that the standard of invention had not changed. The Circuits were divided into three groups. One openly acknowledged that the Patent Office and the Supreme Court were in conflict, and that the standard of invention had been raised by the Supreme Court. It acted to enforce Supreme Court policy on the Office. A second group followed the Supreme Court's lead by maintaining a high level of vagueness, giving lip service to doctrinal continuity, but invalidating a very high proportion of litigated patents. A third group purported to keep its eyes firmly fixed on doctrine, insisted no change had occurred and no conflict existed, and consequently held valid a relatively high share of issued patents.

In one sense the Patent Office had clearly won the war since it continued its operational policies unchanged in the face of Supreme Court opposition. In another sense the Supreme Court had won. It could and did continue to invalidate nearly every patent that came before it and also achieved a very high average rate of invalidation by its circuit subordinates. Of course the total number of patents litigated is small, and, as a percentage of those issued, infinitesimal, so that it could be argued that the Patent Office was winning hands-down on volume. Does it make any difference that the highest court would invalidate when it hardly ever sees a patent so long as it cannot get the Patent Office to invalidate at the point where the mass of patent policy decisions are made, the point of application?

LITIGATION STRATEGY

To answer this question we must enter another field entirely. And again this excursion is not peculiar to patent law but common to many areas of agency–court policy making. The preliminary negotiations between potential litigants, and between the lawyers who counsel and represent them, may be the crucial arena for shaping public policy at any given moment in many areas of government regulation and administration. In antitrust, for instance, the conduct of individual corporations is today shaped less by actual court or Federal Trade Commission decisions than by day to day advice from their own counsel as to how they should shape their actions to avoid getting involved in antitrust proceedings.

The crucial question in the patent field may well be how do the doctrines and actions of the Patent Office and the courts affect the relative bargaining positions of firms that find themselves in dispute over a particular device? Let us begin with a patent holder who discovers what he believes to be an infringer. The patent holder will request the infringer to stop. He may threaten suit, but infringement suits are very long-drawn-out and expensive proceedings, and as things stand he knows that while the Patent Office thinks he has a valid patent, odds are the courts do not. Thus the patent holder's bargaining position is relatively weak. The infringer knows this. The result is likely to be that the patent holder will settle for what he can get, licensing at a very low fee— that is, a small payment from the infringer in return for permission to continue to manufacture, use, or sell the patented item. The infringer will typically offer this fee because the cost of defending an infringement suit would also be substantial, and there is always some risk that he would lose. Assuming for the moment equal financial resources, the impact of the Supreme Court's policy is to create something so near to equality between the bargaining positions of the patentee and the infringer that the infringer need offer very little in return for using the patent. Indeed the infringer's position may be the stronger. If the patent holder has already licensed firms X and Y and is collecting royalties, he knows that if he takes firm Z to court, his patent is likely to be invalidated. If it is invalidated he will no longer collect royalties from X and Y. Therefore he may be strongly pressured to ignore Z's infringement in order to avoid risking his existing royalty revenues. Of course the more clearly valid a patent is—the less close it comes to the grey area where the Court's and the Patent Office's judgment on invention fail to match—the stronger the bargaining position of the patent holder because the more credible his threat to bring suit. In this sense although the Patent Office may control the great mass of official patent decisions against the Supreme Court's few, the Court's position may have a fundamental impact on the really crucial decisions that determine whether a patent once issued is really worth anything.

When we add the dimension of appeal this becomes even more clear. The patent holder is faced throughout pre-litigation bargaining, and the bargaining that continues during litigation itself, with the fact that if the infringer loses, he is likely to appeal. Appeal is expensive to both sides, but the higher the appeal goes the more likely the infringer is to win, given the behavior of the highest court. Thus at any stage of the game, even if he wins at the District Court level, the patentee is likely to settle for far less than he could get if the courts were backing the Patent Office. The Patent Office, by maintaining the conflict, is issuing far more patents but each patent is worth far less. As we have already pointed out, however, since actual impact is hard to measure in specific quantitative terms, the Patent Office may be far more concerned with keeping its volume up than with considerations such as these.

So far we have assumed equal financial resources between the two bargainers. But let us suppose that the patent holder is of very limited means and the infringer is a corporation of vast resources. The patentee knows that even if he were to win an initial suit, the corporation would probably appeal. It can afford to. He can't. And its threat to appeal is made more creditable because it is likely to win an appeal. As a result he will typically be forced to accept the corporation's offer to buy or license the patent for a small sum. The value of the patent is thus reduced to the nuisance value of an infringement suit.

Now take the opposite situation. If a large corporation devises something, the Patent Office might deny it a patent, and the Office has the resources to tilt with the corporation on fairly equal terms. If the Patent Office issues the corporation a doubtful patent, however, it gives the corporation a license to sue the poor infringer. If the rich corporation hadn't been issued the patent in the first place, it couldn't sue anyone. Once it is in a position to sue, however, it can show the poor infringer that it can afford the cost of an initial suit and endless appeals and he can't, even though he stands a good chance of winning in the long run. Winning in the long run and going bankrupt on the litigation costs in the meantime is not very attractive. So the infringer is likely to stop or pay license fees even though both sides know the patent would probably not stand up in court in the long run.

The whole mode of enforcement of patents through infringement suits means that patent matters inevitably show a strong strain of blackmail of the poor by the rich because one can always afford to either mount or defend against an infringement suit far better than the other. But the conflict between the Patent Office and the Supreme Court stacks the deck even more heavily against the poor than it otherwise would be. Surely neither contestant intended this result, but it is an inevitable byproduct of their quarrel.

Thus the policy dispute between the Patent Office and the Supreme Court, and more generally the dual decision making present in this area, cannot be fully understood without a proper appreciation of the impact of court–agency relations on the behavior of participants in the unofficial bargaining that precedes and accompanies official administrative and judicial decision making. It cannot be emphasized too strongly that this is true not only in the patent field but for most of the policy problems upon which dual decision occurs.

THE PATENT ACT OF 1952

From an excursion into the world of litigational bargaining we return to our main story, this time at the year 1952. But the story itself now leads us from Supreme Court and administrative agency to pressure groups and Congress. And again this is not an unusual route peculiar to patent law. Since both court and agency function as supplementary lawmakers under the statute maker, it is hardly surprising that the statute maker sporadically intervenes in the relationships between his two subordinates. It is important to note, however, that such intervention may create a major change in policy, a minor change or, in spite of the passage of a whole new statute, no change at all. In other words, it should not be automatically assumed that the statute maker always makes big policy decisions and the courts and agencies little ones. Each is capable of various levels of intervention in the legal process taken as a whole. The Patent Act of 1952 illustrates an intervention by the statute maker that approaches the zero level.

It is always best to begin the examination of a new statute at the beginning, not with its birth but its conception. By the early 1950s there was a widespread feeling among patent lawyers that the Supreme Court had gone astray and that somehow the good old days as symbolized in the pre-1930 cases had been better and should be revisited. The Patent Office was, of course, both a source and supporter of these sentiments. In 1952 one of those legislative accidents occurred that frequently serve as the catalyst that turns widespread sentiment into concrete political action. Congress was in the process of recodifying the laws of the United States. The U.S. Code is an arrangement in logical sequence of all the laws passed by Congress. But as minor amendments and major changes build up, and are tacked on here and there to the old code, things get more and more confused. Eventually the Congress does a periodic general cleaning and straightening up and then re-enacts its newly ordered arrangement of the laws as a new edition of the U.S. Code. It just so happened that in 1952 the subcommittee of the House Judiciary Committee in charge of going through the entire code and preparing a new edition was the subcommittee which in the normal course of its business, when it wasn't redoing codes, was in charge of proposed patent legislation. So long as the subcommittee had to work over the patent sections of the Code anyway for a new edition—and they badly needed straightening—it might as well take the occasion to improve the law, since that was part of its normal responsibilities—two birds with one stone, so to speak.

At least those forces anxious to undercut the Supreme Court pressed this argument on the members of the subcommittee. They responded favorably and set the subcommittee's professional staff to work on drafting new legislation. The reader will recall that the rather cumbersome term "statute maker" rather than Congress was originally adopted to emphasize that legislation was often a joint product of the executive and legislative branches, not of Congress alone. He should not be surprised to find then that Mr. J. P. Frederico, a leading member of the Patent Office bureaucracy, soon appeared as a counsel to the subcommittee—that is, a member of its staff—and was given the central responsibility for drafting the proposed law. There is nothing improper about this. Experts from the agencies are frequently seconded to congressional committees for such work. But in a very real sense the Patent Office wrote the congressional statute of 1952 as part of its continued battle with the Supreme Court.

It had help. The American patent bar is a relatively well-organized group comprehending most of the lawyers who specialize in patent matters, formed into regional associations with a national coordinating hierarchy. As soon as patent law revision was in the wind, this group created a task force of its most prominent leaders to help shape the legislation. This task force became so active in the statute drafting that in the end Mr. Frederico did not so much draft legislation *for* a congressional committee as *with* the patent bar. Not only did he and three lawyers officially representing the organized patent bar do almost all of the drafting, but the drafts were circulated among all the prominent patent lawyers and revised to conform to their desires.

Political scientists have often pointed out that it is incorrect to view congressional lawmaking as necessarily occurring in the context of various pressure groups fighting it out against one another. Very frequently there is only one pressure group in the field at a time, and it fights *for* what it wants but not *against* any particular interest-group opposition. While patent lawyers of course represent infringers as well as patent holders in court, the bulk of their services to clients consists of helping them obtain and defend the validity of patents. Quite naturally then they tend to identify the good with more patents rather than fewer, just as does the Patent Office for a different but parallel set of reasons. Thus the Patent Office and the patent bar comprise a powerful, "propatent" pressure group.

Because no group of lawyers and no government agency specializes in fighting against patents, and no particular segment of the business community is uniformly harmed by patents, there is no "antipatent" pressure group. The "antipatent" interest in this country is not specialized or concentrated, but consists only of the general interest shared by all citizens that their government not make a bad bargain for them when selling its stock of limited monopolies. Such amorphous interests are notoriously underrepresented in American politics precisely because no organized group and no specialized government agency speaks for them.[31] Indeed, it makes considerable sense to view the Supreme Court's role in this area, as in some others,[32] as the representation of widespread but unorganized public interests that are not ade-

---

31. The nearest approach in the patent field is the Antitrust Division of the Justice Department which is concerned with patents insofar as their manipulation contributes to violation of the antitrust laws, and quite significantly this agency is the only "antipatent" voice in Washington, besides the Supreme Court itself.

32. See Shapiro, *Freedom of Speech, the Supreme Court and Judicial Review* (1965)

quately represented in the executive or legislative branches. This may be the major special reason justifying court intervention in this area of policy making.

In any event the propatent forces had a free hand in writing the legislation unopposed by any countervailing group. Of course the congressman on the subcommittee, and then those on the full Judiciary Committee, all of them lawyers, but none particularly expert on patent matters, did review the draft. But they made few changes, and the Committee's report and "Revisor's Notes," which accompanied and explained the bill, were written by Frederico, either independently or in cooperation with the representatives of the patent bar. One of those representatives has proudly answered the question: "Who wrote the patent laws of 1952? We did."

The bill then had to proceed to the floor of the House where theoretically the whole membership considers it before exercising their legislative will. It was brought up on the unanimous-consent calendar, no one objected, and it was passed without debate; the whole proceedings taking perhaps thirty seconds. It then went to the Senate, where the Senate Judiciary Committee made only a few minor changes. The bill failed of unanimous consent on the floor of the Senate, one senator asking the chairman of the Judiciary Committee whether the bill was simply a new codification or made changes in the law, the chairman replying that it was simply a codification. The bill subsequently passed with no further debate.

There is little question that the general membership of Congress had no idea what it had enacted and was left with the impression that it didn't matter anyway, since the bill was simply a recodification of the previously existing law. The peculiar coincidence which started the whole process off had much to do with this. In a normal year, if a patent bill had been brought to the floor everyone would have assumed it meant some change in the existing law. Committees don't devote energy to bringing in new bills that do nothing. But in the year that Congress was re-enacting the whole U.S. Code, and from the subcommittee that was doing all the re-enactment, this bill must have appeared to most congressmen to be simply another in the stream of re-enactments. It would have taken an alert congressman indeed to remember, if he had even known such a minor thing in the first place, that the subcommittee handling recodification of the whole body of law just happened to also be the subcommittee which had special jurisdiction over patents, and then put two and two together to conclude that this particular recodification might not therefore simply be a recodification but a new law. And even if such a congressman had existed, and he had then bothered to get a copy of the bill and read it carefully line by line, another minor miracle in and of itself since few congressmen have time to do this sort of thing, there are so few hints in the language of the statute that it is anything but a recodification. So much of it is precisely that, that only a superalert congressman, fully briefed by someone on what to look for, would have spotted any changes. There was no someone, because there was no antipatent interest group fighting the bill, and there was no superalert congressman.

LEGISLATIVE INTENT

I have not gone into all this just to illustrate the vagaries of Congress but rather to provide some concrete data on which to base a discussion of "legislative intent" which is frequently a key problem in administrative–judicial conflicts, and also because the specific question of whether Congress intended simply to codify previous law or pass new law becomes the principal vehicle for policy debate in the post 1952 period.

It is one of the small ironies of political studies that the principal source of information for our story of the writing of the patent law by an interest group composed of propatent lawyers and bureaucrats, and its consequent passage by a Congress totally unaware of what it was doing, is the reports of one of the drafters, a noted patent lawyer and leader of the propatent forces.[33] And he makes his revelations in order to prove that the legislative intent of the 1952 laws is to liberalize the standard of invention not codify the old law. What he actually proves is that Congress in passing the legislation thought it was passing a simple codification.

Why then does this distinguished lawyer and judge think he is proving the opposite? The answer lies in the several different approaches to legislative intent that typically lead to conflict in the administrative–judicial sphere.

The lawyer almost instinctively treats a statute as a legal document like a contract. Its meaning is to be derived from its plain words, no matter what those who signed it actually intended. When its words are not entirely clear, one looks to the meaning that those who wrote the words intended them to have. The argument in the patent area then becomes clear. *Precisely because* Congress did not know what it was doing when it passed the statute, and *precisely because* the words of the statute are not themselves absolutely clear, the statute means whatever those who drafted it wanted it to mean. Since those who drafted it meant its words to reduce the standard of invention below that used by the Supreme Court, that is the meaning, i.e., the legislative intent, of the statute.

The legal conventions that grew up around the interpretation of contracts are based on a set of circumstances and considerations that are not necessarily applicable to the reading of statutes. Many administrators and judges today prefer not to pretend that a statute is like a contract, but, shifting to direct and realistic political analysis, to ask what did the Congress really want? This question leads to its own difficulties.

Frequently a statute consists of a set of verbal devices used to compromise between various conflicting interests and purposes rather than specifically furthering one interest. Congress in effect avoids choosing between the interests by using

33. See Rich, "Congressional Intent—Or, Who Wrote the Patent Act of 1952?" in *Patent Procurement and Exploitation* 61-78 (1963)

words that each can interpret as favorable to it. Indeed different congressmen may have voted for the bill for entirely different reasons, some taking the words one way and some another. Realistic political analysis lies not in trying to discover the "true" meaning of such a law, but in taking it as a command by the statute maker to its administrative and judicial subordinates to work out on their own initiative a compromise satisfactory to the interests at play.

Alternatively it may be discovered that Congress as a whole had no intention, in the sense that it was simply approving what one of its committees had done, trusting its committee to have done the right thing. Most congressmen rely heavily on the judgment of the committees and their votes on a bill frequently mean: whatever the committee wanted, it should get. Where this is true judges and administrators will turn heavily to committee reports and statements of committee members as evidence of what the statute meant.

Even when congressmen wish to exercise an independent judgment, they will often make committee reports and committee members' statements the principal basis for those judgments. So here again realistic analysis will rely heavily on such materials to determine what the congressmen thought they were doing when they voted yes. For example when a committee report explains that a bill will do X, there is strong reason to believe that most of the congressmen voting for it wanted X done. The more technical and remote from their major concerns a given bill is, of course, the more reliance congressmen will place on committee information and consequently the more that information reveals what they thought they were getting when they voted aye.

Thus administrators and judges in determining legislative intent are likely to attempt to trace the actual process of decision making in Congress, giving great weight to those materials which give evidence of what the congressmen actually thought they were doing. Frequently such analysis will lead to the conclusion that Congress collectively had no single purpose and that a law was passed by a coalition of congressmen each wanting different things. Since there is no unified

legislative intent in such instances, the administrator or
judge is free to do—indeed has to do—what he pleases within
the broad limits set by the coalition. He will, of course, then
pick and choose among the materials of the legislative history to support his own decision. Such picking and choosing,
emphasizing one senator's statement, ignoring another's, etc.,
will often appear to be an artificial and hypocritical game,
but the game does not alter the fact that where different elements of a winning congressional coalition wanted different
things out of a bill, or did not know what they wanted,
judges and administrators are not only entitled but forced
to choose one thing or another when it comes to specific
enforcement.

The patent laws of 1952, however, offer a relatively rare,
clear situation that neatly dramatizes many of these problems.
We know what the drafters wanted—to undercut the Supreme
Court. Here and there in the committee reports and other
committee publications there are hints, quite obviously put
there precisely so that they could later be used as "legislative
history," that the bill did more than codify existing law. But
it is absolutely clear, and indeed no one has questioned the
fact, that, when the Congress voted, what it thought it was
voting on and, therefore, what it said it wanted, was a simple
codification. Only the most fantastically legalistic and artificial analysis, devoid of all commitment to political reality,
could conclude that the legislative intent was what the
drafters secretly wanted and, as we shall see shortly, expressed
in deliberately ambiguous language, rather than what the
Congress clearly thought it was doing.

What then did the new statute accomplish? The propatent forces had done what many interest groups do when
they lose with one set of politicians; they tried another, Congress. But the propatent forces anticipated that if they tried
to get Congress to explicitly reverse the Supreme Court's
opinions of the late 1930s and 1940s, they might run into
substantial opposition. Posing the real issue openly might
have provided the stimulus, time and opportunity for antipatent forces to rally and counterpressure Congress. Instead

the propatent forces exploited a tactical advantage to slip by an unaware Congress a statute too ambiguous to inspire opposition but one that might subsequently be used to help lever the Supreme Court out of its position. In adopting this tactic, however, the propatent forces paid a very high price to avoid opposition in Congress. They ended up with a statute that did not clearly show a congressional intent to reverse the Supreme Court and thus one that could not be a very effective instrument in forcing the Court out of its position.

For not only did the actual circumstances of the act's passage make it clear that Congress as a whole had simply intended to codify in 1952 whatever the law had been in 1951, without even being aware of a difference between the Patent Office and the Supreme Court, let alone settling it on the side of the Office, but the wording of the statute itself was meaningless as far as the court–agency dispute was concerned. The key passage reads:

> A patent may not be obtained though the invention is not identically disclosed or described . . . if the differences between the subject matter sought to be patented and the prior art are such that the subject matter as a whole would have been obvious at the time the invention was made to a person having ordinary skill in the art to which said subject matter pertains.[34]

This is simply a legislative restatement of the *Hotchkiss* test. The Supreme Court had consistently said that it was following the *Hotchkiss* test in reaching the results it did. The statute does not say that *Cuno* and *A & P* were misapplications of the test. If a statute repeats a judicially created test that has been used continuously, it is normally taken to incorporate into the statutory law the case law that has grown up under the test. Thus the statute of 1952 in this sense actually approves and confirms the Supreme Court opinions in *Cuno* and *A & P*. In short if a statute says we affirm the test that the Supreme Court says it has been using, without specifically condemning the Supreme Court's results in apply-

---

34. 35 U.S.C. Sec. 103 (1964)

ing the test, Congress is declaring its approval of whatever the Supreme Court has been doing.

On the other hand, it can be argued that the Supreme Court had really abandoned the good old test of *Hotchkiss* for a strongly antipatent position, so that when Congress writes the *Hotchkiss* test into the statute, it is really telling the Court to go back to the old propatent position. Aside from the fact that Congress wasn't telling the Court anything because it didn't even know what was going on, the difficulty with this argument is that it simply assumes what is to be proven, that the Court has really abandoned an old pro-patent policy embodied in *Hotchkiss* and that when anyone says the *Hotchkiss* words they really mean a low standard of invention.

AFTER THE STATUTE WAS PASSED

Thus after the statute was over, everyone was back precisely where he started from. The Supreme Court was insisting that it had never deviated from *Hotchkiss* and that *Cuno* and *A & P* are simply applications of *Hotchkiss*. If you begin from this premise then the statute of 1952 is simply a writing into law, confirmation and codification of what the Supreme Court had been doing in the years immediately preceding the statute. The anti-Supreme Court forces were insisting that the Court, while paying lip service to the *Hotchkiss* standard, had really abandoned it in the 1930s and 1940s for a stricter standard. If you begin with this premise, then the statute of 1952 reverses the Supreme Court cases of the 1930s and 1940s and tells it to go back to the *Hotchkiss* standard. Others yet argued that the standard had remained the same but the application had gotten stricter in the 1930s and 1940s. If you begin from this premise the Act of 1952 says nothing, for it simply repeats the standard without saying anything about whether its application should be strict or loose. Thus the statute leaves everyone precisely where he started. Although the statute of 1952 may provide an ex-

treme example, it does illustrate the fact that action by the
statute maker may be of lesser dimensions than those of its
administrative and judicial subordinates and indeed may
have zero impact. It also illustrates that politics is a long and
difficult game and that a pressure group in fighting one government agency with another—in this instance Court with
Congress—may fail by being too cleverly successful.

The propatent forces made a great deal of a line in the
House Committee report on the bill indicating that the new
statutory provision on invention "should have a stabilizing
effect and minimize great departures which have appeared
in some cases." The report, however, was written by an official of the Patent Office, and the line was obviously a ploy
deliberately inserted in the report in language that would
lull the Congress into believing that it was making no changes
but could later be used in litigation as "legislative history"
proving that Congress had intended to reverse the Supreme
Court. Such ploys make good argumentative hooks for those
judges who want to use them, but they are quite rightly
ignored by those who do not, and since those who do not
are precisely those the ploy makers want to put pressure on,
they are largely useless.

Reviewing the political episode as a whole, a fairly clear
picture emerges. The propatent forces wanted to force the
Supreme Court into abandoning its antipatent policy. They
sought to use Congress for this purpose. The Supreme Court's
doctrinal position, and everyone else's for that matter, was
so vague and slippery that only the clearest and most specific
announcement by Congress of a propatent and anti-Supreme
Court stand could prove effective in moving the justices. For
the Supreme Court could interpret any less clear statement
by Congress as approving its position. Two vagues make anything you like. The propatent forces did not feel strong
enough to get a clear statement from Congress and instead
got a very unclear one both in the sense that the Congress
obviously had no clear intention at all and that the statutory
language could be read for or against either side. Thus the
propatent forces did not succeed in their resort to Congress

against the Court. One point to be especially emphasized as of general application to the realm of court–agency–pressure-group–Congress politics is that the state of the technical legal doctrine is not simply an artificial or rhetorical lawyer's concern, but may itself be an important tactical factor in the political campaign. Here the vagueness of the legal standard of invention, whatever its causes, had a direct and major impact on the relative political power of the various political participants, forcing on a pressure group the need for a kind of congressional action it was not strong enough to get.

Because the Supreme Court had been insisting that its most recent cases followed standard X, and because its opposition insisted that they should have but didn't, the congressional statute meant all things to all men. The Patent Office had been insisting that it was following standard X and Congress now affirmed that standard, so it continued to do what it had been doing. The Court of Customs and Patent Appeal had covered its rebellion against the Supreme Court by insisting that the Court could not and had not changed the old standard, so it continued what it had been doing. The circuits which had followed the Court's antipatent tone and actions now read the new congressional statute as confirming their actions by confirming the standard under the banner of which the Supreme Court's tone and action marched. The circuits that had been more obtuse toward the Supreme Court's communications could continue to be so because the statutory message did nothing one way or the other to clarify communication.

The only noticeable and lasting effect of the statute was to change the terminology of political discourse. The argument was now phrased in terms of whether Congress had codified existing law, which would have meant that they had affirmed *Cuno* and *A & P* or alternatively whether the statute had been not a codification but a change in the law, rejecting the case law of *Cuno* and *A & P*, and returning to an older standard of invention. Quite obviously, although the slogans now were transmuted to codification versus change, the issues continued to be exactly the same, and the positions of the various participants, ranging from absolutely ambiguous (Congress) to bureaucratically committed (the Patent Office), also remained exactly the same.

LEARNED HAND AND PATENT LAW

In the years immediately following the statute of 1952, one determined attempt was made to resolve the quarrel between the courts and the Patent Office. It was made by Learned Hand and, for a number of reasons, is worth another of our frequent digressions from the main story. First of all, it illustrates again that the circuit courts play an important role in the relations between the Supreme Court and the federal administrative agencies, and that some circuits may, at any given time, be far more important than others. Secondly, Judge Hand's activities in the patent field reflect his far-ranging and catalytic role throughout the entire realm of federal statutory interpretation. Any student of administrative law or of judicial–administrative relations more generally will constantly run across Hand's influence so that it is important to understand his judicial philosophy and style. Finally, Hand's intervention in the patent field is motivated by a concept of judicial modesty or self-restraint which has historically been a key factor in court–agency relations.

In field after field of federal law as one pushes back from the current cases to discover the origins of recent doctrinal trends, Learned Hand is to be found hard at work first as a judge on the U.S. District Court for the Southern District of New York and then on the Second Circuit. In such diverse fields as obscenity law, immigration, and antitrust Hand was a sensitive and creative sociological jurist who sought to imbue excessively abstract and rigid verbal formulas of law, and age-encrusted doctrinal habits, with a sense of and response to social needs and changing mores. What makes Hand the most challenging and fascinating judicial mind of the twentieth century, however,[35] is not simply his vast store

---

35. Holmes, it seems to me, belongs to the nineteenth.

of reforming energies and highly developed moral sensitivity but the combination of these qualities with a fundamental repugnance for the act of judging. Hand generally knew what he wanted the law to be, his whole life revolved around a concern for public policy, but he did not think that judges should make the policy or even make those of the implementing decisions under that policy for which the tools of the litigational process were not especially suited.

This general reluctance, which at times could reach the stage of total inertia, may be traced to Hand's democratic political philosophy which saw nonelected judges as fundamentally antidemocratic figures. More fundamentally I think it can be attributed to precisely that concern for public policy and moral sensitivity which made Hand an activist. Acutely aware that policy decisions are predictions made on the basis of incomplete data and incomplete understanding of the complexities of the social process, passionately devoted to improving the world, acutely sensitive to the moral responsibility of the decision maker to make the right decision, Hand presented the spectacle of a man too wise and too morally committed to choose. In the face of all the uncertainties of the modern world, it is surely the most stupid and insensitive who are most anxious to make policies and shove them down someone else's throat. Hand represented the other extreme.

This almost pathological condition can be seen clearly in Hand's contribution to patent law. In the 1920s, before many others had become aware of the problem, Hand saw, with his typical foresight, that the traditional formulas of patent law had become excessively rigid, and that through the application of the traditional subtests, particularly the rule against aggregations, the Patent Office was mechanically grinding out decisions that were entirely verbal and artificial without touching base in the social reality of technological and economic practice. Hand's observation of the fundamental transformations of twentieth-century industrial and commercial practice and the startling advances in technology led him to believe that the subtests invented for the nineteenth century would not work in the twentieth. And his observations of the Patent Office led him to believe that the Patent Office had frozen these themes or rules of thumb into its practice. As a result he began writing opinions that tended to ignore the subtests in favor of looking at what the device in question had actually accomplished in the real world. In other words, he began to substitute a general test of social utility for the traditional, detailed subtests.

It is at this point that we can see Hand's fear of judging entering to reinforce his desire to keep patent policy in tune with social reality. Under the old subtests the judge had finally to make the decision based on his own evaluation of the device as described in the claims and the prior art. If, however, the judge would hold patentable any item that had enjoyed wide commercial success and acceptance, he, in a sense, would not make the decision on patentability but would allow the market to make it for him. Whether a device was new and useful and nonobvious enough to warrant a patent need not be decided by a judge relying on his own judgment, but would be decided by the public through its broad acceptance or neglect of the device. And at the same time that the judge avoided the responsibility for judgment, the law would shift from the mechanical application of old verbal formulas to the reflection of real-world practices.

This approach paralleled innovations by Hand in several other areas of law where he had urged, for instance, that a judge decide whether a book was obscene or a man was of good moral character not on the basis of his own judgment but by applying "contemporary community standards." Thus the judge avoided personal moral responsibility for his decision and the law was kept attuned with social reality. Commercial success is the patent-law variation of the community-standards doctrine, with the added improvement of a dollar-and-cents measure of the community standards of technological innovation far more exact and easily discoverable than any available measure of the community's literary or moral standards.

In general, then, Hand attempted to move away from

the stereotyped subtests employed by the Patent Office toward a general standard of invention which looked to the quality of the device as proven by its acceptance in the real world. In the *Cuno* and *A & P* cases the Court accepted with a vengeance the movement to a general standard of invention, but unlike Hand, the justices were more than willing to make their own judgment as to what was worthy of a patent. Indeed in the *A & P* case they invalidated a patent on an item that had enjoyed wide commercial success but which they thought was a trivial contribution to technology. The propatent forces got the worst of both worlds. They lost the old tried and true subtests, and the general standard they got was not Hand's, which was sympathetic to devices of social utility but no great originality, but rather one that placed what was to them an unreasonable emphasis on "genius." Hand had focused on what happened to the device after it was invented, an approach which would save many a mundanity. The Supreme Court emphasized the originality of the invention itself which would lose the patent of many a commercial success.

After the statute of 1952 Hand returned to the fray. For the judicially modest, and particularly for Hand, Congress is even a better entity to which the responsibility for decision can be shifted than is the community at large, for it democratically represents the community and speaks with a somewhat higher level of specificity. Hand, like all the other circuit judges, had been caught in the conflict between the Patent Office and the Court, and, being more sensitive to the obligations of judicial candor and obedience than most, had openly acknowledged the feud and followed the Court. But after 1952 he could say that Congress had made a decision resolving the painful conflict and thus absolving him of the painful task of judging the real originality of patents imposed upon him by the Supreme Court. Congress, he claimed, had decided in the statute of 1952 to repudiate the Court's doctrinal shift and lower the standard of patentability. So, Hand insisted, he was now free to go back to a general standard based on commercial success. Notice the multiple attractions of this position for Hand. First, it placed the responsibility for policy making on the elected Congress rather than the appointed Supreme Court. Second, it removed him from the political conflict between the Court and the agency. Third, it relieved him of the responsibility for enforcing a Supreme Court doctrine that required him to make hard decisions on technological originality. Finally, it allowed him to shift this responsibility for decision to the community.

Hand, then, led the forces that insisted that the statute of 1952 was change not codification, and it looked for a time as if he would be able to swing the 2nd Circuit over to the propatent side. Such a swing would have had a major impact because of the heavy patent case load of that circuit, its high relative prestige among the circuits and Hand's own enormous prestige as one of the most distinguished judges and acute legal minds in America. After some sporadic fighting, however, the 2nd Circuit returned to general obedience to *Cuno* and *A & P* and made no further claims that the statute of 1952 was more than a codification.

I spend the time on this episode partly because it helps to carry our story up to the Supreme Court decisions of the 1965 term, but also so that I may emphasize and illustrate the point that in the sequence of conflict and coalition that marks the process of grinding out legal policy, a circuit court or circuit-court judge may be an important actor to be considered along with the pressure groups, Congressional committees, and administrative agencies we have been adding to the Supreme Court. Such courts and judges do not necessarily act in stereotyped ways or fixed alliances but instead are, like other political actors, partially free to choose sides, allies and policy goals in the light of their institutional interests and social values.

THE SUPREME COURT SPEAKS AGAIN

Fifteen years after *A & P* and fourteen after the statute of 1952, the Supreme Court spoke again on the standard of invention in the cases of *Graham v. John Deere Co.,*[36] *Colmar Inc. v. Cook Chemical Co.*[37] and *United States v. Adams.*[38] The doctrinal content of these opinions is quickly stated. The Court held that the statute of 1952 was simply a codification of the earlier law, including its holding in *Cuno* and *A & P,* and that the standard of invention had never changed; that it had not been raised by the Supreme Court nor lowered by Congress. In short, it stuck absolutely to the doctrinal and thus to the tactical status quo in its conflict with the Patent Office. It is not necessary to repeat here what has been detailed at length previously, that the message "the standard has never changed" means quite different things to different recipients each of whom will presumably interpret it as he has in the past—to support his own position.

The Court did use the language of the opinions to strengthen its stand in some ways, however. It mentions the subtests, with a bow to Hand's attempts at injecting commercial success, but very firmly indicates that they are to be employed as themes under the general standard of invention —in other words, that they may be invoked or rejected as a court finds convenient in supporting its decision. It also seeks to explain away the discrepancy between its insistence that the standard has stayed the same and the general feeling that patents are harder and harder to get through the Supreme Court by saying that the standard has remained the same but technology has advanced so fast recently that it is harder to think of something original.

The Court also read a direct little lesson to the patent lawyers about bargaining with the government. It finally said explicitly what we have earlier seen it saying by its actions. Applicants are now specifically told that they may not narrow their claims to get a patent out of the Patent Office and then broaden them to win infringement suits. The Court thus emphasizes its role in maintaining the fairness of the bargain to the government.

The Court did not neglect a direct lesson to the Patent

36. 383 U.S. 1 (1966)
37. 383 U.S. 1 (1966)
38. 383 U.S. 39 (1966)

Office as well. In a neat bit of rhetoric, although it is nothing more, the Court notes the "notorious difference between the standards applied by the Patent Office and by the Court,"[39] and says that the difference would cease if the Patent Office would strictly adhere to the statute of 1952, which of course the justices have just claimed incorporated the Court's standard. Thus the statute of 1952, which the Patent Office invented to help it against the Court, is neatly turned against it. Similarly the introduction in the statute of a standard of "nonobviousness," rather than invention or genius, which might have been taken as indicating the need of only a modest amount of originality, is treated by the Court as a special Congressional injunction to particularly emphasize the need for a high level of originality in comparison with the previous state of the art.

Perhaps the most interesting aspect of the purely doctrinal layer of the Court's opinions is its insistence that the standards of patentability are constitutional, not statutory. This question had previously been undecided, and Justice Douglas had for years been campaigning to get the Court to declare its functions in this field constitutional. In effect the Court is staking out a position of political strength from which to negotiate in future conflicts with the Patent Office. If patent standards were strictly statutory Congress could do with them what it willed, and thus the propatent forces working through Congress might at some future date undercut the Supreme Court's policy. By stating that patent standards are imbedded in the Constitution, which in effect means they are imbedded in the past and future decisions of the Supreme Court, and that Congress may only legislate standards that are in accord with the constitutional standards, the Court declares that it can and will use its most awesome power—the power to declare statutes unconstitutional—in support of its policies, and that agencies and groups opposed to those policies cannot expect a total victory from Congress even if they were to gain a total victory in Congress.

Incidentally, in terms of some of the things stressed in

---

39. 383 U.S. 1, 18 (1966)

the Introduction, this episode neatly illustrates the artificiality of dividing the constitutional from the nonconstitutional aspects of the Supreme Court's work. For under such a division the Court's patent law jurisdiction, after over 150 years in limbo, would suddenly spring full-blown into the hearts of Supreme Court scholars. Any aspect of the Supreme Court's work is worthy or unworthy of special attention not because it is constitutional or nonconstitutional but because it has an important impact on public policy or does not.

In addition to the doctrinal messages delivered in the 1966 cases, there is another, probably more important set of messages resting essentially on the Court's deliberate choice of these particular cases as its first announcement in fifteen years on the standard of invention. For the Court might have chosen many others from the hundreds that have come to it over the years. It must be stressed again, however, that judicial communications styles are just as complex and subtle as those found in other spheres of organizational life. What follows are the messages that I clearly discern and will clearly be discerned by those who wish to follow and reinforce the Supreme Court's policies or predict its future decisions. On the other hand, given their subdoctrinal status, message recipients who wish to may ignore or distort them to an even greater extent than they do the Court's explicit commands.

For instance it can be argued that the *John Deere* and *Colmar* decisions both involve combination patents on admittedly old elements, that in both, the courts received prior art evidence unavailable to the Patent Office and, therefore, that both are simply instances in which the courts added their institutional strengths to the efforts of the Patent Office in order to achieve a better overall decisional product. Viewed in this light, they deliver no messages about Court–agency conflict.

It is certainly true that the patent involved in *John Deere* possesses so little originality that it would be invalidated under any standard other than absolutely minimal ones and might even have failed the Patent Office's test of mere aggregation if the Patent Office had been fully informed of the prior art. *Colmar*, however, is far more informative. For there the patent holder could persuasively demonstrate a long felt need, repeated failure by others to satisfy that need, and instant and widespread commercial success for his solution, even though the device itself, when viewed outside of the context of its actual history, would strike anyone as a rather crude and simple combination of the most common sorts of previously well-known elements. The Court, even while repeatedly granting the subtests a thematic status as things to be considered in judging invention, seems to have deliberately picked a case in which the patent would clearly meet the subtests relating to need and success and still be invalidated for lack of intrinsic merit. This deliberate emphasis on the Court's very high demands for intrinsic merit is reinforced by the fact that the Court here reverses a finding of validity by the 8th Circuit which has a firm antipatent record. If even those patents that live through the 8th cannot survive the Supreme Court, then things are really tough.

This toughness is, I think, clearly and finally communicated by the interplay between *Colmar* and *Adams*, an interplay that is surely intended by the Court which chose to take two such dissimilar cases and decide them on the same day. For the *Adams* case too involves a combination of old elements, but a combination that functions in such a wonderful and mysterious way that experts in the field at first denied that it could possibly work at all because it violated well-established scientific principles. Indeed it is still not clear why it does work. It is surely no accident that the Court chose a patent showing such a rare level of originality as the first in years that it was willing to say was valid and infringed, nor that it did so at the same time as it found invalid a patent for something that had been long needed, long searched for, and once found was very successful, but was in and of itself quite mundane.

While the Court admits that wording in the 1952 statute was designed to eliminate the "flash of genius" test in its extreme form, and argues that the phrase in reality had never been more than a rhetorical way of summing up accepted case law, *Colmar* and *Adams,* taken together, show that while the Court may have given up "flash," it has gone farther along the "genius" route than ever before. For any of its subordinates who are willing to listen faithfully, the Court is now saying the following: Examine the actual device or process for yourselves, not in the general context of the commercial world nor even in the context of the machine or arrangement as a whole in which it functions, but at the very point that is claimed to be new and different. Viewing that particular point against the whole general background of science and technology, does the thing give you that certain special kick and awe, or does it appear to you to be mundane and pedestrian even if new and useful?

This is not a very exact message, but it is the message that emerges from the cases, and "genius" is about as good a tag as any for it, although the courts will undoubtedly invent a new slogan now that the old one has run into trouble. The 1966 cases represent the Court's continued commitment to a standard of invention far higher than the Patent Office's and a view of the public interest that requires the applicant to give something really special in return for the government granted monopoly he desires.

CONCLUSION

The great Patent Office–Supreme Court war is not over then. But here again what is true of patent law is true of most fields of agency–court relations, and of politics more generally; conflicts and bargaining do not end, they continue indefinitely with each episode marked by some shift in the balance of forces and interests. What is atypical about patent law is that the conflict verges on all-out war on the most central issue of policy. Most court–agency relations more evenly mix conflict and cooperation, involve more frequent, if only partial resolution of conflicts and focus on more marginal and fewer central issues. Patent law illustrates dramatically at the cost of exaggerating. Aside from this repeated caution, I hope it is unnecessary to repeat at length the points that I fear have been repeated too frequently in this chapter. The patent struggle shows the importance of the following:

1. the blurring of court–agency conflict and the frequent tactical advantage to various participants of denying that conflict exists
2. the role of circuit and other inferior courts and of conflicts among the circuits in Supreme Court–agency relations
3. the necessity of focusing on prelitigational bargaining and litigational strategy in order to understand how the law really works
4. the part played by certain key individual judges willing to persistently push doctrinal stances over extended periods of time
5. the complexity of judicial communications networks
6. differing perceptions of the public interest in different political structures, and the institutional conflicts that result
7. the varying institutional contributions of various political actors to the collective product of government decision making
8. the sources of political conflict in genuine policy problems—that is, problems where there is insufficient data and insufficient consensus on intermediate goals to allow easy agreement

If nothing else, the patent story must surely show that judicial review of administrative decision making involves a political setting far broader and deeper than can be encompassed within the traditional modes and categories of "administrative law." The student of judicial review must be prepared for a Supreme Court working within a highly complex decisional process in which its actions are less important as discrete pronouncements on legal–doctrinal questions than as episodes in the evolution of public policy.

The Supreme Court and the F.P.C.

While the Supreme Court–Patent Office relationship illustrates many of the facets of judicial review of administrative decision making, it hardly offers a complete picture. For one thing, the Patent Office is unquestionably empowered to make patent decisions, and the grounds on which it must rest such decisions are clear. A frequent problem of judicial review, however, is whether the agency was empowered to make a certain kind of decision, and even if it were, whether it was free to consider the factors it did. For another, the Patent Office is more or less a "line" agency, while much of the business of judicial review concerns the independent regulatory commissions which have certain peculiar problems of their own. Third, in reviewing Patent Office decisions, courts typically make a final decision on the issues themselves. In other areas of review, judges frequently have the option of remanding the matter to the agency for a new decision guided by the court's pronouncements. Remand raised many interesting tactical questions.

For these reasons, and others that should become clear as the chapter unfolds, I have chosen to supplement the Patent Office materials with an examination of a single Supreme Court case reviewing a decision of the Federal Power Commission.

The case is *F.P.C. v. Transcontinental Gas Pipe Line Corp.*[1] Consolidated Edison, a New York public utility, supplying much of the electric power to the state, had arranged to purchase natural gas from a Texas producer. Such transactions are called "direct" sales, as opposed to indirect sales in which the gas producer sells to a pipeline, and the pipeline then transports the gas and sells it to a local user. As we shall see shortly, the F.P.C. does not have jurisdiction over the buyer or seller in direct sales, but it does have jurisdiction over pipeline transmission in interstate commerce no matter what the nature of the sale. In this instance, because the gas was to be produced in Texas and used in New York, transmission had to be by pipeline in interstate commerce. The F.P.C. refused to issue the certificate necessary for such transportation, not because it objected to the transportation, but because it objected to the sale itself—a direct sale over which it had no jurisdiction—and to the effect the sale would have on other production and sales. The issue then was whether a government agency can use its power over one phase of a transaction to in effect regulate other phases over which the statute maker has not assigned it jurisdiction.

REGULATION AND REGULATORY COMMISSIONS

Before squarely facing the specific issue, however, some general things must be said about regulation and regulatory commissions. Government regulation of private business represents the intersection between American ideology and

---

1. 365 U.S. 1 (1961)

real world economic interests, practices, and demands. At the level of ideology we believe in the free market, the laws of supply and demand, freedom of choice for seller and buyer and the whole intellectual baggage of laissez faire. In practice, however, various interest groups have always sought and received various governmental protections from the vicissitudes of the free market on the grounds that no matter what the general virtues of the laissez-faire model, it yielded bad results or could not be made to work at all in certain instances. Government regulation typically seeks to preserve as much as possible of the free market while seeking to "correct" its particular faults in a given area. The free-market model, however, presupposes an almost infinite number and complex pattern of interdependent feedback loops in which every market transaction affects every other. Indeed the collective effect of all is supposed to insure that each will harmonize with and benefit the system as a whole. To cut into any one of these loops is, therefore, to court unanticipated and disharmonious results elsewhere in the system, which will then have to be corrected by further regulation, which will cause further unanticipated results, etc., etc.

Government regulation is, as a result, always uncertain, frequently sloppy and irrational from a "pure economics" point of view, and always in incipient collision with the prevailing ideology. Moreover, as a necessary sop to the ideology, government regulation almost invariably leaves business initiative and most of both the major and minor decisions in private hands while seeking to influence private business interests through occasional negative interventions. Instead of telling businesses what to do, the regulatory agencies only tell them what not to do, so that regulation often gives the appearance of a harassed mother yelling "No, no," a tactic that only frustrates the child without inducing him to really be good. Regulation constantly tries to plug up holes, undo damage or make last-minute saves *in response to* rather than in direction of, the private decision maker's initiatives. All of this is not to condemn regulation but to warn the reader that regulatory action necessarily has about it a kind

of fragmentary and sporadic quality that is far less estheti-
cally pleasing than the neat models of either laissez faire or
socialism.

PUBLIC CONVENIENCE AND NECESSITY

The phrases with which the statute maker has typically
chosen to symbolize his cross-grained acceptance of the ideology, *and* the necessity of tinkering with the system, are
"public convenience and necessity" or "public interest."
Statutes typically authorize an agency to grant a license, for
instance, if the service to be provided would serve the public convenience and necessity, or to consider the public interest in approving rate proposals. These phrases obviously
allow the agencies a thematic approach in which they may
weigh nearly any and all factors, allowing none to be independently decisive. The agency is thus free to make nearly
any decision it wishes. For if it merely says in each of its
decisions that it has considered factors *A, B, C, D, E*, and *F*
(all possible factors), and that in this particular instance
they add up to deciding in favor of *X*, it would be difficult
to say that the agency had violated a statute that invokes so
vague an expression as public convenience and necessity.

Of course a reviewing court might go through the whole
weighing process again and reach a different decision, but
usually there is no particular reason to engage in this double
decision making because there is no reason to believe that
the court will make a better decision than the agency. Indeed, when a court so markedly disagrees with an agency's
judgment on a convenience and necessity question that the
judges are willing to overthrow it, they are typically quite
embarrassed by the obviousness of the substitution of their
judgment for that of the agency. Unwilling to acknowledge
that dual decision is justified, they are likely to hide their
policy disagreement with the agency behind a smoke screen
of technical findings and analytical distinctions without differences. Very frequently the judges will compromise by

remanding the case to an agency with the suggestion, properly couched in legal jargon, that they wish the agency would weigh things a little differently. In such instances the agency simply can (and very often does) go through the motions and reach the same decisions all over again.

This thematic approach, while authorized by the statute maker, and increasing the scope of their supplementary lawmaking powers, nevertheless entails great costs to the agencies. Agency hearings are already extremely long and their records voluminous. An agency using a purely thematic approach invites endless and shapeless testimony, for petitioners will seek to cover every point that the agency might plausibly consider. If the agency simply says that it weighs all factors, or in one case emphasizes one and in another a second, it gives no direction to private parties or its own staff and hearing officers as to how to ration their time and attention.

Thus in order to economize the scarce resource of decisional time, agencies are tempted to develop rules of thumb within this basic thematic approach. At one extreme they may adopt certain absolute subrules. We shall shortly examine one: that burning natural gas under boilers is always against public convenience and necessity. Note that such a subrule still leaves the agency free to use themes on all uses of natural gas except the one covered by the rule. Alternatively, an agency may openly declare or communicate by its pattern of past decisions that it gives far more weight to some factors than to others or that when factor X and factor Y are equally present X will always win over Y.

When an agency invokes such rules, in order to give better shape and guidance to decisional participants, it pays a price in reduced freedom. For now reviewing courts may insist that the agency itself abide by its own past rules of thumb. Courts make this insistence partly because it provides them a hook on which to hang their dual decisions when they do wish to intervene: the agency's past practice becomes "a question of law" open to courts. There is another reason, however, based on considerations of equity. If an

individual has relied upon an established agency rule of
thumb in shaping his conduct, it is difficult to subsequently
condemn that conduct because the rule no longer suits the
agency.

This intimate interweaving of thematic and rule-of-
thumb approaches in an attempt to balance considerations
of freedom and efficiency, so typically present in the realm
of public convenience and necessity, leads to many of the
problems of "long-standing practice" and estoppel discussed
earlier.

These problems are further complicated when the statute maker combines convenience and necessity with various
restrictions or boundaries on the agency's discretion or the
scope of its authority. There is a great logical thrust toward
ultimate expansion in the doctrine of convenience and
necessity. Each factor immediately important to public convenience on a given matter is in turn affected by other factors, and these in turn by others ad infinitum until, having
begun with the question of whether to lay a mile of railroad
track, and gone on to the price of steel track, and then steel
in general, one ends up evaluating the potential defense
demand for steel and guessing what the Russians are going
to do next. If in addition the statute maker has commanded
that the agency not consider certain factors or leave the regulation of certain matters to other agencies, the expansionist
forces of convenience and necessity are constantly pushing
against and threatening to overthrow these boundary fences.
For instance, how can the I.C.C. decide whether the public
convenience and necessity requires that the 6:02 stop at
Podunk without considering whether flight 7B stops there
or perhaps should stop there. Yet the statute maker gives
jurisdiction over airlines to another agency entirely.

The courts, as keepers par excellence of statutory limits, are frequently involved in these boundary conflicts.
Again, they may use these conflicts as the opportunity for
direct reconsideration of the policy question. Alternatively,
the courts may be acting for the statute maker, keeping their
fellow subordinate within the proper boundaries. Such prob-

lems of jurisdiction, scope of authority, legally relevant or permissible considerations, delegation, and the like arise in many areas, but because of its expansionist quality they are particularly acute in the realm of convenience and necessity.

THE LIMITED JURISDICTION OF THE F.P.C.

The powers of the Federal Power Commission on matters of convenience and necessity are perhaps the most limited of those granted any of the regulatory commissions over its major area of concern. For while Congress in a sense aimed at the regulation of the entire natural gas industry, the commission was specifically denied the power to regulate "direct" sales, that is those made by producers to consumers as opposed to indirect sales in which producers sell to pipeline and pipeline to consumer. In addition, however, the Commission regulates all interstate pipeline transportation even where the gas being transported is involved in a direct sale.

This pipeline-centeredness of the federal power statute is awkward and essentially artificial. It is the whole pattern of natural gas production and consumption that is really of public concern. Transportation is only one facet, and not the most important or troublesome facet, of the problem. The federal power act is in a way a burlesque of the indirectness of government control inherent in all regulation. For in this area a government agency is supposed to regulate an entire industry by its negative control—its power to refuse a license or a rate, not over the industry as a whole but over one small facet of it—its transportation.

This pipeline-centeredness is, however, understandable. Federal regulatory agencies have traditionally been concerned with transportation and communications media. In establishing the F.P.C. it seemed least radical to also make its subject matter transportation. The commissions operate under the interstate-commerce power of Congress, and pipeline transportation is the facet of the natural-gas industry that most clearly falls in interstate commerce. When the F.P.C. was founded there was still a hot constitutional debate about whether production and final local sales were interstate commerce. Finally, the states had long been in the business of regulating the production of natural gas. It was not patently obvious, as it was with railroads and radio, that the states could not do this job for themselves.

In short, in the political struggle to establish the F.P.C., bows were made to the regulatory tradition, to the constitutional myth, and to the hallowed canons of federalism in order to reduce opposition. The paradox is, of course, that while the I.C.C. was given power over *railroads* because *railroads* were a central problem, the F.P.C. was given power over *pipelines* because *gas* was a central problem. The forces in and outside of Congress that wanted federal control of natural gas hoped that the F.P.C. would be able to regulate the whole natural-gas picture through its control of the pipelines. The forces that opposed federal regulation hoped that the scope of the regulation they finally had to accept could be narrowly limited by confining the F.P.C. to the regulation of pipelines. Thus the F.P.C., unlike the I.C.C., the C.A.B., the F.C.C., and the S.E.C., has been faced not only with the problem of making the essentially negative and indirect power of regulation over an industry effective but of making such negative and indirect power over one part of an industry effective over the rest of the industry.

Moreover since pipeline-centeredness was a compromise between forces within the statute maker that wanted much federal control and those that wanted little, and each hoped that the final statutory provisions would achieve its desires, the problem of proper subordination of a supplementary lawmaker to the statute maker is raised in acute form. May the agency use its pipeline powers as a lever for expanding its real jurisdiction to other facets of the industry or should it confine itself strictly to pipeline matters? Obviously this is a question of degree, but that the question arises indicates that judicial review is likely to focus not only upon whether the agency's policies are excessively parochial but on whether they are properly subordinate.

THE COMMISSION SEEKS TO EXPAND ITS JURISDICTION

From the passage of the Natural Gas Act in 1936 until 1942 the F.P.C. took a generally conservative view of its powers. It denied any overall responsibility for the end use of natural gas. Congress did not intend the Commission generally to weigh the broad social and economic effects of the use of various fuels.[2] Denials of this sort, although they were little more than a tactical reassurance to anticommission forces designed to smooth the advance of the Commission in other areas, later proved of considerable embarrassment to the Commission when it did attempt to assume such responsibilities.

In 1942 the advances that the Commission had been trying to make succeeded in the form of amendments to Section 7 of the Natural Gas Act which granted the Commission authority over the extension of natural gas facilities into areas not previously served by other such facilities. Under the original act the Commission only had jurisdiction over proposed facilities that would compete with existing ones, and such a limitation had thwarted any Commission ambitions toward comprehensive regulation.

Once its pipeline-centered jurisdiction had at least been extended to all market areas, the Commission also began to gingerly extend its jurisdiction in both directions from the pipeline, that is to field production and end use. Where "indirect sale" is involved the Commission has always had jurisdiction over the prices paid by the pipeline for the gas. Consequently it has always exercised major control over field prices and thus inevitably over all the production practices that are effected by price. In the 1950s there began to be some hints that the agency was beginning to move toward considering price in direct sales as well through the medium

---

2. *Kansas Pipe Line and Gas Co.*, 2 F.P.C. 29, 57 (1939)

of hearings on transportation certificates for direct sale gas.[3]
By increasingly taking into account the impact on production practices of various pricing arrangements, the Commission has become a major participant in setting production
policy. The Commission has also begun considering the impact of natural-gas marketing on competing fuels such as
coal, thus looking beyond natural gas to the whole spectrum
of fuel production. And finally, from a gingerly start in the
1940s, the Commission in the 1950s had come consistently
to consider end use as a factor in certification proceedings.
While the Commission had not asserted a general conservation authority, and had never made end use the decisive
factor in withholding a certificate, it had repeatedly argued
that the most wasteful end use, that of natural gas as boiler
fuel, was so undesirable as to be permissible only under a
positive showing of convenience and necessity.[4]

By the late 1950s, then, the F.P.C. was tentatively and
by use of thematic approaches pushing its convenience and
necessity jurisdiction outward toward greater power over
field pricing and more control over end use. The Transcontinental case was its next step forward in both these directions. For in this case the Commission refused a certificate
for transportation on three grounds: (1) that the intended
end use of the gas was "inferior"; (2) that direct sales such
as the one contemplated would drive up field prices; and
(3) that direct sales to major industrial users would preempt
pipeline capacity to the detriment of the needs of other
consumers.

No one really seems to have taken the third ground seriously. It is actually dependent on the other two because
if there were no objection to direct sales in terms of their
effect on prices or their intended end uses, there could be
no objection to the use of pipeline capacity for a transmission of gas just as worthy as other transmissions. This ground
is interesting, however, because it shows that the Commis-

---

3. See *Northern Natural Gas Co.*, 15 F.P.C. 1634 (1956)
4. id.

sion is still trying to touch base with the pipeline centeredness of its parent statute. It was obviously added in an almost touchingly sophistic attempt to give the appearance that even while driving on to the production fields and the end uses, the Commission was still firmly astride the pipeline to which Congress had attached it. At the very least it might serve as a hook on which courts, favoring the Commission's policy aims, but queasy about its subordination, or lack thereof, could hang their judicial consent. In the actual event the ground was largely ignored by the courts which went to the central issues.

FIELD PRICES

The first of these was field prices, and this seems really to have been the crux of the matter for the Commission. Indeed, the Commission may have felt fortuitously blessed when the direct sale it wished to fight for price reasons turned out to also have an inferior end use. In politics, however, what looks like fortuitous blessing often has something less than divine about it. It is not improbable that the Commission staff chose to make its great stand against direct sales to large industrial users in this particular case precisely because in this one they could bolster their concern for prices with a concern for end use. Two debatable grounds for decision are often stronger than one.

Just as important, the attachment of end-use concerns to a Commission drive basically aimed at greater control over field prices gave the Commission another political advantage. Quite typically the politician seeks to agglomerate various interest groups into a coalition more strongly supportive of his policies than any single group would be. In striving to keep field prices down the Commission was seeking to further the interests of household consumers against those of gas producers. The producers are a relatively well-organized and politically articulate group. The household consumers are not. By adding the end-use element the Commission recruits the coal industry and unions to its side of the struggle because resting a decision on the grounds that use of natural gas under boilers is necessarily inferior halts an incursion of gas into one of the few remaining major markets for coal.

Finally, the natural gas statute so clearly prohibits the Commission from exercising control over direct sales that a very thematic approach is particularly desirable from a tactical point of view. The more grounds the Commission can wave about, and the less specific it has to be about exactly what policy goal it is pursuing, the more likely it is to achieve its policy goals without the adverse judicial and Congressional reaction to be anticipated from a direct, specific, and concrete assertion of an expansion of its powers beyond those contemplated in the statute.

Commission regulation of prices and/or rates in a basically open market where independent buyers and sellers retain the initiative in offering and accepting prices is always difficult. Moreover, in an economic system the parts of which are highly interdependent and which retains a fair degree of fluidity, Commission intervention at one point may have all sorts of unforseen consequences elsewhere, and those who wish to circumvent Commission policies may find many paths around the point blocked by regulation. These problems would be serious even if a single Commission held regulatory power over the whole of a single commodity market. They are enormously complicated in the instance of the F.P.C. which controls the indirect, but not the direct sale, gas market. It is not easy to see how the F.P.C. could effectively regulate the field prices, and thus the eventual price to household consumers, of indirect sale gas if the gas producer is free to channel his product into direct sales whenever he wants to and at whatever prices he can get. Thus of necessity the F.P.C. views the expansion of direct sales practices as a major challenge to its regulatory authority.

In the Transcontinental case, as in many Supreme Court opinions, the realistic crux of the matter is to be found in the footnotes. To understand them, however, the reader must know that utility companies providing electric power from steam generators typically fired by coal have for some time bought relatively small quantities of natural gas on an interruptible-service basis. Because they could not be assured of a steady supply, they could only use gas as a supplement to their regular coal operations. Transcontinental, however, had begun to offer a noninterruptible service labeled "X-20" that would have allowed utilities to use gas as their regular rather than supplementary fuel. It was this X-20 service for which the F.P.C. had refused a certificate. Here are the telltale notes:[5]

> The Commission has recently set field prices for sales for resale in the area where this gas was bought at 18 cents per Mcf. . . . The sales price to Con. Ed. in this direct sale was 1¼ cents per Mcf. over the line at which the Commission is trying to hold field prices. Any reading of the Commission's opinion which does not keep this fact in mind is, we believe, bound to be incomplete.

> The *amicus* briefs of two California public utilities, Southern California Gas and Southern Counties Gas, reveal that the competitive bidding of California Edison Co., a large industrial user, for direct purchases in the field has already forced up the prices to domestic consumers in California. . . . Several other industrial users are also contemplating taking advantage of an X-20 type service. . . . In fact, the record reveals that Transco has suggested the possibility of providing X-20 service to its other customers, and several of these customers are negotiating for such service. . . . It is interesting to note that an Assistant to the Vice President of Con Ed testified that the producers sold the gas directly to Con. Ed. with a limitation on resale because "they (the producers) were allergic to proceedings before the Federal Power Commission."

> The Commission stated that certification would have the adverse effect of: "(M)aking it more difficult to meet the requirements of smaller purchasers *in the event arrangements of this type become widespread.*" (Emphasis added.)

---

5. 365 U.S. 1, 23 n. 18, 29 n. 23, 25 n. 21 (1961)

LOOPHOLES

In short, the F.P.C. felt that a gigantic loophole was being developed through which producers and electric companies could carry a significant share of the natural-gas business out of the reach of the Natural Gas Act and the Commission's regulatory powers. This problem of loopholes is a constantly recurring feature of judicial review of administrative decision making. It is most familiar, of course, in the field of taxation, but it is also to be encountered frequently in many of the regulatory areas. Given the ambiguity of language, the complex interrelation of various provisions of the same statute, the even more complex relations between the provisions of different statutes passed at different times, unanticipatable economic and technological developments, and the fertile minds of lawyers and businessmen trying to wring every ounce of advantage out of the statutory provisions, each year there are thousands of instances in which individuals or business firms are able to make at least a plausible legal case for doing something that to a detached observer would seem to violate the spirit if not the letter of the law. If Congress had to close every loophole that was discovered it would spend most of its time in a nightmarish patching race. Given the necessarily slow Congressional processes, new loopholes would develop faster than it could close old ones. Thus the federal legal system simply would not work unless the regulatory commissions and other administrative agencies were allowed to exercise their supplementary lawmaking powers to routinely plug most of the loopholes themselves. They do so both by issuing rules and regulations and deciding specific cases relying on the intent of Congress. In a sense this reliance is pure fiction. Typically Congress was not aware of what form a specific loophole would take, and therefore had no specific intent as to how it should be closed. It does seem relatively certain that the general intent that agencies try to make the statutory scheme work effectively is embodied in most statutes. The specific form of plugging a loophole, however, what interests are sacrificed to which, what goals of the statutes emphasized and what de-emphasized is more a matter of agency than congressional intent.

The difficulty is that the question is always one of degree. Thousands of small holes must be plugged by the agencies without reference back to Congress if the legal process is to work. On the other hand, an agency, particularly a regulatory agency, is likely to view as a loophole any situation in which the law does not allow it to do what it wants to do. Many of these situations involve such major extensions of regulatory power or such major changes in government policy, or such evident statutory hesitancy to grant greater power, that quite obviously they ought to be returned to the statute maker for further decision rather than handled by the agency on the fictional assumption that the statute maker intended that it do what it pleased. In between these two extremes are the thousands of situations in which a genuine question exists as to whether this is the kind of statutory hiatus that ought to be pointed out to the statute maker with the request that he make his pleasure known, or the kind of unintended loophole that ought to be handled by supplementary lawmakers.

Courts tend to exercise their half of the dual decision-making process frequently in this area because of the complex problems of subordination involved. First they feel themselves in a better position than the agency, plunged into the heat of the regulatory struggle, to determine fairly which statutory blanks must be referred back to the legislature and which the agency may handle on its own. Put another way, the courts as loyal subordinates of the statute maker seek to insure that the kinds of decisions that it thinks the statute maker would have wanted referred back to it by subordinate lawmakers are indeed referred back to it. Secondly, even where supplementary lawmaking to fill loopholes seems desirable, the courts may intervene as they do in other supplementary lawmaking situations if they feel that the substance of the supplementary law made is in violation of the statute maker's intentions. Finally, there seems little doubt that the more the Court dislikes the substantive policy that the agency is evolving, the more sensitized it becomes to suggested insubordination.

RULES OF THUMB VERSUS THEMES

Transcontinental illustrates this problem of subordination rather neatly. If the F.P.C. had clearly stated as a matter of general policy that it would use whatever powers it had to block any and all direct sales, the judges would have uniformly held that it was acting insubordinately. For such a position would be clearly contrary to the statute's exemption of direct sales from F.P.C. jurisdiction. On the other hand, if the F.P.C. says that in granting certificates of public convenience and necessity for transportation, it will take into account all factors affecting public convenience, including impact on field prices, it seems to be following the statute. However, what if the Commission then says that in the process of certificating transportation it will consider transportation of direct sale gas as per se not in the public interest? That is, no matter what the other factors present, this factor when present is always decisive. Agencies engaged in evaluating various factors frequently go on to establish that certain behavior is per se illegal because its evil always outweighs any possible benefits. But if the Commission says that direct sale is per se against public convenience and necessity, has it not really come back to the first, and clearly illegal position, that it will block all direct sales even though, indeed *precisely because,* the statute maker has exempted direct sales from its jurisdiction?

In fact the Circuit Court and the Supreme Court dissenters found the Commission to be saying the first and/or third thing, and found it to be insubordinate. The Supreme Court majority, obviously viewing this question as crucial, labored long and hard to show that the Commission was using field price as only one factor among many to be considered in determining convenience and necessity and so was acting within its statutory powers.

Were the judges then simply saying that if the Commission used rule-of-thumb decisional techniques, it was acting illegally, and if it used thematic techniques its actions were valid? If so, this exercise of judicial review was essentially artificial and futile. The agency in future need only go through the ritual of saying, "We have weighed all the factors," to cover its real internal decisional rule of thumb, "direct sales are per se against public convenience and necessity." As in case after case the ritual wording is invoked, but direct sale always loses, the bad man's law will become clear enough. Indeed, after a sufficient number of cases the agency will begin to say, "It is the long-standing practice of this agency to deny transportation facilities to direct-sale gas," with a good chance of getting the Supreme Court to acknowledge the long-standing practice, thus writing it into the statute. In short, if the agency can get away with using the rule of thumb long enough under the pretense of balancing all factors, it will eventually get the rule of thumb written into the statute by the very court that said it couldn't use the rule of thumb in the first place.

I think this is precisely the situation created by the *Transcontinental* decision. The majority of the Court not only refuse to penetrate below the pretense of weighing of factors to the quite obvious attack of the Commission on direct sales, but they scurry desperately to cover up the various slips the agency made that rendered perfectly clear that it was direct sales and nothing but direct sales that the agency was after. Even the dissenters wished simply to return the case to the Commission, slapping it on the wrist for so obviously attacking direct sales, and instructing it to consider the impact of this particular direct sale on field prices as simply one of the factors to be weighed in deciding whether convenience and necessity warranted this particular transportation. Such a remand is little more than an invitation to the agency to parrot the verbal formulas approved by the Court and then make exactly the same decision for exactly the same reasons it had before. All it need say is that in balancing all the factors the impact of the direct sale on field prices tipped the scales against granting the certificate. The only way to prevent this sort of response is for the Court to clearly prohibit the Commission from giving any weight to the direct sale aspects on the ground that direct sales are outside its jurisdiction. None of the justices were willing to do this.

STATIC DELEGATION AND ORGANIC GROWTH

Why then did the Court issue such a decision? Was it simply failing in its duty to the statute maker? The crux of the matter lies in an issue that underlies a wide range of the relations between courts and commissions. One way of visualizing a regulatory statute like the Natural Gas Act is as a concrete, although rather general, statement of what the statute maker wants and then as an assignment to a regulatory commission of certain powers to enforce the statute maker's will. The other view is that in passing legislation creating a regulatory commission or assigning an existing one new jurisdiction, the statute maker has deliberately set loose into the political process a new political actor who is given something of a license to make his own way. The first of these is an essentially static view which seeks to discover what policies the statute maker intended the day the statute was passed. The latter sees the statute maker as having initiated a process of organic growth, as having created a commission precisely because commissions have the tendency to expand their jurisdictions and change their policies to meet changing conditions or more receptive climates of opinion.

The structure of the Natural Gas Act suggests that the statute maker was constructing a comprehensive system of regulation by leaving some of the regulation to the states while assigning those matters that the states could not handle to the F.P.C. At the time the act was passed, direct sales were almost entirely intrastate and it reasonably could have been anticipated that the states could effectively regulate this area. It was precisely indirect sale through pipelines that in 1938 was beyond the reach of effective state regulation and so was assigned to the F.P.C. If twenty years later the situation in the industry has changed, and a new practice of direct sale has arisen that is beyond effective state control, the courts can take one of two positions. They can say: "When the statute maker passed the statute, he assigned direct sale regulation to the states. If the situation has now changed so that some elements of direct sale should be assigned to the F.P.C., it is up to the statute maker to change the statute. Until he does, we shall enforce the statute as it was passed." On the other hand, the courts may say: "The statute maker desired comprehensive and effective control of natural gas. At the time the statute was passed, the specific devices for achieving this purpose under the conditions then present included emphasizing state control of direct sales. As conditions have changed, however, this particular device is not meeting the purposes of the statute. To the extent that a subordinate agency can use its regulatory powers to meet the new situations, it should not be hamstrung by a literal and mechanical enforcement of the original specifics of the statute if, in the court's opinion, the statute was designed to allow for growth through agency interpretation. The proper role of the subordinate given authority in relatively general language is to use that authority to meet new situations. To restrict it to the exact patterns at the time the statute was passed would be to refuse to allow the statute maker to invent devices for anticipating problems and would shackle him to a constant round of new legislation to meet each and every change in economic and technological conditions. If the statute maker feels that his subordinate agency has acted wrongly, he can always correct the error by new legislation. In the meantime, it is better that someone regulate according to some line of policy than that hiatuses in regulation appear because the old specifics do not meet the new circumstances. Since the F.P.C.

has the statutory power to regulate pipeline transmissions
for the public convenience and necessity, it should use that
power to meet new situations that would otherwise threaten
the whole functioning of the regulatory system envisioned
by the statute, even if such use should thrust against the
initial specifics of the legislation."

Quite typically broad-gauge regulatory statutes like the
Interstate Commerce Act, the Natural Gas Act and the Motor
Carrier Act contain a mixture of general sections that declare
the need for regulation, create a regulatory commission to
do the job and provide general guidelines for its future development, and more specifically worded sections applying
whatever particular rules and practices seem best at the moment. Twenty years later courts must decide whether to give
full sway to the institutional invention in the statute—the
creation of a new agency or the vesting of new general powers
in an older agency—or to enforce the old specifics, inviting
the statute maker to change them if he likes. Moreover only
the most politically naïve court could fail to realize that
frequently the general provisions of regulatory statutes represent the hopes of those most favorable to regulation that the
agency once created will be able to do things that they could
not get Congress to specifically authorize, while the specific
provisions embody the desires of those least favorable to regulation to curb the agency as much as possible.

LARGE-STEP AND SMALL-STEP CHANGES

Thus a court that adopts any but the most mechanical
and literalistic interpretation of a regulatory statute, and
such an interpretation will almost always generate so many
loopholes as to make the statute totally unworkable, faces a
curiously subtle problem in determining where true subordination lies. Its solution is frequently the one to be found
in both the majority and dissenting opinions in the Transcontinental case. Courts will frequently in effect say to
commissions, "You may treat the powers originally given

you expansively, using power in some areas to lever your way into others, as long as you proceed slowly, one small step at a time. What we will prevent as insubordinate is large-step changes that suddenly freeze new policies into law." In short, it is not simply the agency that is to grow organically but the whole system of regulation. The agency must proceed in such a way as to allow, rather than prematurely cutting off, opposition, persuasion, political bargaining and private initiative.

What had happened in *Transcontinental* was that the F.P.C. had been gradually pushing its pipeline-centered jurisdiction outward for years. Faced with the development of a major new loophole through X-20 direct sales, it took the giant step of holding that direct sales of this sort were per se against public convenience and necessity because they allowed large quantities of gas to escape Commission regulation. It is always a little dubious for any agency to say that what is against public convenience is for you to be clever enough to find a legal way to escape the jurisdiction that I have been busily trying to expand. So the Commission, in taking the giant step, threw in all sorts of ambiguous language, pretending it was not such a giant step after all—that the evasion of its jurisdiction was not the sole reason for denial of certification but simply one factor to be weighed.

It is a favorite tactic of courts under such circumstances to take the verbal smoke screen seriously. By repeating and emphasizing it, and holding that if the judges did not believe in the smoke screen they would reverse the agency, courts may actually prevent the agency from taking the bigger step and confine it to the smaller one. In *Transcontinental*, the majority opinion pretends that the Court did not see the giant step, warns that if it saw such a step it would prevent it, and piously congratulates the agency on taking the smaller step of simply considering the jurisdictional and price problems of direct sale as one factor to be weighed. The dissent openly sees the giant step, condemns it and returns the case to the agency allowing it to consider price–direct-sale–jurisdiction matters only as one factor among many, knowing full well that the Commission can reach exactly the same decision as it did before.

The effect of both opinions is roughly the same, however, and both are aimed at slowing down but not preventing the agency's jurisdictional growth. The Commission gains a partial victory. The whole gas industry will note that it has succeeded in blocking one major direct sale and been authorized by the courts to consider direct sale as a negative factor. The Commission does not, however, gain a full victory, because the Supreme Court opinions prevent it from claiming in the future that direct sale is per se illegal. The Commission has succeeded in moving in that direction, but the Court prevents that policy from yet being frozen into the Agency's formal policy—i.e., into law. It thus keeps the political situation more fluid, allowing the opponents of the policy more time and room to maneuver for its reversal either in the Agency itself, in Congress or by another round of Court decisions.

Of course it would be naïve to assume that the F.P.C. will loyally follow the Court's orders and impartially weigh favorable factors involved against the loss to its own jurisdiction in future direct-sale cases. It would be equally naïve, however, to assume that an agency that has to take the official position that it is weighing will not have to behave differently than an agency that can proudly proclaim that its preference for viewing one factor as decisive has now been approved by the Supreme Court and thus is a part of the law of the land. For under the Court's decision the Commission's hearing officers are commanded to weigh factors rather than hold direct sales per se invalid, and the hearing officers are sufficiently independent and imbued with the lawyer's ethic that their behavior will be affected by these commands. The Commissioners themselves will have to formally say "weigh all the factors" even if they mean "we hate direct sales," and their formal statements will affect the behavior of their agency subordinates. The presence of the Supreme Court opinions and the need to pay lip service to them will reduce the clarity of the agency's internal communication and thus its zeal and efficiency in pursuing its goals. Even if the Commissioners in their own minds defy the Court and resolve to strike down direct sales no matter what, they will be hampered by subordinates who take at least somewhat seriously the "official law."

At the very least, the Court opinions mean that direct-sale proponents will be allowed to continue to introduce evidence and argument favorable to direct sales at certification hearings of the Commission rather than having that opportunity cut off as it would be if direct sales were held by the Commission to be illegal per se. Thus the Court assures the proponents of direct sale better access and lobbying conditions before the Agency. It should not be assumed that the Commission is absolutely obstinate, stupid and self-aggrandizing at all costs. As long as it cannot proclaim that direct sales are per se against public convenience, and must constantly hear evidence that shows that some such sales are in the public interest, it may eventually be persuaded to modify its position. Most "lobbying" consists of trying to persuade bureaucrats, and the crucial problem is frequently to gain access to them in order to persuade them before policies get frozen. The Supreme Court decisions in *Transcontinental* allowed the proponents of direct sale just such an opportunity.

Finally, the Supreme Court opinions in *Transcontinental* can be clearly read by all the participants in the policy struggle as proclaiming that the Court knows where the Commission is heading, does not disapprove of the direction, but will not let it go all the way yet. Such a proclamation signals to the Commission's opponents that they still have time to mount a major campaign, perhaps in Congress, but that they do not have forever. Put another way the Court solves the subordination problem by allowing the subordinate agency to continue the institutional momentum granted it by the original statute, but slowing it sufficiently and signaling its movements loudly enough so that the statute maker and the political process as a whole have time to issue the agency new commands if they want to.

END USE

The second major issue in *Transcontinental* concerned
end use. We have already noted that it was a stroke of luck
for the Commission that the direct sales that it wished to
prevent by a rather novel extension of its jurisdiction involved an end use as boiler fuel. For the Commission had
for some time opposed such end use. Thus by stressing the
end-use factor the Commission could give a greater sense of
routineness and continuity to a decision that was actually intended as a great leap forward to close the yawning new
jurisdictional loophole created by direct sale and X-20 service. But even while employing end use primarily to bolster
its expansion of jurisdiction into the gas fields, the F.P.C.
was also attempting some expansion at the other end of the
pipeline. For *Transcontinental* is the first case in which the
Commission purports to find inferior end use a decisive factor
in denying certification.

It is generally accepted that the use of gas under boilers
violates ideal conservationist practice. Natural gas is a scarce
resource that is exceptionally well adapted to certain uses
such as household cooking and heating, while less scarce
materials less well adapted to household use, such a coal and
fuel oil, are adequate boiler fuels. It is also true that there
is some conservationist thrust to the Natural Gas Act. Here
again, however, general and complete conservation powers
were not given to the Commission. Its initial pipeline-centered jurisdiction left the basic control over end use to the
states. Unlike pipelines, each end-use operation occurs solely
within a single state. Each state has a strong interest not only
in how, where and under what conditions gas is burned, but
in conservation of the resource in order to assure its own
citizens the steady and adequate supply they require as
consumers.

Nevertheless the typical situation is one in which one
state is asked to regulate end use in such a way as to conserve
the natural resources of another. Under these circumstances

the using state's desires for cheaper fuel or a greater proportional cut of the total interstate gas supply may lead it to subordinate the general interest in conservation to the immediate demands of its own citizens. In *Transcontinental* we find the added factor of a state's special concern for the peculiarly pressing problem of air pollution in New York City moving it away from any general concern for conservation.

The F.P.C. has in recent years been prone to argue that, contrary to expectations at the time of passage of the Natural Gas Act, the states have not actually been able to completely carry out the conservationist philosophy of the statute maker. Thus in order to fulfill the purposes of the statute, the Commission itself must gradually expand its concerns to augment state conservationist practices. Here again the thematic approach is used as a vehicle for institutional growth, with the Commission asserting that end use is simply one factor to be considered in determining the public convenience of any given request for pipeline transportation, but in fact moving further and further toward the position that certain end uses invariably and in and of themselves will result in refusal to issue a certificate.

Transcontinental was not quite a final step in this direction. End use was one of two, rather than the only, decisive factor, and the Commission made a few very brief bows toward weighing such other factors as air pollution. Nevertheless it is indicative of the state of movement in the Commission's policy that its staff urged that end use be a major consideration, but that its own hearing officer refused to consider it at all. The hearing officer did, however, say that if he were authorized to consider end use he would have decided against certification. The Commission held that end use could properly be considered and did decide against certification. Such uncertainty and pulling and hauling within the Commission itself is good evidence that the agency was in the process of changing its policies and expanding its jurisdiction. There is always some confusion during the march forward.

The Supreme Court's treatment of end use is a particularly illuminating example of the problems it faces when dealing with an old statute and a regulatory agency's attempt to grow to meet new circumstances. It also provides a neat illustration of the continuous interaction of Congress, Court and agency in the structuring of public policy.

The Court admits that when Congress passed the Natural Gas Act in 1938 it "intended the states to be the primary arbiters of conservation problems."[6] The Commission immediately began to lobby hard to get this and other limitations on its jurisdiction eliminated. Its particular target was Section 7 of the act. The F.P.C. drafted an amendment to 7, primarily designed to extend its control to gas entering areas where it had not previously been sold. But there is no reason not to try to kill more than one bird. So into its draft amendment the Commission also packed a good deal of ambiguous language that might—or might not—mean that the Commission's jurisdiction might also be extended in many other ways, including some responsibility for conservation and end use. It backed its attempt to push the amendment through with all sorts of arguments, including many to show that it needed control over end use in order to achieve better conservation.

The Congress adopted the amendment, but neither the wording of the amendment nor anything in the legislative history of the bill (committee reports, floor debate, and so on) specifically indicate or even strongly suggest that Congress wished to extend the Commission's jurisdiction over end use. The amendment was primarily designed to extend the geographic jurisdiction of the Commission to cover "virgin" areas where gas had not previously been sold. Congressmen apparently had their eyes firmly fixed on this purpose, and there is no indication they wanted to do anything more than this. Yet in *Transcontinental* the Supreme Court argues that when Congress adopted the amendment, it did extend Commission jurisdiction over end use and conserva-

---

6. 365 U.S. 1, 9 (1961)

tion, *because the Commission had asked for such powers in the course of pushing for the amendment.* In short, what the statute maker intended when he adopted the statute is to be defined by what one of the pressure groups lobbying for the statute said it wanted. In one sense this is patently ridiculous; it is the argument that whatever X wanted when he suggested Y, he got when Z chose Y.

On the other hand, this episode in statutory interpretation illustrates why I have resorted to the rather awkward, and in a sense fictional, device of the "statute maker." For here an administrative agency has drafted a statute, pushed its draft in Congress, and Congress has accepted its draft. The drafter and the acceptor may not have been in perfect communication on what the statutory wording was supposed to convey. Indeed it is typical of congressional politics that there is considerable ambiguity involved in such communication. Does the statute mean what the drafter wanted it to mean, or what the acceptor thought it meant? A politically realistic court must answer, "a little of both." The intent of the statute maker must be a kind of rough summing and averaging of the intents of the various units that in reality constitute the statute maker. Of course in doing the calculation, any court has, and cannot avoid exercising, considerable discretion in how it runs the figures. In *Transcontinental* we get an extreme instance of such discretion, with the court arguing that because the drafter loudly and repeatedly said he wanted something, he must have been given that something when his draft was passed, even though there is no specific, concrete evidence anywhere in the congressional proceedings to indicate that the congressmen were listening to the drafter on this point.

After the 1942 amendments, the Commission did not rest on its laurels. Having gotten part of the extension of jurisdiction it wanted, in a rather ambiguous way and not without a little sleight-of-hand, it next tried a frontal assault. Subsequent to 1942 it sought further amendments to the Natural Gas Act that would openly and fully give it comprehensive power over conservation. At this point a slight political embarrassment arises. If the Commission had really been given power over end use in the 1942 amendment, why would it subsequently need more amendments in order to control end use? Having gotten such power in at best a very ambiguous and incomplete way in 1942, the Commission now wanted it openly and directly. It became natural then for the F.P.C. to argue, in trying to persuade Congress to give it new amendments, that the 1942 enactment had not given it the power at all, and that was why new amendments were necessary. But the Commission did not get the new amendments it wanted. When it failed in its frontal assault, it went back to the position that the 1942 amendment had really given it what it wanted anyhow.

This is where the embarrassment arises. For the whole set of proclamations that the F.P.C. made to the effect that the 1942 amendment did not give it conservation power—proclamations made in the context of trying to get more amendments—came back to haunt it, and the Supreme Court, when the Commission had lost its attempts at new amendments and was again trying to rest its self-expansion of jurisdiction on the slender reed of the 1942 statute. The Circuit Court in *Transcontinental* quite boorishly insisted that the Commission must have really meant what it said in 1944 when it denied it had conservation jurisdiction in order to get Congress to give it some. The Supreme Court was more charitable to the tactical needs of political discourse. While having to strain our credibility a little, and their own, the justices' opinions, after considerable struggle, manage to ignore these proclamations altogether. They permit the Commission to go back to the indirect tactics of expansive interpretations of old statutes without forcing it to continue hauling around the casualties it incurred in the failure of its direct assault for new statutes.

I suppose at this point the question is: Why does the Court adopt a rather fantastic interpretation of the Act of 1942, and a totally evasive treatment of the Commission's own later pronouncements, in order to support its jurisdictional expansion into the conservation field? Perhaps it is best to let the Court answer in its own words:[7]

> There is a broader principle here which also stands in opposition to respondents' contentions. When Congress enacted the Natural Gas Act, it was motivated by a desire "to protect consumers against exploitation at the hands of natural gas companies." To that end, Congress "meant to create a comprehensive and effective regulatory scheme." It is true, of course, that Congress did not desire comprehensive *federal* regulation; much authority was reserved for the States. But, it is equally clear that Congress did not desire that an important aspect of this field be left unregulated.
>
> *   *   *
>
> It is questionable whether any State could be expected to take the initiative in enforcing this type of "economic" conservation. A producing State might wish to prolong its gas reserves for as long as possible but producing States have no control over the use to which gas is put in another State. Consuming States may control the end use of gas, but the deficiencies of this system in the present context are apparent—unless all States cooperate in enforcing a common regulation, the producer may pick a State which is sufficiently anxious for this scarce resource that it will take gas irrespective of the use.

In short, the Court is taking the position that in the area of end-use conservation, an organic development of the institution established by the statute maker is desirable even when the statute maker has not given his specific approval to new policies, because the states have not been able to do the part of the conservation job that the statute maker had originally anticipated they could do. The Court must choose whether to freeze the specific arrangements that seemed best to the statute maker at the time or to implement what it believes to be the statute maker's general intention. It chooses to allow the Commission to expand its jurisdiction to meet conservation problems as they have actually developed.

---

7. 365 U.S. 1, 19-21 (1961)

Here again the question of what is and what is not in-subordination is a difficult one. Just as in the field-price area, however, the Court couples its expansive views of proper subordination with efforts to insure that the political situation does not become frozen to agency desires too rapidly. In view of the F.P.C.'s obviously weak position vis-à-vis the 1942 act, and the embarrassment of its later denials of conservation jurisdiction, the Court cautions that while it may give great weight to end use when granting transportation certificates it may not yet go all the way to asserting general conservation jurisdiction. The Court will not permit the agency to do immediately by statutory interpretation the whole job it hoped but failed to do by lobbying Congress for further statutes. The Commission and its opponents are thus left with a still relatively fluid situation in which to carry on their political campaigns. The Court allows the Commission a major step forward, or rather outward, from its pipeline centeredness toward the control of gas before and after it enters the pipe. On the other hand it leaves the Commission in the position of having to proceed by steps, and indeed in its opinion language gives the Commission's opponents some ammunition with which to fight against any Commission assertion of general conservation jurisdiction. Here again by saying, "We are sure the Commission did not mean to do more than weigh end use as one factor among many, for to do otherwise would be illegal," the Court imposes certain restraints on both the internal and external functioning of the agency. Hearing officers must continue to accept evidence and argument on other factors that counterbalance inferior end uses. The Commission itself must continue officially to proclaim that inferior end use is not per se against the public interest. Thus the access to the Commission of views contrary to those of the agency is maintained. Subordinate agency officials, mindful of their duty to "the law," must withhold total commitment to the agency's drive for expansion and thus maintain a higher receptivity to nonagency views than they otherwise would. The Agency is redirected to Congress for any immediate assumption of general conservation powers and thus held within the orbit of political forces that are involved in congressional action. The Commission's opponents are encouraged to continue to test for the outer boundaries of the Agency's jurisdiction by devising more new marketing practices, so that the arena of litigation remains open.

MAJORITY AND MINORITY OPINIONS

It is worth turning now for a moment to the policy difference between the majority and minority of the Court. We have already noted that the principal difference between Justices Harlan, Frankfurter, and Stewart and the majority was that the minority were unwilling to overlook the political reality that the Commission had taken a giant step forward and was attempting to eliminate direct sales altogether in order to force all gas into its full indirect-sales jurisdiction. The minority condemned this action outright, chastised the Commission for seeking to establish a general policy beyond that permissible under the statute, and remanded the case to the Commission with the instruction that it consider direct sale only as one factor among many in each individual case. The majority, of course, had adopted a policy rather like that of a mother who sees her child pulling the dog's tail and says: "I see that you are only petting the dog now, but if you should ever pull its tail, I will severely punish you." Hopefully this discourages the child from pulling the dog's tail again without all the fuss that would follow from directly accusing him. Since the dissenters knew full well that after a remand of the sort they wished to make, the F.P.C. could decide against *Transcontinental* again, so long as it publicly proclaimed a thematic approach, the majority and the dissenters simply use slightly different routes to the same conclusion. Either way the Agency continues its progress toward greater and greater jurisdiction. Either way the Court proclaims, and forces the Commission to proclaim, that it still must use a thematic approach and has not yet pushed far enough to get away with a blanket condemnation of non-jurisdictional, direct sales.

If the dissenters' opinion had become the binding pronouncement of the Court only two rather minor, although perhaps important, differences in result would have occurred. The more anti-F.P.C. tone of the opinion might have encouraged the Commission's opponents to struggle harder within the litigational arena, although the conditions in the arena remain the same under either opinion. Secondly, in later years, as the F.P.C. moves further in extending its jurisdiction, it will find it easier to cite the majority opinion than it would the dissent as evidence of the unbroken support of the Court for its expansions. Thus the majority opinion gives the Commission a certain marginal advantage in future litigational campaigning.

The most striking similarity between majority and dissenters is, of course, that both agree with the Commission on the substantive policy embodied in *Transcontinental* and both oppose the Commission only on the delicate question of what constitutes proper subordination. *Transcontinental* offers some modicum of proof for the proposition that Court consideration of jurisdiction and other subordination questions is not simply and invariably a cover for judicial disagreement with the substantive policy the agency is pursuing. Of course if either the majority or the dissenters or both had been in serious disagreement with the F.P.C.'s substantive policy, perhaps they might not have confined themselves to allowing the F.P.C. only a small instead of a giant step forward but would have actually pushed it slightly backward. In the process of dual decision, questions of whether the agency's substantive policies are excessively parochial and questions of subordination to the statute necessarily interact. Nevertheless it would be simplistic to equate the two.

The majority and dissenters did disagree on one substantive policy question—that of air pollution. The majority brushed this consideration aside. Perhaps here again the crux of the matter is buried in a footnote.

At the time certification for the X-20 service was sought, Con. Ed. was using gas on an interruptible basis at a rate that averaged 78,578 Mcf. per day. A substantial amount of this gas was fired under Con. Ed.'s boilers, although not under the boilers at the Waterside station. No reason appears in the record why Con. Ed. could not have used the gas it was then receiving under its Waterside boilers to alleviate, if not solve, the air-pollution problem.[8]

Obviously the Court felt that the invocation of the public concern for air pollution was something of a ploy to cover Consolidated Edison's pursuit of its own corporate interest in cheaper fuel.

The minority obviously felt that the Commission had treated air pollution considerations too cavalierly in its headlong rush to prohibit all direct sales.

. . . [I]ts previous consideration of . . . [the "end use" factor] . . . seems to leave much to be desired, doubtless because of the over-all mistaken premises on which the Commission proceeded. In a reconsideration of the case upon correct premises, the air-pollution problem may take on a different significance, and whatever conclusions the Commission may reach on this score should in any event be accompanied with more convincing particularized findings.[9]

This passage illustrates still another aspect of judicial–administrative relations. Too frequently judicial review is thought of as only some sort of club with which the Court beats the agencies, or perhaps a guillotine which suddenly descends to lop off an agency decision as the executioner proclaims "This is illegal." Very frequently, however, review consists of the very common and widespread political phenomenon of asking someone to consider something, hinting at how you would like them to look at it, and mildly and vaguely threatening some indefinite and unspecific reprisal if they do not do what you ask. The whole process is low-keyed. In effect one political actor asks another to look at

---

8. 365 U.S. 1, 30 n. 25 (1961)
9. 365 U.S. 1, 41-2 (1961)

things in a little different light. When courts remand to
agencies for a second decision because the first was based on
inadequate grounds or a faulty interpretation of a legal
standard, they are frequently doing just this. Both the agency
and the court know that the agency can simply go through
the motions. It can pay lip service to the court's remand
instructions and come up with exactly the same decision
again. The agency knows that if it does this, in most instances
the court will give in gracefully. It also knows that such per-
formances reduce its political credit with the remanding
court. Moreover, politicians, including agency personnel, are
not necessarily and invariably single-minded and rigid. A
reasonable man, taking a second look, and prodded in a
slightly different direction by another reasonable man, may
modify his judgment not under threat or compulsion but because the new look really changed his mind.

In *Transcontinental,* the dissenters, finding themselves
in substantive disagreement with the Commission on the air-
pollution question, wished to resort to this mildest form of
judicial review. It should not be overlooked because of
excessive preoccupation with the clamor and clash of direct
confrontation between courts and agencies. Mild persuasion
is an integral part of this sector of politics as of most others.

CONCLUSION

The process of dual-decision making then may not only
involve a second decision on the merits of substantive policy
but a judicial reassessment of the agency's actions in terms of
proper agency subordination to the statute maker. This problem can be a peculiarly complex one for a number of reasons,
particularly when independent regulatory commissions are
involved. Regulation is itself an awkward and ambiguous
device. Regulatory statutes with one hand impose responsibility for a certain sector of the economy on a given agency,
while with the other leaving ownership, initiative, and nearly

all the actual decision-making power in private hands. The agency is apparently intended to get the private decision makers to act in the public interest not by telling them what to do but only by sporadically intervening to tell them what not to do. Furthermore, the statute maker typically invokes the public interest or public convenience and necessity without saying what he means. Just as typically he mixes a number of specific limitations on jurisdiction and a number of concrete policy standards with these rather open directives to the agency to use its discretion and take its own initiatives to meet new circumstances. In short, regulatory statutes represent an uneasy compromise between laissez faire and government-control visions of the economy. As such they are likely to embody the ambiguity and internal contradictions of contemporary economic philosophy. More specifically such statutes will almost invariably set up an internal tension between the tendency toward self-expansion inherent in the agency's general commission and the static boundaries embodied in the specific provisions of the statute that grants the agency its powers.

A regulatory statute may in one sense create an agency and direct it to solve a problem not at a single blow but by a dynamic process of yea- and nay-saying that grows and changes with the private initiatives of the economy rather than freezing in a single mold. On the other hand, a regulatory statute may be viewed as a specific and concrete, although generally worded, solution to a given problem as it existed at a given moment. The duty of the agency then is to fulfill the typical supplementary lawmakers chores of filling in with specifics the generally stated commands of the statute maker.

Quite obviously most regulatory statutes combine both visions. The Supreme Court, faced with the difficult problem of enforcing subordination, is therefore likely to arrive at intermediate solutions. *Transcontinental* is quite typical of such solutions. The F.P.C. is allowed to continue its constant and single-minded campaign to expand its jurisdiction, but not quite at the pace it wants to go. The Court attempts to maintain a relative openness and fluidity in the process of institutional expansion not only for the agency but its opponents as well. If the agency wishes to plead the institutional-growth vision, it itself must not freeze each new step forward into law so hastily as to avoid fully submitting itself to the arguments and tactics of the other political participants is this growth process. The Court thus provides a peculiar solution for the peculiar problem of subordination posed by the regulatory commissions. As the Commissions claim they are supposed to grow dynamically, they are subordinated by the Court to the dynamic process of politics—that is, required to move slowly enough to allow all participants in the process full opportunity to affect one another's behavior by the mixture of persuasion, bargaining, threat, and coalition building that we call politics.

Transcontinental also represents the very tip of the iceberg of judicial deference to administrative decision. For, when all is said and done, the Commission's decision not to grant the pipeline certificate stands. Of the hundreds of thousands of issues that arise before administrative agencies each year, over 99 per cent are settled by informal negotiations between the agencies and the parties and so are totally beyond judicial cognizance.[10] Of the many thousands of formal administrative decisions reached each year, probably only one or two per cent are appealed to the courts.[11] Of those that are appealed, relatively few are reversed by the judges. For instance, a recent study of administrative agency cases that were appealed from the circuits to the Supreme Court shows that the circuits had backed the agency in 95 out of 124 cases. Moreover, the Supreme Court is far more likely both to grant certiorari and then decide for the agency when the lower court has found against the agency than it is to

---

10. See Woll, *Administrative Law: the Informal Process* (1961)
11. It is impossible to calculate the exact percentage because, while it is possible to count the number of appeals from administrative agencies considered by the courts, it is impossible to determine the total number of formal administrative rulings made in any given year.

either grant certiorari or eventually decide for the private party when the lower court has supported the agency.[12]

Transcontinental, of course, is an instance in which the Supreme Court did intervene, if only marginally, in agency affairs even while affirming the agency decision. Far more typical, however, are the instances in which the Court affirms an agency decision per curiam—that is, without any written opinion of its own, thus allowing the agency position to stand completely, or those in which the Court adopts as its own the reasoning of the agency thus fully affirming it. Indeed, *Transcontinental* is interesting precisely because it marks the very edge of judicial intervention, beyond which lies either the full affirmation or refusal to reconsider agency judgments that is typical of judges' relations with administrators and follows naturally from the dual-decisional situation in which they find themselves.

---

12. See Loeb, "The Role of the U.S. Courts of Appeals in Administrative Agency Cases," a paper presented at the Annual Meetings of the Western Political Science Association, March 17, 1967.

Conclusion

The two preceding chapters present something near to the two extremes of judicial review of administrative decision making; one at which the Supreme Court persists in major opposition to agency policy, the other where the Court acquiesces in the agency position, imposing only a very marginal check on its actions. It bears repeating, however, that these materials may be somewhat misleading, for they direct the reader's attention away from the thousands of instances in which the circuit courts simply approve the agency position completely and the Supreme Court refuses certiorari, and the hundreds more in which the Court accepts certiorari and then totally supports the agency view. At least during the last twenty years the federal court system has devoted the vast bulk of its energies to simply giving legal approval to agency decisions.

It is fashionable these days to follow what I have just said with the proclamation that the chief role of the courts then is to "legitimate" agency decisions. Indeed, whenever in recent years investigators have found courts acquiescing in anything and everything put on their judicial plate by the rest of government, the response has been to say that courts are legitimating instead of saying that they are doing nothing. Among students of courts there remains a certain romantic reluctance to admit that courts frequently do nothing. And among systems-and-process-analysis-oriented social scientists, a similar reluctance to admit that a distinct and readily identifiable subunit is there but often plays no real part.

Thus when a court says yes or says nothing so that the agency rolls along as if the court has never existed, we pretend that the court has done something politically significant —it has legitimated the agency decision, that is it has proclaimed that the decision is legal and thus endowed it with greater power to extract obedience from the population than it otherwise would have. The difficulty with the legitimation argument, at least when applied to court–agency relations, is that the administrative agencies have been sufficiently recognized as supplementary lawmakers in their own right, that their decisions independently have all the legitimacy they need. Litigants do not go to court because they are not sure whether they must obey an agency decision until a court gives it the judicial imprimatur. They go to court precisely because they know they should and must obey the agency unless they can get the court to intervene in their behalf. When the court says no or says nothing to the individual litigant, it has simply refused to help him. There is little use dressing this negative up in the positive language of legitimation.

Yet somehow it seems disturbing to admit that courts typically let the agency do what it pleases. This disturbance no doubt arises because deep down most of us still carry the vision of courts as omnipotent and omni-competent protectors of the individual against the machinations of government. Once it is recognized that a court is simply one political actor among many, it should not be disturbing or even surprising that it typically says no to the individual. For every political actor typically says no in the sense that each can intervene against its fellows in only a limited range of circumstances; and even where and when it is possible to intervene, a political actor will honor only a few of the individual requests it receives to do so.

I offer no apologies then for concentrating in this book on what the Supreme Court can and does do vis-à-vis agencies when most frequently it can or does do nothing. What is politically interesting about an agency of government is what it does do, or at least what it could do if it wanted to. One would not write a book about the House Appropriations Committee which concentrated on its inability to control promotions from Captain to Major or its helplessness to affect cattle-grazing practices in Wyoming.

Perhaps it is largely because court-agency relations were traditionally viewed as the intersection of two inherently different, hostile, and competing bodies that there is a tendency to abruptly dismiss courts as unimportant when it is found that they rarely reject an agency decision. For if courts and agencies are inherently at odds, then court approval of agency decisions must be judicial "surrender." Once the vision of inherent judicial–administrative conflict is abandoned, this overreaction will disappear. For roughly the past twenty-five years the federal government has enjoyed a relatively broad post-New Deal consensus. The statutes to which courts and agencies are subordinated have embodied policies that most judges and administrators approve. Judicial and agency personnel have themselves entertained quite similar policy views. Under these conditions, and bearing in mind that judicial review involves two essentially similar decisions —the first by administrators, the second by judges—it is hardly surprising that the federal courts are today rarely found in opposition to the agencies.

For a series of reasons having to do with the evolution of jurisprudential thought in the United States, much of what has simply been a high level of policy consensus between courts and agencies has been expressed by the Supreme Court in terms of judicial self-limitation. Instead of saying, "We agree with the agency's decision," the justices have very often

said, "We will not interfere with the agency's decision."
Where a low level of policy consensus has existed, however,
the Supreme Court has hardly been timid. Where it has
strongly disagreed with other governmental authorities on
such questions as the treatment of Negroes, the rights of
accused persons, apportionment, and obscenity, the Court
has not pleaded institutional incapacity. Admittedly these
instances largely involve state authorities, but the Court's
policy views on obscenity and accused persons have been
enforced just as vigorously on federal as on state authorities.
The patent dispute does indicate that even within the federal
sphere the Supreme Court will not modestly defer to an administrative agency with which it is in fundamental policy
disagreement.

Moreover a substantial share of judicial "deference" to
agencies is undoubtedly the result of twenty-five years of
agency experience in cultivating consensus by throwing issues
up to the courts in forms and degrees that will elicit judicial
approval or at least acquiescence. In short, the agencies know
what will play in court and what won't. As in many other
political relationships that are essentially harmonious, each
participant has a tendency to screen out in advance demands
or actions that he feels would tend to disrupt the harmony.
And, as the Transcontinental Pipe Line case shows, even
when an agency pushes a bit too hard the Court has ways of
gently telling it to move a bit more slowly without disturbing
the outward calm. The administrative agencies are not likely
to press claims on the Supreme Court that the Court will
not accept. The justices are unlikely to press for open confrontation with an agency if they are assured that the agency
will moderate its conduct according to the Court's doctrinal
communications. Thus the rule of anticipated reaction operates on both sides as both seek to maintain a harmony which
is built upon and facilitates their general policy consensus.
Each participant exerts influence on the other, although few
open confrontations will occur.

The study of judicial–administrative politics in the
United States, like the study of other sectors of American

politics, is essentially the analysis of marginals. Most American politics, and particularly most governmental activity, involves a high degree of acquiescence on the part of one participant in the actions of others—or perhaps a high degree of agreement that whomever has been assigned major political responsibility for a given job should be allowed to do it with minimal outside interference so long as he stays within certain generally acceptable limits. The dual decision-making aspect of administrative–judicial politics undoubtedly exaggerates this general tendency of American politics. Nevertheless those politics fall well within the range of the typical American situation in which one actor, agency, or interest is assigned primary responsibility for certain tasks but with sufficient overlap and interdependence that marginal conflict is usually present and major conflict is always potential.

Judicial review of administrative decision making is then marginal in the sense that, at least in the current Washington situation, policy differences are unlikely to arise in most of the instances in which review is theoretically possible. Thus most of the relations between agencies and courts are relations of acquiescence, consent, or compromise arrived at by anticipation of the other participant's position before even a tremor of conflict arises. While acknowledging this great area of harmony, an area that also exists in the relations between the Armed Services Committee and the Defense Department, the Bureau of the Budget and the Treasury, the President and the State Department—in short, in nearly every interesting American political interplay—the political analyst necessarily focuses on areas of actual or potential conflict. Looking at the potential conflict involved in judicial review of administrative decision making, I think it is possible to make several general points. The Supreme Court is unlikely to make a second decision unless it is convinced there is some special reason to do so. Most frequently that special reason, when it does occur, involves the parochialism of the agency against which the Court sets its generalist outlook. Another major clump of special reasons involves those situations in which the agency is attempting to make the statutes it administers, and thus its own powers, grow at a perhaps too-rapid rate. Here the principal question is subordination, not policy, but of course the two can never be fully separated.

The Supreme Court, faced as it is with the same questions of agency policy and power as the agency itself, using roughly the same decisional methods and exposed to roughly the same data, also, like the agency, confronts Congress, pressure groups and other participants in the policy-making process who can be expected to react to whatever decisions it renders. The Court, like other politicians in this situation, is not limited to, or often capable of, a thundering yes or no. Indeed the persistent tendency of American political analysis to either view the courts as a great dictator or dismiss them as powerless, or do both at once, is partly due to a failure to appreciate that courts are not confined to a simple yes or no. The Supreme Court may issue opinions that influence policy by altering the bargaining positions of potential litigants. It may refuse the agency a per se rule, thus preserving access to the agency for groups who wish to argue points and present evidence that the agency would prefer not to hear. The Court may help to plug a loophole or help to leave it open just a little or a whole lot. It may impose delays on an agency attempting to extend its jurisdiction or work a major shift in policy, delays that give the agency's opposition more time to muster congressional support. The Court can create legal positions that would require major congressional intervention to change, or only minor intervention or no intervention. Once intervention has occurred, the Court may favor one or another of the various policy preferences which are uneasily combined in the congressional coalitions that bring off such an intervention. The Court may delay decision or send ambiguous or contradictory messages to the circuits which handle the vast bulk of agency cases, thus creating a far different litigational terrain than might otherwise exist. It may simply urge an agency to take into account matters that the administrators have ignored, and its request carries a certain force, given the needs of the agency to maintain long-run good relations with the judiciary. Or the Court may introduce or exclude or facilitate the entry or exit of rivals to the agency as it sets jurisdictional boundaries not only between federal agencies but between national and state governments.

In setting the verbal formulas that define phrases like "ordinary and necessary business expenditure," "auxiliary and supplementary" rail–trucking services, "reserve gate picketing," and "public service" broadcasting, which are the common coin of administrative decision making, the Supreme Court helps to set the terms of debate and trade in the bargaining that constantly goes on between those who administer and those who are administered. It does the same when it refuses to define at all, as it has for instance when the Internal Revenue Service asked for a set of rules to determine what was or was not a gift. Both the F.P.C. and Consolidated Edison could have written Supreme Court opinions in the *Transcontinental* case that each would have liked better than the one they got, opinions that would have more fully facilitated their own and hindered their opponent's maneuvers in the politics to come. It is precisely this power of the Court to choose doctrines that will favor or impede the positions of various participants in the administrative arena that is difficult to quantify in terms of yes–no decisions, but remains at the heart of judicial influence over administrative politics. It is in these terms that judicial legitimation should be thought of—judicial doctrines become the legitimate bases for discourse and negotiation in the administrative process.

Thus in most instances where judicial review of administrative decisions is theoretically available, the Supreme Court will not review at all, for there is no general reason for a second government agency to make again a decision already made by another. Where special reasons do exist, the Court, having gone through the process of decision making again, is quite likely to arrive at roughly the same decision as the agency has. Even when it cannot agree with the agency, its difference of position is likely to be expressed in something other than a clear-cut no. The student of judicial–administrative politics must be prepared for a world of mutual influences rather than sovereign commands. This is only to say that in studying courts he must be prepared for the same kind of politics he finds elsewhere. Judicial review is the power to say yes or no. It is also the power to say many things in between. And it is the in-betweens that are the stuff of political life. The study of judicial review of administrative decision making offers a peculiarly rich insight into the workings of the Supreme Court and courts in general precisely because it points us to the everyday world of bargaining, persuasion, concession, and compromise which is central to an understanding of the actual process of American politics.

A Note on Further Reading

The full texts of Supreme Court Decisions
are reported in United States Reports (U.S.), the official
publication printed by the government, The Supreme Court
Reporter (S.Ct.) which provides a digest and indexing system, and the Lawyers Edition (L.Ed.) which, in addition to
text, digest, and indexing system, contains notes on many of
the leading cases that analyze the decision in terms of the
precedents. The Table of Cases gives all three references for
each case cited in the main portion of this volume. If the
student has a law library available to him, he will discover
all three series. Most college and public libraries acquire
only one. The two nonofficial series provide considerably
more analytical paraphernalia, particularly for linking one
decision with others on the same subject, but all three contain exactly the same text.

The study of judicial review of administrative decision
making necessarily flings the bibliographical doors wide,
for it places the scholar squarely at the intersection of two

enormously complex institutions—courts and bureaucracies—
and also at an even more famous and confused intersection,
that of law and politics. Perhaps the best place to begin, if
the suggestions I have put forward in Chapter 1 have any
merit, would be with organizations; for theories of the
structure and behavior of organizations should shed light
on both courts and agencies, particularly on their interrela-
tions. Amitai Etzioni, *Modern Organizations* (Englewood
Cliffs, N.J.: Prentice-Hall, 1964) and James G. March, ed.,
A Handbook of Organizations (Chicago: Rand McNally,
1965), the former designed as an elementary introduction
and the latter far more ambitious, are good starting points
although both are themselves representative of certain limited schools of thought rather than comprehensive surveys.
Organization under another name is spelled *bureaucracy,*
and here two recent works, Michael Crozier, *The Bureaucratic Phenomenon* (Chicago: U. of Chicago, 1964) and
Anthony Downs, *Inside Bureaucracy* (Boston: Little, 1967)
not only make major original contributions but comment
widely on earlier work. All of the above works contain
useful bibliographies. Yet another approach to this whole
subject area falls under the rubric *decision making.* I have
relied heavily on Richard M. Cyert and James G. March,
A Behavioral Theory of the Firm (Englewood Cliffs, N.J.:
Prentice-Hall, 1963) and David Braybrooke and Charles
Lindblom, *A Strategy of Decision* (N.Y.: Free Press, 1963),
but the beginner should be warned that the decision-making
literature is vast and that the theories of incrementalism
presented in these works are hardly the definitive word.

    As to the particular participants in the process of dual
organizational decision making described in this book, there
is no better place to start on the administrative agencies than
a standard text such as Merle Fainsod, Lincoln Gordon,
and Joseph C. Palamountain, Jr., *Government and the
American Economy* (New York: Norton, 1959). The independent regulatory commissions have been the subject of
numerous investigations, one of the most recent and comprehensive of which is James M. Landis, *Report on the
Regulatory Commissions* (Committee Print, Senate Judi-

ciary Committee, 86th Cong., 2d Sess. 1960). Earlier studies are cited and commented upon in Kenneth Culp Davis, *Administrative Law Treatise* (St. Paul: West Pub., 1958), which, with its pocket supplements, is the most exhaustive and up to date treatment of administrative law in the narrow sense. It should be compared with Louis L. Jaffe, *Judicial Control of Administrative Action* (Boston, Little, 1965). Samuel Krislov and Lloyd D. Musolf, eds., *The Politics of Regulation* (Boston: Houghton, 1964) provides a good brief introduction to the general problem of regulation.

My own *Law and Politics in the Supreme Court* (New York: Free Press, 1964) and "The Warren Court and the Interstate Commerce Commission," 18 *Stanford Law Review* 110 (1965) provide some concrete data on the role of the Supreme Court vis-à-vis administrative agencies; but, for a series of reasons explained in the earlier of these two works, neither lawyers nor political scientists have done much with this area of the Court's work. The interested student will have to accustom himself to ferreting out relevant data by consulting the substantive law headings (natural gas, transportation, etc.) of the *Index to Legal Periodicals* as well as its administrative agency, administrative proceedings, and administrative law headings. The survey of the Court's last term published in the November issues of the *Harvard Law Review* and Phillip Kurland, ed., *The Supreme Court Review* (Chicago: U. of Chicago) provide annual reviews of the justices' work which do not confine themselves to constitutional issues. The work on the attitudes of Supreme Court justices, which can be most conveniently approached through Glendon Schubert, *The Judicial Mind* (Evanston, Ill.: Northwestern U. P., 1965) and the works cited there, also sheds much light on Court–agency interactions.

It would give some scholarly satisfaction to conclude with references to those works that integrate the justices' relations with the agencies into an overall anlaysis of the role of the Supreme Court in American politics. Unfortunately there are none. Perhaps the series of which this book is a part will provide a basis for taking a few steps in this direction.

Table of Cases

Index